Ch. Lochinvar of Ladypark
*Born 1947*

# THE
# COLLIE

## MARGARET OSBORNE

ARCO PUBLISHING COMPANY, INC.

*New York*

Published in the United States
by ARCO PUBLISHING COMPANY Inc.
219 Park Avenue South, New York, N.Y. 10003

Fourth edition, First printing, 1975
Second edition © Margaret Osborne 1960
Third edition © Margaret Osborne 1962
Fourth edition © Margaret Osborne 1975

Library of Congress Catalog Card Number 74–82130
ISBN 0–668–00943–8

*Printed in Great Britain*

To

## CLARE MOLONY

who allowed a novice to pick her brains!
Without her knowledge the 'Shiels' would
not have come into being, and this book
therefore never written

# CONTENTS

# CONTENTS

# ILLUSTRATIONS

## IN THE TEXT

*The line drawings are by Prudence Walker,*
*to whom the author is greatly indebted*

# AUTHOR'S INTRODUCTIONS

★

## TO THE FIRST EDITION

It has seemed to me for some time that there was a great need for a new book on the Collie. In common with almost all Collie fanciers, I have combed the bookshelves from time to time and found nothing except a very old book or two on the breed, and it was on the assumption that many other people were also looking for similar literature that I set about writing this book.

In it I have tried to offer something for everyone, the complete newcomer to the breed and the older hand. As a specialist breed club secretary and breed correspondent to both the canine weeklies, I am constantly receiving letters posing queries of all kinds relating to the breed. The variety of questions is weird and wonderful, but all point to the same thing: that there is no real book on the breed which is a guide to those breeding and showing Collies today.

Although my own personal experience with Collies covers only about a decade, it is now thirty years since I accompanied my first show dog, a Sheltie, to his first show, and during those years dogs of several breeds have been mine, and I have also been fortunate in that I have had friends whose knowledge of my favourite breed was far greater and longer established than my own and who were willing to teach me, and for my part I tried to learn! One great point about this pastime of ours —you never stop learning. If you have had your first dog for thirty days or for thirty years, there is always something new cropping up, and the intense interest in building up a strain of one's own is a lifetime's work and a work that is most absorbing.

In Chapter 3 I have remarked that the lines and families in our breed were first classified only four years ago. I was the person who made that classification, and who did the work necessary in such a detailed task. I can honestly say that every moment of the work was more than worth while, if only because I personally learned so much about the breed. In the course of the work I collected pedigrees of thousands of Collies, and today have in my files the details of the breeding of almost any Collie ever shown, and of a great many which were unregistered and used as breeding stock only. Furthermore, there is on my bookshelves a copy of every book on the breed which, as far as I can discover, has ever been published in this country, as well as many from abroad, and to crown what is undoubtedly the most complete record of the breed in the world, my bookcase also houses an entire set of *Kennel Club Stud Books*, beginning with the first volume published in 1874 and covering the years from 1859.

If any reader wishes to take advantage of these records to fill a 'missing link' in a pedigree, or to discover information of some of the old dogs, I shall be only too willing to help if possible.

Provided *The Popular Collie* gives as much pleasure to you who read it as it has to me whilst writing it, I know the publishers and I will be well satisfied.

## TO THE FOURTH EDITION

I am delighted to find myself already introducing this, the fourth edition. The charts have again been brought up to date (April 30, 1965) and certain new information has been incorporated. I still hope that someday someone somewhere will come across some old pedigrees which may help me to tie up some loose ends; particularly do I want to know the pedigrees of Kinnersley Allegro (ex the unregistered bitch Seedley Lassie) about 1910, and of Yellow Primrose, about the same date, as well as the Irish bitch Clanrole Daisy (1927 approximately), and Mountshannon Mona (again unregistered), born about 1920.

## TO THE SIXTH EDITION

The fact that the sixth edition is already upon us, enabling me to bring the charts up to date to 31st May 1969, delights me. But also I am depressed because so many new C.C. winners, including the latest name in the illustrious line of Launds, Ch. Laund Livia, now tie into the families on which I am still seeking information. I appeal to you all again to search any old records you can possibly get your hands on, to try to find the pedigrees of the bitches. Yellow Primrose and Seedley Lassie

were both unregistered, and born, I would think, in the first
ten years of this century; Mountshannon Mona must have been
born in the very early 1920s and the Irish bitch, Clanrole
Daisy, even more recently (about 1928). It *must* be possible to
trace these four ladies, and I certainly shan't be happy until
we do.

## TO THE SEVENTH EDITION

My plea in my introduction to the last edition for information
on four bitches has, sad to say, brought no result. Because we
now have so many C.C. winners tracing back to the family
which, so far, I have designated by a '?', I have made an
alteration in this new edition. Those winners which, in earlier
editions, were marked as belonging to Family ——, are now
designated YP (for the unregistered Yellow Primrose) and
those who were marked '?', are now designated SL (Seedley
Lassie). I am not prepared to give these two families new
numbers, for I am absolutely convinced that they must both
be branches of one or other of the existing families. Do please
try to fill the gaps for me before I start work on the eighth
edition; it is so unsatisfactory for me to leave this job un-
completed.

## TO THE EIGHTH EDITION

The fact that I undertake the revisions for the eighth printing
less than eighteen months after the seventh edition gives me
great pleasure, for it proves that this book is of value to all the
newcomers to our breed.

I'm sad, however, that no one has yet been able to help in
my search for the pedigrees of the four bitches which are
needed to complete the families. It would be expected that
the older hands would be more likely to come up with this
information, but maybe one of the newcomers might, accident-
ally, drop on some old pedigrees somewhere. If you do, please
keep your eyes open; I do so want to close the gaps!

*Shiel*                                                    M. O.
*Stockbury Vale*
*Sittingbourne Kent*

# CHAPTER I

# ORIGIN AND HISTORY OF THE BREED

No one has ever been able to solve the question of the origin of the breed. It would seem that the Collie must be the result of intermingling the various breeds known of old, and then making a careful selection from the results. Whilst minute descriptions of dogs exist in manuscripts as much as 2,000 years old, nowhere can a description of a Collie be found until well into the nineteenth century, and all descriptions of farm dogs of earlier centuries are far removed from the picture of the Collie we know today.

If only we had proof that the Collie is a descendant of the ancient Sheepdog we would then be able to trace his history back to Roman times with the greatest of ease; probably further, for have we not evidence that in the time of Job[1] there were Sheepdogs tending the flocks? Further, it is most probable that at the time of the Roman invasion the Sheepdog was introduced into England, for rarely does an army travel without some canines, either 'on the pay-roll' or as stowaways. These dogs would probably remain in this country and later, when the Britons were invaded by the Picts and Scots, it is only sensible to conjecture that, with the herds and cattle we know they plundered, they took the dogs as well.

From there the next step looks easy—the interbreeding of the plundered dogs with the farm dogs they must have had at home.

All this, of course, is pure conjecture. We have absolutely no proof at all, and there can be as many suggestions as there are breeders of Collies and no one person can be more right than another. However, one thing is sure: the selection which would have been carried out would have been solely for working and herding capabilities and instincts. Type, if there was one, would have been given no consideration, and it was not until the second half of the last century that much attention was

[1] Job xxx, 1.

paid to this aspect, when dog shows first came into being. At the same time it should be realized that there was almost certainly an overall *physical* type which would be the most suitable for the work, so that to a certain extent it is probable that the selection for usefulness carried with it, fortuitously in all probability, a certain amount of selection for physical characteristics as well.

In the very early days, even as far back as Roman times, there was a classification of dogs, and one of the groups was always 'shepherd dogs'; beyond this there was virtually no further distinction, but assuredly the progenitors of our beautiful breed must have come from that group.

The name 'Collie' does not help us much, either, in tracing back the breed's origins, for the history of the word is as obscure as that of the dog itself. The word has been spelt in many different ways at different periods, 'Coll', 'Colley', 'Coally', 'Coaly', to mention only a few, and the derivation of these words is as mystifying as anything else. The most accepted origin is that the word 'Col' in Anglo-Saxon meant black, and that the dogs were so called after the black-faced sheep which was the most common in Scotland in those times.

In the *Canterbury Tales* Chaucer, in the Nonnes Priores Tale, says 'Ran Coll, our dogge', and if this is used as a specific name of the dog then it is reasonable to assume that the dog was black. But the line goes on, 'Ran Coll, our dogge, and Talbot and Gerlond'. Talbot might have been a hound, in which case the three words were more likely to be describing the types of dogs than to be individual call-names of the dogs themselves.

By the end of the eighteenth century the breed was well enough established to have a name, and the name was Collie, however it may have been spelt.

Unfortunately, far more recently than this date infusions of different blood were introduced into the Collie, usually to satisfy a whim for a special point: the cross with the Gordon Setter was made to enrich the tan; with the Irish Setter in a misplaced attempt to enrich the sable; with the Borzoi to increase the length of head. As a result of the Irish Setter cross the words 'Setter red most objectionable' came to be included in the earlier standards of the breed, and even today we all too often see the horrible results of the Borzoi cross in the receding-skulled, roman-nosed horrors which masquerade under the name of Collie.[1]

Fortunately these crosses have not been practised for many, many years, but such are the tricks of heredity that their presence can still make itself felt.

Today, although the enormous prices that the breed raised in the early part of this century are no longer reached, the Collie is in a peak period, and it can only be hoped that a new craze to improve some point will not result in the crossing with some other breed in order to 'improve' a Collie characteristic.

The history of the Collie as a show dog is almost as old as the history of dog shows themselves. The 'first ever' dog show was held in Newcastle in June, 1859, and it was a show confined to Pointers and Setters. The next show, at Birmingham in November of the same year, was again for Sporting dogs only. However, in 1860 Birmingham was the only show to be held, this time in December, as it is today, and it was a show for Sporting and Non-Sporting dogs. For the first time at any show there was a class for 'Sheepdogs'. This meant, of course, that the Collies, if any were shown at all, were lumped in with the Bob-tail, the herder's dog and any other type which might come into the classification. The first prize on this occasion was awarded to an exhibit of which we have no further information than 'ıst Mr. Wakefield's bitch'! Really a very sad state of affairs for such an epoch-making occasion! Was she a Collie or was she something else? A question which must for ever remain unanswered. But in those early days there was no Kennel Club; registrations were not compulsory; and even when the Kennel Club came into being and the first Stud Book was published it contained numerous entries of dogs for which there were no particulars available. How confusing we find, today, such an entry as that for Manchester Show in 1867, where we had the following Stud Book entry: 'Sheepdogs. ıst Palethorpe's Rover, 2nd Percival's Rover, 3rd Horsepool's Rover!' How very difficult pedigrees must have been in those early days and what a pity there was no established authority in a position to visualize the enormous expansion of dog breeding and showing, so that registration could have been

[1] See note on page 23.

B

made compulsory from the first. It would have been so much
more interesting for us today had this been so.

From the early show records available it is apparent that
the Sheepdog classes were very popular ones and almost every
show scheduled them with varying success. Quite soon the same
owners' names began to appear with great regularity, and one
of the very earliest Collie enthusiasts was apparently a Mr.
J. Siviter. His first win seems to have been at Birmingham in
1861 although his dog does not appear in the Stud Book and is
described in the show awards as Jeho (Scotch Dog)—just that
and no more. But Mr. Siviter was certainly keen, for we find
him still showing and winning as much as twenty-five years later.

The entries in the Stud Book varied between Colleys, Sheepdogs and Collies, over a number of years, according, presumably,
to the whims of the Kennel Club. But in quite early days they
became divided into three sections, Rough-coated, Smooth-
coated, and Short-tailed, this latter being, of course, the Old
English Sheepdog, which at that time was shown together with
both coats of Collies, in general Sheepdog classes. The Old
English achieved its own section in the Stud Book, under its
correct name, rather earlier than did our breed, and it was not
until the volume published in 1895 that the breed became
permanently known as Collies (Rough) and Collies (Smooth).

This apparent indecision on the part of the Kennel Club
had not stopped some of the shows from using the name Collie
in their schedules, and the first to do so was 'The First Annual
Grand National Exhibition of Sporting and Other Dogs'—
what a wonderful title!—held in Cremorne, Chelsea, in
March, 1863. But in May of the same year, at Islington, they
returned to being Scotch Sheepdogs. In the following year
Cremorne tried breaking new ground again; this time they
were Sheepdogs, Scotch and English, presumably the first
attempt to separate, in the ring, the Bobtail from the Collie.
After this little burst of originality they settled down to being
Sheepdogs, and this continued with no further change until
the show held at the Crystal Palace in 1870 where there were
classes for Sheepdogs Rough and Sheepdogs Smooth; so, for
the first time, we had a division by coat. Sad to relate, the
results sheet shows, in Smooths, 'Dogs: Prize not awarded,
want of merit'—I think a rather more outspoken comment than

it would dare to receive today in similar circumstances! It was not until a show held in Nottingham in October of 1872 that there is the first record of a Smooth winning in separate Smooth classes, and this was Mr. W. R. Daybell's *Nett*. We know no more of this exhibit, not even its sex!

At Belfast, in June, 1875, the breed was classified as Sheepdogs or Collies, but at all the succeeding shows they again became Sheepdogs, until, oddly enough, another show was held in Ireland, just over a year later, when Cork scheduled Colleys, and at Brighton two months later they became Collies, and from then the breed seems to have settled down under the appellation by which they are known today.

However, even before the breed settled into its proper classification some of the dogs to which we owe so much were making their mark on the breed. Mr. S. E. Shirley, founder of the Kennel Club, can lay claim to having also had a very big hand in the founding of the Collie as a show dog, for he bred and owned the great *Trefoil*, the dog to which every one of our present-day C.C. winners traces his or her ancestry in direct tail male. Can any other breed claim this descent of all its dogs from one male line only?

Two dogs whose names became a household word in Collies were *Old Mec* and *Old Cockie*, and both made their debut at Birmingham in 1871. It is most interesting that, whilst they were always known as 'Old' Mec and 'Old' Cockie, neither was entered in the Stud Book in this way, simply as *Mec* and *Cockie*. One must assume, I think, that the adjective was a term of endearment, and probably a measure of the esteem in which the old fanciers held these two dogs. *Cockie*, in fact, appears in several different ways in the Stud Book; in 1871 he was shown as *Cockie*, in 1872 as *Cocky Boy*, but in 1873 he became *Cockie* again! Apparently dogs were not disqualified in those days if they were entered in the wrong name!

On the occasion of the debut of *Old Mec* and *Old Cockie* they were placed first and second respectively in a class of 17. In the opinion of the fanciers who saw these two great dogs, and who have left some comment on them, *Old Cockie* was by far the better of the two and there is no doubt that he had a great deal of influence on the improvement of the breed at that time. Both of these dogs, however, played a big part, and more will be said of this later. *Old Cockie*, in one name or the other, dominated the ring for the next three years.

Steadily the Collie gained in favour, helped considerably by the interest taken in them by Queen Victoria, who succumbed to their charms on one of her visits to Balmoral.

From the 17 exhibits at Birmingham in 1871 the entry had risen to 39 dogs and 23 bitches by 1875. Names to conjure with in Collie history, names both human and canine, began to fill the records. *Trefoil* was just beginning his show career, *Scott*, his son, also. A year later the names of J. and W. H. Charles of Wellesbourne Kennels first came into prominence, and with the word 'Wellesbourne' there are evoked pictures of the great Collies of the past. Mr. J. Bissell, owner and breeder of the grand dog *Ch. Charlemagne*, made his first appearance in the ring in 1877. Mr. W. W. Thomson, already exhibiting for several years, showed here with great impact, his dogs on this occasion being *Old Hero*, *Marcus* and *Bess*, and they are traced in the pedigrees of dogs from which our present-day winners descend.

The year 1878 saw one of the fathers of the breed take his place in the ring for the first time, for the Rev. Hans Hamilton became a competitor, again at Birmingham, which seemingly was the cradle of the Collie race. On this occasion he showed *Tricolour II* without any success, but, together with this dog, he had purchased from the Hon. Everard Digby *Captain*, *Eva* and *Ruby*, these latter both daughters of *Nellie*, from whom over 50 per cent. of today's C.C. winners are descended. It will be seen what a strong foundation this reverend gentleman was laying—the prefix 'Woodmansterne' quickly became one to be reckoned with.

Mr. A. H. Megson, famed for years as the owner of the greatest Collies of his day, made his debut in 1882, and for many years held sway in the breed. He was in the fortunate position of being able to pay record prices for the dogs he wanted and almost every first-class Collie of the time was owned by him for some part of its career. Rarely, however, did he breed any of his own winners. On this occasion his exhibit was *Chieftain*, later to become a Champion, but he was to own, amongst others, *Ch. Rutland*, *Ch. Metchley Wonder*, *Ch. Caractacus*, *Ch. Edgbaston Fox*, *Ch. Southport Perfection*, *Edg-*

*baston Marvel* and *Ch. Ormskirk Emerald*, for which he paid Mr. Tom Stretch the then unheard-of price of £1,500.

About this time Mr. C. H. Wheeler had been exhibiting a number of dogs with considerable success, and Mr. S. Boddington had purchased, as a puppy, *Rutland* from the Rev. Hans Hamilton. In 1883 Mr. Boddington decided to branch out still further and purchased all Mr. Wheeler's dogs from him, on the oral agreement that this last-named gentleman would not exhibit for a period of three years. It is therefore with some surprise that we note Mr. Wheeler showing *Smuggler* in 1885!

Three years after Mr. Megson had entered the ranks Mr. Tom Stretch led his first Collie into the ring, and in a very brief space of time the 'Ormskirk' prefix was known to Collie lovers all over the world.

Blue merle history started to be made in this year, too, for it was now that, for the first time, a blue merle won in open competition against all comers and all colours. Mr. W. Arkwright produced his two famous merles, *Ch. Blue Ruin* and *Blue Sky*. More of their history, and that of the blue merle generally, will be found in the chapter dealing with Collies of this colour.

Mr. Hugo Ainscough's is the next name to remember. He came into the game in 1886. It was not long before his 'Parbolds' were holding top places in the prize lists, and many of his dogs' names are to be found in today's pedigrees, the greatest, undoubtedly, being *Ch. Parbold Piccolo*, whose influence on the breed was very marked indeed.

Two years later the 'Barwells', owned by Mr. J. Powers, began to be noticed and the following year two new names were added, those of 'Wishaw' (Mr. R. Tait) and Mr. H. E. Packwood's 'Billesleys', this latter being particularly noted for his great interest in blue merles. Mr. W. E. Mason and the 'Southports' were only a year behind, and in *Ch. Southport Perfection* there surely lived one of the greatest of all time.

After this, eight years were to pass before another addition, which had great impact, was made, and this was Mr. R. H. Lord, with his 'Seedley' prefix—the earliest granted prefix which is still in existence today, although now in different ownership, for on Mr. Lord's death in the early 1920s he passed his Kennel name to his friend and manager, Mr. Rudman, and today the Seedley prefix is held by Mrs. M. Rudman. Almost sixty years of unbroken succession of breeding in the same lines is going to take some beating!

Only one more name was added to the roll before the turn of the century, and that was Mr. W. T. Horry, whose 'Tyttons' have writ large their name in Collie history.

A dozen years of the new century were to pass before any illustrious newcomers made their mark. In these early years, in fact, the breed was to lose a number of its most ardent supporters. Then came the name of 'Treffynon' and Miss I. Jones, who is still with us, and in 1913 Mr. W. W. Stansfield wrote the word 'Laund' on the scroll from which it will never be erased as long as the Collie breed exists. Today the great 'Stanny' is no longer with us, but many of us owe much to him, and it is nice to know that the 'Launds' still go on in the ownership of his daughter, Mrs. Ada Bishop.

What a year 1913 was, for in addition to the Launds the 'Edens' came into being too, and all of us showing Collies today feel we have not had our money's worth if the bright, cheerful and ever-young countenance of Mr. Fred Robson[1] is missing from the ringside at a big show. These two breeders both had very big Kennels and were in constant competition over the next thirty years.

Then came the war. In its early years it did not stop the showing and breeding of dogs entirely and in 1916 Mr. A. Ray bred *Ch. Poplar Perfection* who gained one C.C. before the showing of dogs was banned. This dog quickly gained his title when shows were resumed again after the cessation of hostilities.

In 1917 the food shortage was such that the Kennel Club, in order to discourage dog breeding, placed a ban on all dog shows and refused to register any puppies born after September 27th of that year, unless bred under licence. These restrictions were not lifted until January, 1919. Just before the ban was imposed one or two dogs, afterwards to become Champions, were born, and these included the two Launds, *Logic* and *Legislator*.

Naturally it took some time for things to get back to normal, and a number of the pre-war fanciers disappeared for ever, having dispersed their stock, but their places were soon taken in the early '20s by new names which again made a substantial

---

[1] It is sad to record that Mr. Robson died in April 1966

mark, and many are still with us today. Mr. Ball's 'Backwoods', Mr. Hughes' 'Treflans', Mr. Bennett's 'Sedgemoors', Mr. Hayter's 'Athelneys', and Mr. Robert's 'Ashteads' have been and gone, but Miss Molony's 'Westcarrs' came into being in 1923, and in the same year Miss Grey showed the first 'Lady-park'. Three years later Mrs. George's 'Beulah' prefix was first registered. At the same time came Mr. and Mrs. Newbery with the 'Alphingtons'. In 1930 the 'Mariemeau' prefix of Mrs. James was first introduced, but she had previously exhibited for some years in the name of 'Beaulieu', and this brings us to little more than a decade ago. Most of the successful Kennels started since that date are with us today, and their influence can be traced in the ensuing pages.

*Note* (see page 17):

The reference to the alleged Gordon Setter and Borzoi crosses has caused some consternation, particularly abroad, and it should be stressed that, although there is fairly definite proof that, at some time in the history of the Collie, the blood of both these other breeds enfiltered, there is no suggestion of proof that any such crossing has taken place within the last 100 years! In *The Book of the Dog* (Vero Shaw, 1881), this question of the Setter cross is discussed at some length. The Gordon Setter is virtually the national Setter of Scotland, and it is agreed by all authorities that the honour of its production should be bestowed upon the Duke of Gordon. It is certain that, in the early part of the nineteenth century (about 1820) the Marquis of Huntly, (later Duke of Gordon), possessed a strain of Setters he was anxious to improve. He heard of an extraordinarily clever Collie bitch, the property of a neighbouring shepherd. This bitch had been taught to set birds, and her steadiness in this respect had won her great fame. History relates that, on hearing of this wonderful Collie, the Marquis immediately purchased her and put her to one of his most successful Setter sires. It is to this Collie bitch that many hold the Gordon Setter owes his origin, and the story is well authenticated. The year 1880 was well in advance of the date of the first dog show, so obviously the Setter × Collie was made, not with the intention of 'im-proving' the colour of the Collie—as has been held—but, in fact, to improve the working capabilities of the gundog. In those far off days dogs were looked upon solely for their abilities to work in various fields, and not for points of 'beauty' so much sought after today. It is, however, more than probable that some of the progeny of the original Collie used in this cross may well have been mated later back into the Collie line, and from this source, and this alone, arose the erroneous statements about the introduction of Setter blood into our breed.

# CHAPTER 2

# THE GREAT ONES OF THE PAST
# AND OF TODAY

## *Male Line*

ANYONE writing at the present day must of necessity rely on the writings of the old breeders who have left records and impressions of the dogs they knew, and all one can attempt is to try to strike a mean between the different, often conflicting, comments we have about the same dogs by different people! Occasionally it has been necessary to take a 'majority vote' on a certain dog, and the official details are also frequently different from other descriptions left us. It would seem, in fact, that some of the early breeders supplied most peculiar details to the Kennel Club!

The writer to whom undoubtedly we owe most is Mr. H. E. Packwood, for in his book, published in 1906 and now long since out of print, he has left us the most complete record we have of the early show dogs of our breed. Before the publication of Mr. Packwood's book we also had *The Collie* by Mr. Hugh Dalziel, which, published at an uncertain date but certainly prior to 1876, for in that year Mr. Dalziel died, gives us some interesting, but naturally very early, information. The only other books which have been of any real value to students of the breed are those of Mr. Baskerville and Dr. O. P. Bennett, the latter published in U.S.A. Both these authors quoted liberally from Mr. Packwood's book.

During approximately the first ten years of shows, no dogs appear to have been shown which made any stamp on the breed, and it was not until the 1870s that we begin to record great names on the Collie rolls.

Dealing first with the dogs which have established and maintained the breed, pride of place must go to *Old Cockie*. This extraordinary dog, of whom unfortunately we have only a photograph taken after the age of ten years, is one about whose merit there has been no doubt, and the almost unanimous description is that he was a very handsome animal and a real ornament to the Sheepdog section at any show. He was a rich sable, one of the first of his colour, and to him we owe the whole of the sable colour today. *Cockie* had a full white collar and the usual white markings. His legs, however, were spotted with brown, in the manner of a Cocker Spaniel and frequently seen today in the Sheltie. He had a good head and nice ear carriage. He was a sturdy, sound dog, and his coat was dense and of excellent texture, with a very profuse undercoat. One is led to believe that he was not a big dog, though I have been unable to discover his actual measurements. I have seen it mentioned that his son, *Ch. Cocksie*, was 'a little bigger than his sire', and it is recorded that Cocksie was $21\frac{1}{2}$ inches at the shoulder, so presumably Old Cockie was not over 21 inches.

*Cockie* had a wonderful show career and his greatness in this field was equalled by his amazing influence as a stud dog. It is particularly interesting to note this influence and to bear in mind that he was very little used indeed until he was over eight years of age! What he might have done had he had a normal stud career is almost impossible to assess, for even as it is it is quite impossible to trace back the pedigree of almost any winner at the end of the last century, and the beginning of this, without finding several lines leading to this grand old man.

It has been impossible to trace the antecedents of this dog, as his original owner, Mr. White, refused to disclose where he got him, so the beginning of all that is best in Collies as we know them today must for ever remain in obscurity. *Old Cockie* was born in 1868 and died in 1882. To him a big 'thank you' from the breed which owes him so much.

Two years after the birth of *Old Cockie*, *Old Mec* came into the world, and these two were frequent protagonists in the show-ring. *Old Cockie* is certainly considered to have been the better of the two, though the first time they met 'Old Mec' won the day. It would appear that things have always been much the same in the ring!

'*Mec*' was black and tan with a white chest and narrow white blaze. He, too, had a wealth of coat, which was inclined to wave, and though his head was of good length his expression apparently left a lot to be desired, being somewhat sulky and never kindly like that of Old Cockie. Again, we know little of this dog's parentage, except that he was by Mr. Haslett's dog ex Mr. Gerrard's bitch, the dam being Scottish.

Tomlinson's *Scott*, born in 1876, was probably the best of Old Cockie's descendants. This symmetrical, bright sable and white dog, with good legs and feet and grand movement, had a coat of great density, if not over-long. He had a magnificent mane and frill which off-set his beautiful head and good ears. Unfortunately he was never shown as he was badly scalded by a kettle of boiling water, but through his children, principally his son *Duncan*, his name is to be found in most pedigrees, for Duncan was the great-grandsire of the wonderful and well-named Ch. Metchley Wonder.

*Trefoil*, younger than Old Cockie by five years, is the dog to which all our present-day winners trace their pedigrees and therefore he deserves special mention. He was outstandingly successful as a show dog, but even this great record was eclipsed by his wonderful success as a sire. A tricolour, with a coat of great length, but which lacked somewhat in density, this was a shapely dog, gay and attractive, with a fair head, good eye and ears which he carried well. He had the ability to hand on to his children his great length of coat, as did his younger brothers, *Tartan* and *Tricolour*, but the coat, whilst long, was not sufficiently weather-resisting. However, the fact that Trefoil's 'frill' almost touched the ground was a point on which many of the early breeders were very keen.

Here, then, were the sires in the strain which contributed most to the production of coat, but the best and most typical type of head was established by Old Cockie, Duncan and through the bitch line springing from Elsie, Ch. Madge and Old Bess.

One other dog of the period remains to be noted. This was Mr. Brackenburg's *Scott*. Born in 1873, another of unknown pedigree, he played an enormous part in the history of the blue merle, as he was responsible for the lovely colour for which Mr. Arkwright's blue merles were so famed. More about this dog will be found in the chapter devoted to the blue merles.

This completes the list of the early dogs which had a great effect on the Collie race, and now it is proposed to continue and bring us to the notables of the present day.

In 1879 the great *Ch. Charlemagne* was born, by Trefoil ex
Maude (by Old Cockie ex Meg by Old Mec). Another very
showy sable and white, with a profuse coat of great length; his
head, however, coarsened early. Charlemagne was five years
old before he sired the next link in the chain, *Sefton*, who
claimed Ch. Madge as his dam. This tricolour had a stong head
and only middling ears, and his show career was undistin-
guished, but while still a junior he made his mark by siring an
'all-time great' in *Ch. Metchley Wonder*, and establishing himself
for posterity. Ch. Metchley Wonder was, in fact, the result of
a very early mating on the part of both his parents, for whilst
Sefton was only just out of puppyhood at the time of the
service, the dam, Minnie (by Loafer ex Catrine) was but seven
months old! This great dog was sable and white, and well
named, for he became the wonder of his age. He was a very
big winner and a great sire. No dog of the time ever earned
anything like the amount he brought in in stud fees, and Mr.
Megson is reported to have received much more than the £500
he gave for him—and that took some doing in the days when
stud fees were around the 30s. mark!

*Ch. Christopher*, the best-headed Collie shown to date, was
the next in the line; he was a son of Ch. Metchley Wonder
ex Peggie II (by Ruthven ex Madge). This lovely-headed dog
with good coat was a typical Collie; nevertheless he left much
to be desired behind the head. However, faultless or not,
Ch. Christopher left, among other numerous progeny, two sons
who demand our attention, *Ch. Stracathro Ralph* and *Edgbaston
Marvel*; the former out of Stracathro Fancy who was by
Scottish Hero ex Broadford Duchess by Smuggler ex Sweet
Lassie; the latter ex Sweet Marie by Smuggler ex Sweet Fairy,
so these two dogs were of very similar breeding.

Although Ch. Christopher is reported to have been prick-
eared, both these dogs were low-eared, doubtless owing to their
Smuggler blood, as he was a very heavy-eared dog. Both were
sable and white. Ralph was a quality dog with a lovely head
and his low ears did not detract very much, it appears, since
he gained his title. Marvel, however, though exhibited once,
was not a show specimen because of his ears, but apart from this
he was probably the most perfect Collie seen up to that date
(1888). Mr. Wheeler recognized his potentialities as a stud

dog and paid £30 for a non-show specimen, but after proving his value as a sire he sold him to Mr. Megson for £500!

Continuing this line, we come to *Ch. Southport Perfection*, born in 1892 ex Tabley Rose, by Ch. Metchley Wonder. Another sable and white of quality, with good body, legs and feet, and good head and ears, but he failed somewhat in eye placement. A son of his, *Wellesbourne Councillor* (ex Wellesbourne Christabelle by Ch. Christopher), a dog who did not have much of a show career but who, through his son, *Ch. Wellesbourne Conqueror* (ex Wellesbourne Beauty by Edgbaston Marvel), became grandsire of Ch. Parbold Piccolo. As may be seen, Conqueror was the result of a very careful piece of line-breeding, and his place is undoubtedly a result of superlative breeding which enabled him to make his reputation as a sire, and *Ch. Parbold Piccolo* was his most distinguished descendant.

*Piccolo* was a most attractive, showy dog, excelling in coat, good bone and shapely body. He had exceptionally good ear carriage and his ears were very small. He was, however, a shade deep through the muzzle. This dog left three sons which are of importance to us today, *Ch. Ormskirk Olympian, Ch. Anfield Model* and *Parbold Pierrot*. It was a very sad day when Piccollo, after gaining world-wide fame as a show dog, left this country for the States and was lost en route.

Of the three sons already named, it is particularly interesting to note that Mr. Packwood, writing at the time when these three dogs were in the middle of their show careers, says of Ch. Anfield Model: 'To the writer's mind the hereditary influence of this dog will be great indeed.' Today his only C.C. winning descendant is Ch. Delwood Meryl, whilst Ch. Ormskirk Olympian and Parbold Pierrot, particularly the latter, have had a far greater influence on the breed.

*Ch. Ormskirk Olympian* (ex Ch. Ormskirk Ideal), a dark-shaded sable with very little white, was an outstanding dog for his time and, except for a trace of coarseness in head, seems to have been difficult to fault. In a very brief stud career in this country before going to the States he became the sire of *Ch. Wishaw Leader* (ex Hartwood Lady by Ch. Wishaw Clinker), a big, upstanding tricolour dog with a profusion of coat. Continuing the line from Leader, *Wishaw Dazzler* (ex Wishaw Prunella by Ch. Parbold Picollo), *Wishaw Baldy* (by Dazzler

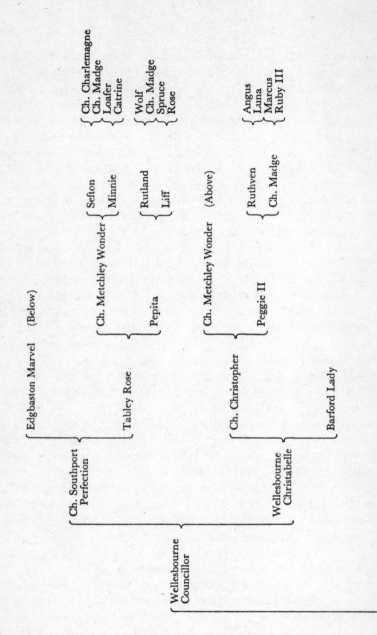

Ch. Wellesbourne

Wellesbourne Councillor
  Ch. Southport Perfection
    Edgbaston Marvel (Below)
    Tabley Rose
      Ch. Metchley Wonder
        Sefton
        Minnie
      Pepita
        Rutland
        Liff
  Wellesbourne Christabelle
    Ch. Christopher
      Ch. Metchley Wonder (Above)
        Ch. Charlemagne
        Ch. Madge
        Loafer
        Catrine
      Peggie II
        Wolf
        Ch. Madge
        Spruce
        Rose
    Barford Lady
      Ruthven
      Ch. Madge
        Angus
        Luna
        Marcus
        Ruby III

Conqueror 1895
└─ Wellesbourne Beauty
   ├─ Edgbaston Marvel
   │  ├─ Ch. Christopher (Above)
   │  └─ Sweet Marie
   │     ├─ Smuggler
   │     │  ├─ Tramp II
   │     │  │  ├─ Tramp
   │     │  │  └─ Moss
   │     │  └─ Sable Plume
   │     │     ├─ Glen
   │     │     └─ Jessie
   │     └─ Sweet Fairy
   │        ├─ Rutland
   │        │  ├─ Wolf
   │        │  └─ Ch. Madge
   │        └─ Strawberry Girl
   │           ├─ Ch. Charlemagne
   │           └─ Sinico
   └─ Ryland Jennie
      ├─ Caractacus
      │  ├─ Cremorne
      │  │  ├─ Rutland
      │  │  │  ├─ Wolf
      │  │  │  └─ Ch. Madge
      │  │  └─ Patience
      │  │     ├─ Clydesdale
      │  │     └─ Maude
      │  └─ Barby Rose
      │     ├─ Cliftonian
      │     │  ├─ Staffa
      │     │  └─ Rose
      │     └─ Gazelle
      │        ├─ Champagne
      │        └─ Brenda
      └─ Olton Pride
         ├─ Ch. Christopher (Above)
         └─ Sweet Lassie
            ├─ Young Cockie
            │  ├─ Champagne
            │  └─ Patience
            └─ Lady Macbeth
               ├─ Wolf
               └─ Leila

ex Miss Stormer) and *Wishaw Victor* (by Baldy ex Wishaw
Polly) lead us to Victor's son *Ch. Wishaw Rival* (ex Kennis-
head Lassie by Southport Shah). Born in 1911, this sound,
handsome sable dog was undoubtedly noteworthy for having
very few faults indeed. He had an outstanding show career,
and left several offspring which we must note. His two sons
*Wishaw Ben* (ex Wishaw Mary) and *Craigside Chieftain* (ex
Craigside Corona) were neither very distinguished in themselves, and to Chieftain only one dog traces back today—
this is Ch. Alphington Nigger King. Ben, however, became the
grandsire, through *Wishaw Bendigo* (ex Kildean Laura), of
*Ch. Wishaw Reliable* (ex Wishaw Nancy by Wishaw Ben), a
big tricolour with much to commend him. He contributes to
the plan with *Netherkeir Reliable* (ex Netherkeir Maisie) and
*Corella Don* (ex Netherkeir Doris). Netherkeir Reliable sired
*Ch. Netherkeir Starboy* (ex Netherkeir Queen by Wishaw Ben),
and he in turn through his son *Fleetway Fearless* (ex Ashtead
Artiste) became grandsire of *The Rajah* (ex Mariemeau
Chrystabelle by Ashtead Aristocrat).

By far the most important Piccolo son, however, from our
point of view, was the 'uncrowned' one, *Parbold Pierrot*, sire of
*Ch. Parbold Paganini* (1904) (ex Parbold Pleasance by Ch.
Balgreggie Baronet), a dog of great merit but lacking somewhat
in refinement in skull. In 1907 Paganini's son *Ch. Ormskirk
Foxall* was born (ex Ch. Ormskirk Adair by Ch. Ormskirk
Clinker by Ch. Wishaw Clinker). Another dog with a great
reputation in the ring which was to be enhanced by his great
merits as a sire. A sable and white, with almost all the essentials
and particularly excelling in the desired almond eye. Foxall
sired many notable winners, but of main interest to us is his
son *Parkside Pro Patria* (ex Parkside Paulette by Parbold Prior),
sire of the lovely *Ch. Seedley Sterling* (1911) (ex Seedley Sylvia),
a sable and white of great quality and ·character. Sterling,
through his son *Eden Eric* (ex Eden Eileen by Ch. Parbold
Picador), became grandsire of *Ch. Eden Extra* (ex Alloway Ideal
by Broomoor Bayard), who, through *his* son *Eden Eldred* (ex
Oswald Lady by Ch. Poplar Perfection), was grandsire of *Ch.
Laund Lindrum* (ex Glenack Juliet by Ch. Laund Latto). This
dark sable dog was bred by Mr. C. F. Pyle and owned at first
by Mr. W. W. Stansfield, who sold him to Mrs. 'Mariemeau'

Tramp II
*Born 1880*

Ch. Charle-
magne (at 10
years of age)
*Born 1879*

Sable Plume
*Born 1880*

Smuggler
By Tramp and
Sable Plume
*Born 1884*

Ch. Metchley Wonder
*Born 1886*

Ch. Christopher
*Born 1887*

James in whose hands he gained his title. Two Lindrum sons keep the line going, *Ch. Knight of Monaster* (ex It's-a-Gift by Grimsby Sepoy) and *Seedley Study* (ex Ch. Seedley Sequence by Ashtead Approval). Knight was a rich sable and white excelling in head properties, and can be taken today as the example of the true Collie eye placement and expression. He did a great deal of winning and sired two dogs which are of much interest as links in our chain, *Ch. The Laird of Killartry* (ex Killartry Vanessa) and *Thane of Mariemeau* (ex The Ladye of Mariemeau by Mariemeau Brilliantine). Both these dogs were sable and white. Thane, unshown owing to an accident to his tail, is the sire of *Ch. Gunner of Mariemeau* (ex Patricia of Mariemeau)[1] who in his turn has so far sired one Champion dog in *Cragienure Chancellor* (ex Cragienure Crystal by Sensation of Bellrenia), a sable dog who shows his Knight of Monaster blood in his lovely expression. Chancellor sired *Ch. Danvis Drifter* (ex Eden Golden Queen of Riglea), and this dark sable dog produced a dark sable Champion son in *Danvis Driver* (ex Danvis Daphne by Eden Excellent), and a golden sable in *Ch. Alexander of Arcot*.

The Laird did not sire any champions himself, but through his son *Kay of Killartry* (exKillartry Queen of the May by Ashtead Aristocrat), who was mated to a Smooth bitch, he is directly responsible for a number of today's Smooth champions. Another son of his, *Lyndene Fantail* (ex Lass of Saxlingham by Ashtead Aristocrat), sired *Lucky of Ladypark* (ex Lyric of Ladypark by Ch. Beulah's Golden Favor), and from this line are descended almost all today's C.C. winners in the Wearmouth Kennels.

Returning to the other Lindrum son, *Seedley Study*, he left a Champion son *Walford of Waldemar* (ex Seedley Spec), and Walford's son *Waldorn* (ex Pool's Bett by Ch. Marimeau Fantail) sired *Ch. Cezar of Corbieux* (ex Golden Queen of Bellrenia), a dog which unfortunately died young; and another

---

[1] Ch. Gunner of Mariemeau also sired *Ch. Gunner of Glenturret*, sire of the tricolour champion, *Andrew of Arcot* (ex Ch. Antanette of Arcot), and of the history-making *Ch. Danvis Damascus* who, in July 1961, became the first Rough Collie ever to win best in show all breeds at a British Championship Show. Gunner also sired *Ch. Jefsfire Strollaway*, sire of four Champion daughters and the Champion brothers, *Chateauroux Caesar* and *Chateauroux Flawless*; whilst through his son *Craiglyn Commander* he is grandsire of *Ch. Larkena Rabelias*, sire of *Ch. Larkena Vanara Golden Victor* who has two Champion sons in *Antoc Vicar of Bray* and *Larkena Rebais*. *Ch. Danvis Damascus* produced *Ch. Danvis Duffer*, sire of *Ch. Danvis Camanna Golden Sensation* and *Ch. Jefsfire Gold Token*.

Heather Ralph

Stracathro Ralph

{ Ch. Christopher

Ch. Metchley Wonder (Below)
{ Ch. Charlemagne
  Ch. Madge
{ Loafer
  Catrine

Peggie II
{ Ruthven
  { Angus
    Luna
  Ch. Madge
  { Marcus
    Ruby III

Stracathro Fancy

Scottish Hero
{ Scottish Tweed
  { Tramp II
    Sable Plume
  Lucky Spy
  { Young Cockie
    Lady Macbeth

Broadford Duchess
{ Smuggler
  { Trefoil
    Maude
  Sweet Lassie
  { Marcus
    Ruby III

Apple Blossom

Ch. Metchley Wonder

Sefton
{ Ch. Charlemagne
  { Chang
    The Lily
  Ch. Madge
  { Bonnie Laddie
    Bonnie Greta

Minnie
{ Loafer
  (Above)
  Catrine
  { Trefoil
    Maude

Grove Daisy

Eclipse
{ Ch. Charlemagne
  Flirt

Lady Clare
{ Wolf
  { Old Cockie
    Lorna
    Tricolour

Ch.

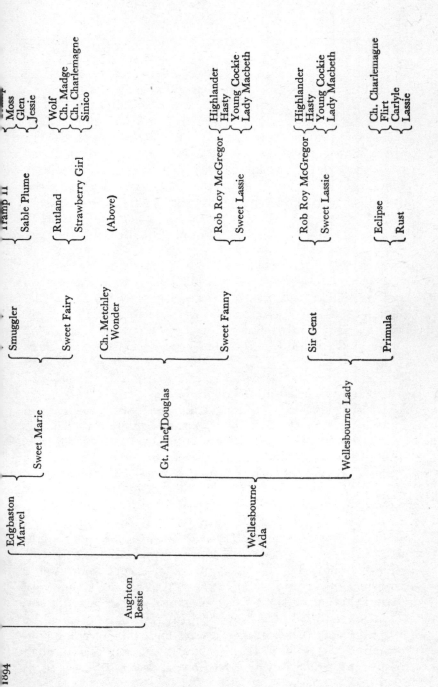

1894

C.C. winning son, *Walhost of Waldemar* (ex Yvette of Waldemar.)

To continue this story in the same line we must return to Ch. Christopher's other son, *Ch. Stracathro Ralph* (1888) (ex Stracathro Fancy by Scottish Hero ex Broadford Duchess by Smuggler ex Sweet Lassie), for he was grandsire, through his son *Heather Ralph* (ex Apple Blossom by Ch. Metchley Wonder), of that outstanding show dog *Ch. Ormskirk Emerald* (1894) (ex Aughton Bessie by Edgbaston Marvel). Emerald was heralded as the most perfect specimen of the breed yet seen, and this he undoubtedly was, but unfortunately his merits as a stud force were negligible, undoubtedly because, although he was not exactly 'chance got', he sprang from coarse beginnings on both sides of his pedigree, yet most of his blood, differently mingled, was that which had been 'producing the goods' until this time. Already is clearly seen the amount of care and study which was going into the plannings of matings with a special emphasis on line- and in-breeding as we know it today. Emerald left only one son which we need be concerned with, and this was *Ormskirk Galopin* (ex Ch. Ormskirk Memoir by Ormskirk Chris, who was by Ch. Christopher), sire of *Heachum Galopin* (ex Wisbech Dolly), a sable and white of merit but lacking in coat qualities. There followed *Ch. Wishaw Clinker* (1898) (by Ch. Heachum Galopin ex Last Rose by Ormskirk Amazement ex Bridesmaid by Ch. Metchley Wonder), and Clinker through *Ch. Balgreggie Baronet* (ex Old Hall Duchess by Kirkdale Patrick ex Old Hall Real Gem by Ch. Balgreggie Hope) was grandsire of *Ch. Squire of Tytton* (1904) (ex Helle of Boston by Ch. Parbold Piccolo), a sable dog of the very greatest merit with lovely head, eye, ears and expression, and good body, legs and feet; he had a grand show career, and sired a great number of winners, but the only son to concern us is *Seedley Squire* (ex Southport Sissie by Ch. Anfield Model) who sired *Ch. Seedley Superior* (1906), a reallly lovely sable of exceptionally sound construction. Superior sired *Clarksfield Superior* (ex Countess of Clarksfield) and he sired *Tonge Admiration* who became the sire of the one and only *Ch. Magnet* (1912) (ex Southport Seal by Parbold Picador). *Ch. Magnet*, a sable and white of grand conformation and style, made his mark in the ring and through his progeny, principally his lovely son *Ch. Poplar Perfection* (1916) (ex Pickwick Peeper by Parbold Privateer). This wonderfully headed and expressioned sable and white has been of the greatest possible value to the breed and no dog born has ever had more influence than he, through his two sons *Ch. Backwoods Fashion* (1921) and *Ch. Eden Emerald* (1922). These two brothers (ex Ch. Eden Elenora by Eden Extra ex Eden Emily) were both sable and white and both excellent representatives of the breed, with Emerald probably slightly the better in expression. Fashion, through *Backwoods Feature* (ex Ch. Backwoods Famous by Eden Extra), was grandsire of *Ch. Backwoods Fellow* (ex Backwoods Fritter), a sable excelling in head properties, with excellent ear carriage and expression. Fellow is considered by many to be one of the greatest Collies ever born. His influence was very considerable, and had it not been for the Second World War, when breeding plans were of necessity curtailed, we should owe him even more than we do today. Fellow sired *Beulah's Golden Shade* (ex Beulah's Nightshade by Ch. Glenack Kingfisher) and *Beulah's Nightmail* (ex Ch. Eden Electora by Eden Electron). The latter sired only two litters, I believe, but one of these gave the breed two Champions in Ch. Beulah's Golden Favor and Ch. Beulah's Golden Feather (ex Beulah's Golden Florida by Backwoods Farrier) and it is a great pity that he was not more used. Golden Shade has the honour of having sired the last pre-war Champion dog in *Ch. Beulah's Golden Future* (ex Beulah's Golden Florida), and he in his turn sired the first post-war Champion dog, *Beulah's Golden Futureson* (ex Ch. Beulah's Golden Feather). Futureson sired *Ch. Beulah's Golden Fusonkin* (ex Beulah's Golden Kiska) and he, too, sired a Champion in *Beulah's Golden Sunfuson* (ex Beulah's August Princess).

Back then to Ch. Eden Emerald, a dog of outstanding qualities who made his mark for posterity through his son *Eden Educator* (ex Eden Endive by Eden Extra), and through Educator's two sons, *Eden Extreme* (ex Eden Elvira by Eden Extra ex Sonnenburgh Sumptuous by Ch. Seedley Squire) and *Eden Electron* (ex Eden Enid by Ch. Laund Latto) we trace today no fewer than 245 Champions or certificate winners, almost 75 per cent, in direct descent today. Extreme sired *Ch. Glenack Kingfisher* (ex Glenack Silver Cloud by Laund Landseer) and this lovely blue merle dog through his son *Beulah's Nightshadowing* (ex

Beulah's Nightshadow) became the grandsire of *Beulah's Night-victorious* (ex Ch. Beulah's Silver Merienda by Ch. Backwoods Flutter ex Beulah's Silver Tern by Ch. Glenack Kingfisher). This tricolour was born, unfortunately, in the very early years of the war, so he had no show career worth mentioning. He was a dog with very little white, but with a body, legs and feet of excellence, a good coat of correct length and texture and a most glorious head and expression with the true Collie eye. With few opportunities, this dog has sired a number of outstanding sons and daughters and the present-day Collie probably owes more to him than to almost any other dog born in the last twenty years. Apart from his particular influence on the blue merle lines, to which more reference will be made later, he also made his mark on the sables and tricolours principally through his two sons *Lyncliffe Landseer* (ex Ch. Lyncliffe Blue Lady) and the sable *Shiel's Beulah Golden Viceroy* (ex Beulah's Golden Fantasy, litter sister to Ch. Futureson).

Nightshadowing produced a son to whom the breed also owes a lot, the blue merle *Am. Ch. Beulah's Silver Don Mario*. This dog was 'evacuated' to America on the outbreak of hostilities, and so left only one litter in this country, but this included *Lyncliffe Lancer* (ex Leyland Lima), a beautiful tricolour with coat of grand texture; another 'war baby', he was little shown but he sired one Champion son in *Woodlands Wanderer*, and his most outstanding son was without doubt the C.C. winner *Eden Examine* (ex Seagull). A dark sable dog, this, of true Collie type and unlucky not to gain his title—his head and expression greatly appealed. Examine sired three Champion sons: *Selstoma Safeguard* (ex Danethorpe Dairymaid) and *Lad* and *Lochinvar of Ladypark* (ex Ch. Beulah's Golden Flora by Ch. Beulah's Golden Futureson). Though brothers, Lad was a year older than Lochinvar. Undoubtedly the most outstanding of these was *Ch. Lochinvar of Ladypark*. This big, upstanding golden sable was born in 1947. He was all 'Collie' with the most beautiful head and expression, and one of the few with the correctly placed almond eye. Beyond question a pre-eminent dog of his period as a sire, and though beaten in the ring from time to time nevertheless a most worthy Champion. But it is as a sire that his name will be written in gold on the Collie roll of honour. Admittedly he served more bitches than any other dog of his time, but he was extremely prepotent, and had that rare ability of producing his like from the less good bitches as well as from the top-class ones. It is almost always easy to spot 'Lochinvar' descendants, even if one is only his great-grandchild, and in my opinion no other dog in recent years has had such marked ability, except perhaps Beulah's Nightvictorious. Lochinvar bred two Champion daughters in his first litter and in his second a Champion son, *Westcarrs Whistler* (ex Beulah's Nightglamorous by Beulah's Nightvictorious). Since then he has sired no fewer than seven Champion sons, *Walbrooke Stormy Petrel* (ex Tessa of Riglea), *Laird's Galway Sun* (ex Laird's Rose), *Eden Rip of Ladywell* and *Lena's Golden Son* (ex Ch. Lena of Ladypark by Lucky of Ladypark ex Lilac of Ladypark) and *Ch. Loyal of Ladypark* (ex Dawn Duchess of Ladypark). The seventh Champion son of Lochinvar was *Ch. Leonertes of Ladypark* (ex Ch. Eden Estrella). Add to this his daughters, Maid and Rose (ex Laird's Rose), Ch. Danethorpe Wistful of Wessingvil (ex Wessingvil Kay's Playmate by Eden Excellent), Ch. Lilt of Ladypark (ex Ch. Lena), Ch. Danvis Dyllorna (ex Ch. Danvis Deborah by Ch. Gunner of Mariemeau) and Ch. Sudborough Lochdorna (ex Lassie of Sudborough by Eden Esquire) and he has already established a record which will surely remain unchallenged for some time to come. Another Lochinvar son, *Libretto of Ladypark* (ex Ch. Lena of Ladypark) has played a great part in the breed's history by leaving us the champions *Legend* (ex Ch. Maid of Ladypark) and *Liberty* (ex Lindy Lou of Ladypark). Legend has given the breed two Champion sons as well as three Champion daughters. Liberty has also sired a Champion son, *Alphington Sociable* (ex Leonie of Ladypark) and seven Champion daughters. *Pattingham Kismet*, yet another C.C. winning son of Lochinvar, has his own special place, for he sired *Ch. Pattingham Pacemaker* (ex Ch. Pattingham Gay Lady of Glenmist) who wrote a glorious page in the breed's history when he won the Non-Sporting Group at Crufts 1964— the first time this award had ever gone to a Rough Collie. *Kismet* also sired *Ch. Debonair of Glenmist*, sire of the brothers, *Ch. Pattingham Gay Legend of Glenmist* and *Ch. Golden Legacy of Glenmist*. Lochinvar himself is, alas, no longer with us, nor is *Kismet*.

Ch. Lad of Ladypark sired one Champion son, *Ugony's Golden Son o' Lad of Rifflesee*, a most showy golden sable and white excelling in coat, and who sired a number of winning offspring. His most valuable son, however, from a point of view of the breed's history, was the tricolour, *Rifflesee Royalist* (ex Beulah's Night Flare) a most neglected dog. Used only three or four times in his life he produced what was undoubtedly the best blue merle sire the breed has ever seen in *Ch. Westcarrs Blue Minoru* and his C.C. winning sister Westcarrs Blue Minerva, and the Ch. litter sisters Lovely Lady of Glenmist and Pattingham Gay Lady of Glenmist.[1]

Eden Examine gave the breed yet another son, *Rimington Kittieholm Pilot* (ex Homeward Treasure), who has carried on the line through his son *Mywicks Monitor* (ex Rimington Panda), sire in his turn of the sable *Ch. Mywicks Meadow Lancer* (ex Shoinemaw Sheena), and Meadow Lancer sired *Ch. Rhodelands Boy* (ex Seftonian Sunshade) himself the sire of *Ch. Carramar Boy Blue* and his litter brothers *Carramar Blue Prince* and *Carramar Midnight Raider* (ex. Westcarrs Blue Myrobella), the latter the sire of *Ch. Lowerpark Black Buccaneer*, the only tricolour male Champion in the breed in Britain today.[2] *Meadow Lancer* also sired *Ch. Duntiblae Dog Watch* (exCh. Duntiblae Doorknocker), sire of *Ch. Ralvera's Meadow Marquis* (ex Ralvera's Meadow Maid) and the Champion daughters Swintonian Model, Inglebrooks Melody Mischief, Mywicks MyLady Fair, and the litter-sisters Ch. Mywicks Satine of Simbastar, Ch. Danvis Sheba of Simbastar and Ch. Deborah of Dunsinane.[3]

---

[1] The influence of *Blue Minoru* is still strong in the breed, for his son, *Ch. Bridholme Crosstalk Silver Rambler*, is sire of *Ch. Fourjoys Blue Danny*, and *Ch. Fourjoys Blue Minstrel of Whitelea*, and through *Lacemaker of Ladypark* he is four generations behind *Ch. Asoka Clayswood Blue Venture*, himself sire of two winning daughters.

[2] *Ch. Carramar Boy Blue* sired *Ch. Carramar Blue Tweed*, in turn sire of *Ch. Clickham Night Superior* who has a champion son in *Clickham Ciraveen Black Cavan.*

[3] Ch. Pattingham Peaceable and Ch. Deloraine Dinah-Mite. *Meadow Lancer* himself, though now dead, is still a big influence in the breed for he has two Champion sons, the litter brothers *Jefsfire Happy By Name* and *Jefsfire Lucky By Name* (ex Jefsfire Fashion), and another C.C. winning son in *Ares of Cressbrook* (ex Affinity of Cressbrook). The line to *Eden Examine* is again very much to the fore through a different branch. His son, *Abbot of Arranback*, gave *Dunsinane Alaric of Arranbeck*, and in direct line from him comes *Ch. Defender of Dunsinane*, sire of *Ch. Dorgano Demander of Dunsinane* who sired *Dazzler of Dunsinane*, sire of *Ch. Royal Ace of Rokeby* (and his Champion sister Romney of Rokeby) as well as the *Ch. Ramsey of Rokeby* (ex Ch. Romney). *Ch. Royal Ace* is sire of *Ch. Dorgano Double Ace of Rokeby*, whilst *Ramsey* has produced *Ch. Shane of Skellvale*, and his C.C. winning brother

Returning to Educator's other son, *Eden Electron*, we find the line which has given a number of the Scots champions and C.C. winners. Electron sired *Bruce of Waldemar* (ex Pelton Blue Frisetta) and his son *Waldo of Waldemar* (ex Seedley Ideal by Ch. Seedley Sepia) sired the gorgeous headed *Ch. Chapelburn Ivor* (ex Chapelburn Golden Gleam). Ivor could undoubtedly have been of even more value to the breed had he carried a little more body and bone behind his lovely head. Nevertheless he sired two Champion sons in *Helengowan Superior* and *Helengowan Starboy*, both ex Helengowan Shirley but from different litters.

Waldo also claims two other sons of note in the Chapelburns, *Stormer* (ex Chapelburn Pansy) and *Ronald* (ex Backwoods Flower Girl by Backwoods Flutter). Stormer sired *Ch. Netherkeir Dulwych Diolite* (ex Dulwych Debutante by Chapelburn Ronald) and *Laund Dewshill Banner* (ex Dulwych Lassie also by Ronald), who was the sire of *Ch. Laund Ebony of Killartry*, another who crossed the Atlantic after gaining his title here. Ronald sired *Ch. Dewshill Dynamite* (ex Chapelburn Morag by Stormer), so it will be seen how successful the intermingling of the blood of these two half-brothers proved to be.

Electron's other son, *Blue Mischief*, established a line, through Hewburn Blue Boy, which produced a number of Smooth champions.

And so the story reaches the present day, with sons of these champions now beginning to make their mark, and their history will write new pages in the Collie chronicles.

---

*Rossheath Seeker of Skellvale* and two more champion sons, *Ch. Rauno of Rokeby* and *Ch. Geoffdon Westlynns Wayside Boy*. Royal Ace has three more champion sons, *Ch. Jefsfire Falkenor of Joywil* and *Chs. Bririch Gold Edition* and *Gold Emblem*, the latter now in U.S.A. *Ch. Jefsfire Lucky By Name* is sire of *Ch. Thistleblue Bluelands Boy*.

# CHAPTER 3

# THE GREAT ONES OF THE PAST
# AND OF TODAY

## *Female Line*

IT is more than unfortunate that the first serious attempt to classify the families in our breed was only made in 1949, for by then many of the roots of the families were lost in the mists of the past. Had registration always been compulsory, matters would be quite simple today, but, as has already been said, this was not so, and to complicate matters still further, until quite recent years it was possible to change completely the registered name of a dog, so that he no longer bore any resemblance to himself, or provided any clues as to his origin! Except for Family 1, which we have fortunately been able to trace back to its known beginnings in approximately 1860, the other families all fall more or less short. It is almost certain that there are NOT 14 families in the breed, and several of those listed may prove to be a branch of one of the other families, if only the necessary extensions of pedigree can be found. If the publication of this book leads to any more information being discovered it will be received most gratefully by the author.

Possibly because of 'blanks' in the other families, Family 1 appears to be the most prolific in producing C.C. winners. Starting from a bitch, *Fly*, born about 1860, who produced a great-great-grand-daughter, *Eva* (1878) (by Tricolour).

*Eva* has an astonishing number of winning descendants, and these stem from *Seedley Sagacity* (by Ch. Seedley Statesman). Sagacity, not in herself a winner of any note, was the dam of *Seedly Sombre* (by Ch. Seedley Sterling) and Sombre, mated back to her grandsire, Statesman, produced that tremendously prolific and wonderful bitch *Denny Lively Bird*, whose merits as a brood cannot be too loudly sung. To Ch. Poplar Perfection she had the sable and white *Denny Dinah*; from her, eight generations later, there stemmed directly another outstanding brood bitch in *Beulah's Night Black and*

*Beautiful* (by Am. Ch. Beulah's Silver Don Mario). Her two daughters' *Beulah's Nightglamorous* (by Beulah's Night-victorious), herself a C.C. winner, and *Beulah's Golden Kiska* (by Beulah's Golden Fanfarist by Ch. Backwoods Fanfare) have carried on the family. Nightglamorous had only two litters; and the first of these to Ch. Beulah's Golden Futureson gave us *Ch. Westcarrs Whitethroat*. Ch. Whitethroat's daughter, *Westcarrs Black Ballet* (by Ch. Westcarrs Whistler) produced *Westcarrs What* (by Ch. Legend of Ladypark) and she became the dam of *Ch. Duntiblae Doorknocker*, dam of Ch. Duntiblae Dog Watch. Her second, to Ch. Lochinvar of Ladypark, produced a Champion son in Westcarrs Whistler. Kiska, however, with more opportunities, has proved the more successful of the two, for she is the dam of *Ch. Beulah's Golden Flora* and her litter sister *Shiel's Beulah Nightflower* (by Ch. Beulah's Golden Futureson). The latter was the dam of *Ch. Beulah's Night-so-Neat* (by Shiel's Beulah's Golden Viceroy), but Flora goes down in history as the dam of Ch. Lochinvar of Ladypark (by Eden Examine). She has also produced a number of daughters who have carried the line down: *Linda of Ladypark* (by Eden Examine) who was dam of *Lucibel of Ladypark* (by Lupin of Ladypark); Lucibel produced two C.C. winning daughters in *Lucretia* and *Little Mary*, both of Ladypark and both by Ch. Lochinvar. These two bitches are, however, lost to us, for both left the country after each had won a certificate. Another daughter of Flora, *Lass of Ladypark* (by Eden Examine), produced *Levity of Ladypark* (by Ch. Chapelburn Ivor) and she was the dam of *Cathanbrae Gaiety* (by Lumley of Ladypark) who in turn was the dam of *Ch. Prue's Golden Regina* (by Shiel's Beulah's Golden Viceroy).

Returning to yet another daughter of Denny Lively Bird, *Denny Darkie* (by Seedley Secure), we find a line which, six generations later, gave *Miss Muffet of Faux* (by Netherkeir George) who was responsible for three daughters of note, *Mignon, Maureen and Miss Mischief*, all of Faux and litter-sisters (by Masterpiece of Faux). Maureen is the dam of *Lassie's Return* (by Chapelburn Ronald) who was dam of *Ch. Selstoma Whitelea Wildcat* (by Rimington Kittieholm Pilot by Eden Examine), *Whitelea Winniepoo* (by Stantree Squire) who was dam of *Ch. Hewburn Irene* (by Longmeadow Lancer), and

*Whitelea Wyne*, litter-sister to Winniepoo, who was the dam of *Ch. Whitelea Why Gal* (by Whitelea Why Lad). *Miss Mischief of Faux* had two daughters who carry on in *Moselass of Faux* (by Hawkridge White Eagle by Masterpiece of Faux) and *Alphington Glamour* (by Ch. Alphington Achievement). Alphington Glamour was dam of *Helengowan Shirley* (by Air Commander) whose daughter, *Helengowan Sequence* (by Ch. Chapelburn Ivor), gave us *Ch. Campsieglen Wendy* (by Lyncliffe Lancer). A litter-sister of Sequence, *Helengowan Sapphire*, was dam of the C.C. winner *Hallmarsh Bloom* (by Meanwood Magnate).

Back now to Denny Lively Bird's third daughter, *Eden Emily* (by Ch. Laund Limit by Ch. Parbold Picador), and we find a further branch of this family still strongly represented today. Emily had two noteworthy daughters, the lovely *Ch. Eden Elenora* (by Ch. Eden Extra), a sable and white excelling in almost all points, and her sister, *Eden Embrace*, who is ten generations behind *Danethorpe Laugh of Ladypark*, dam of *Ch. Pattingham Lullaby* and *Ch. Pattingham Prelude*, the latter, in her turn, dam of *Ch. Pattingham Pheasant*. Laugh also gave *Pattingham Polka* (by Pattingham Kismet), dam of the Champion litter sisters, *Deloraine Decorative* and *Distinctive*, the latter, in her turn, dam of *Ch. Clanayre Chiffon Princess*. Ch. Elenora gave the breed the beautiful dog Ch. Eden Emerald (her son by Ch. Poplar Perfection) and his litter-sister *Ch. Eden Enrapture*, but Enrapture does not figure in the lines today. However, there was an older sister of these two, *Ch. Eden Etiquette*, whose direct descendants carry on today, and yet another daughter of Eleanora in *Eden Esme* from whom, in direct female descent, we have today *Ch. Shearcliffe Golden Queen* (by Lyncliffe Loadstar by Lyncliffe Landseer).

Family 2, as already mentioned, starts with the unregistered *Billesley Bluey*, and continues for eight generations without doing anything very startling, and then produced that absolute gem of a brood bitch the C.C. winner *Westcarrs Blue Moon* (by Lucas of Sedgemoor). Blue Moon, a beautifully coloured blue merle bitch, must be regarded as a pillar of the breed. Her daughters, the sisters (from different litters) *Westcarrs Blue Moonlight* and *Westcarrs Blue Minuet* (by Ashtead Blue Ensign), have both a share in today's winners, but the most outstanding of all was yet a third sister, *Blue Dawn*. Dawn's daughter *Blue Poppy* (by Backwoods Fireman by

Backwoods Feature) was the dam of the strongest links in the chain, *Backwoods Flower Girl* and *Silver Bouquet* (both by Ch. Backwoods Flutter). Flower Girl, through her daughter *Chapelburn Heatherbell* (by Waldo of Waldemar), was the grand-dam of the three good winner-producing sisters (by Chapelburn Ronald) *Dulwych Lassie, Dulwych Debutante* and *Alphington Sally.* Debutante's daughter, *Dulwych Decorous* (by Chapelburn Stormer), produced *Ch. Helengowan Cornriggs Catriona*, and Decorous' litter-sister gave *Netherkeir Dulwych Dancing Lady* and her brother Netherkeir Dulwych Diolite, both of whom gained their titles. From *Alphington Sally's* daughter *Alphington Lass* (by Alphington Shepherd's Boy), are descended directly *Ch. Mywicks Fashioness* (by Eden Examine) and *Ch. Ugony's Golden Fablelita* (by Ralda's Beulah's Golden Fable).

*Silver Bouquet* was dam of two daughters who carry on the family, *Silver Emblem* (by Radiant Knight) and *Radiant Princess* (by Round Robin). The most important of these is Emblem, who produced *Mystic Maid* (by Round Robin). Mystic Maid, mated to Air Commander, gave *Laird's Rose*, who gave the breed two Champion daughters in one litter, *Chs. Maid* and *Rose of Ladypark* (by Ch. Lochinvar of Ladypark), and their Champion brother Ch. Laird's Galway Sun. *Ch. Rose of Lady-park* was dam of the unfortunate Ch. Rifflesee Resplendence (by Ch. Lad of Ladypark) and *Maid* is dam of Ch. Legend of Ladypark and grand-dam of Ch. Loyal of Ladypark, also by Ch. Lochinvar. Rose also produced the Champions *Rifflesee Regality of Dunsinane* and *Rifflesee Reward of Glenmist* and she in turn produced two champion daughters, the litter-sisters *Sapphire* and *Sceptre of Glenmist* (by Ch. Liberty of Ladypark).[1]

Family 3 starts with yet another unregistered bitch, *Leila*, born about 1890, and passes through no fewer than 16 generations before a bitch, *Redevalley Dinkie*, who makes ripples on the surface of the pond, is born. Dinkie produced two daughters, the sisters *Redevalley Rosette* and *Warbreck Blue Bubble* (by Blue Mischief). Rosette, mated to Waldorn of Waldemar, whelped that lovely tricolour bitch *Ch. Bapchild Floss.* I personally consider her the best tricolour bitch we have had

---

[1] Their younger sister is *Ch. Spellbinder of Glenmist.* Sapphire, in her turn, has produced the champion daughters *Pattingham Gay Lady of Glenmist* (by Rifflesee Royalist), and her sister, *Lovely Lady of Glenmist.*

since the war. Unfortunately Floss proved a very doubtful breeder and left little progeny of note. In another litter, Rosette produced *Longscar Luscious* (by Rex of Grenoside) and she was the dam of *Waitress of Wearmouth* (by Longscar Leader). Waitress is the dam of *Whatagirl* (by Wearmouth Lucky Lukey of Ladypark) who gave the C.C. winner *Whatabird of Wearmouth* (by Whataspec of Wearmouth) and a Champion son, Whatastar of Wearmouth (by Lucky Laddie of Rokertop).

Rosette's other daughter, *Warbreck Blue Bubble*, produced four daughters, each of whom have played a part in carrying on the line, and from Blue Bubble we have today in direct descent *Ch. Lyncliffe Lucinda* and *Ch. Raybreck Golden Gloria*.

Family 4 again starts with an unregistered bitch, *Yieldshields Bute*, and again proceeds through many generations (13, to be exact) to produce *Biddy of Daddystown* (by Golden Rufus). Biddy, an Irish bitch, is dam of four bitches who have each played a useful part. First, the C.C. winner, *Lass of Daddystown* (by Jerry's Choice), then *Eden Edwina* (by Killartry Rex) and her sisters, *Mariemeau Colleen* and *Eden Epaulette*. Lass, mated to Don of Oldpark, produced *Foxlyn Poppy of Daddystown*, who died of poison soon after winning her first C.C. Colleen produced two C.C. winning daughters, *Mariemeau Maureen* and *Crystal of Mariemeau*, both by Thane of Mariemeau but from different litters. Edwina gave *Eden Engraving of Shoinemaw* (by Eden Extra Model) and she in turn whelped the very nice *Shoinemaw Sheena* (by Lyncliffe Thyland Lad) and Sheena is the dam of the sensational young dog Ch. Mywicks Meadow Lancer (by Mywicks Monitor by Rimington Kittieholm Pilot).[1] Eden Epaulette, gave *Black Ricky* (by Alstonian's Normington) dam of *Silver Flame* (by Blue Boy) and *Ch. Crosstalk Silver Belle*, dam of the C.C. winning sisters, *Kingsville Corviross Gay Silver* and *Corviross Silver Joy*, dam of *Ch. Tilehouse Thistle*, whilst Gay Silver produced *Dream Baby of Kingsville*.

*Ladysmith*, also unregistered, starts Family 5. She was the great-grand-dam of that beautiful star of the past, *Ch. Seedley Sapphire* (by Ch. Parbold Picador), and Sapphire, in her turn, was grandmother of *Sweet Mary* (by Parbold Pierrot) who was

---

[1] Engraving's other daughter *Shoinemaw Sheila* (by Eden Excellent) was grand-dam of *Sheildon Shani*, dam of *Mywicks Sheildon Marigold* (by Ch. Mywicks Meadow Lancer) dam of *Mywicks Mylady Fair* (also by Ch. Meadow Lancer).

dam of *Hallwood Serene* (by Ch. Seedley Stirling). Serene had two daughters, both by Ch. Magnet, *Hallwood Secret* and *Hallwood Secure*. Secure was dam of *Ch. Laund Laud* (by Almondbank Bummer by Ch. Seedley Stirling) and Laud's descendant, in the seventh generation, is *Old Mill Duchess* (by Bruce of Waldemar). Duchess had two daughters, sisters, by Blue Mischief, *Redevalley Freda* and *Redevalley Favourite*. Of these only Freda need concern us; her daughter *Redevalley Rita* (by Eden Electrician) produced *Danvis Favourite* and this bitch bred on in the following manner—her daughter *Danvis Delta* (by Longscar Leader) produced *Ch. Danvis Deborah* (by Ch. Gunner of Mariemeau), and Deborah was dam of *Danvis Daytime* (by Ch. Cezar of Corbieux), and, in one litter, of *Ch. Danvis Dyllorna* and her C.C. winning sisters *Danvis Devotion* and *Lottery of Ladypark* and their C.C. winning brother Danvis Diadem! It is sad that both Daytime and Dyllorna left this country for Italy after gaining their titles but at least Dyllorna left a very lovely pair of daughters to take over from her.[1]

*Hallwood Secret*, through her daughter *Hallwood Shine* (by Craigside Chieftain), had two grand-daughters *Hallwood Serf* and *Hallwood Sensitive* (both by Ch. Eden Extra) and these two shoots still produce C.C. winners today.

Another most important family is Family 10. It is all wrong that this family, too, cannot be traced to its source, for *Mountshannon Mona*, the latest source to which it can at present be taken, was born as recently as 1918. Mona is only four generations behind the great bitch *Ch. Backwoods Folio* (by Ch. Freshfield Freedom), and Folio's daughter, *Backwoods Florabella* (by Backwoods Feature), produced *Beulah's Golden Florida*, responsible for so much that was good in the Beulah strain. Florida (by Backwoods Farrier) produced *Ch. Beulah's Golden Feather* (by Beulah's Night Mail) and Feather's daughter, *Beulah's Golden Fantasy* (although she left this country while still fairly young, to go to Sweden), holds an exceptionally strong place in this line. She was mated twice to Beulah's Nightvictorious, the first time producing *Ch. Beulah's Night Fame* and *Beulah's Night Flare*, and a year later *Beulah's Nightvivid*. Flare became the

---

[1] Delta's other daughter *Danvis Daphne* produced the champion *Danvis Deanna* (by Danvis Diadem) and through her became grand-dam of *Ch. Danvis Derna* (by Laudable of Ladypark).

dam of that amazingly successful brood bitch *Lilac of Ladypark*
(by Maroel Blue Mandarin) and Lilac's C.C. winning descendants are almost legion. Starting with two Champion
daughters, *Ch. Lena of Ladypark* (by Lucky of Ladypark) and
*Ch. Silvaseabear from Shiel* (by Westcarrs Black Bisley), she also
gave us another daughter in each of these litters, *Letty*, sister
to Lena, and *Lobelia of Ladypark*, sister to Silvaseabear, who have
both carried on the family as well as their more illustrious sisters.

*Ch. Lena* had a Champion daughter, *Lilt of Ladypark*, one of
the best bitches of recent years, and two Champion sons in the
same litter, by Ch. Lochinvar. *Lobelia of Ladypark*, in her first
litter, produced the C.C. winning blue merle *Westcarrs Blue
Minerva* and her Champion brother Westcarrs Blue Minoru.
*Ch. Silvaseabear*, in each of three litters, produced at least one
C.C. winning daughter, *Silvaseagull from Shiel* (by Beulah's
Silver Don Mero), *Silvastarjoy* and *Silvastartime from Shiel* (by
Ch. Sombresextens from Shiel) and *Silvacymbal from Shiel* (by
Ch. Westcarrs Blue Minoru). *Silvaseagull*, in her first litter,
whelped *Ch. Silvasceptre from Shiel* (by Ch. Westcarrs Blue
Minoru). Minerva, mated to Mywicks Monitor, gave the
Champion bitch, *Westcarrs Blue Mygirl*.

One thing which strikes one very forcibly is how few, comparatively, of the Champion bitches of the breed are playing a
part in carrying on; so often it is the less glamorous sister, or
near relation of the Champion, who has had the bigger part
to play. The unusual situation arose recently when *Leecroft Ladyfair* produced three Champion daughters in one litter, *Mywicks
Satine of Simbastar*, *Danvis Sheba of Simbastar* and *Deborah of Dunsinane* (by Ch. Mywicks Meadow Lancer). This poses a little
problem! For, tracing back fourteen generations in tail female,
one comes to *Kinnersley Allegro* (by Ch. Magnet ex *Seedley
Lassie*, who was unregistered) and here I am faced with a blank
wall and do not know into which family to tie these children!

*Note.* Family 13, which, in the past, has never been very prolific, has, in recent
years, burst to life, particularly in giving the breed so many Champion bitches. In
direct descent we have, *Ch. Sudborough Lochdorna*, her daughters Ch. *Girley of Whitelea*
and Ch. *Whitelea Watastra* and her daughter Ch. *Jefsfire Amber Linnet* had two Champion daughters in Ch. *Jefsfire Tudor Queen* and Ch. *Jefsfire Phares Forever Amber*. Other
branches gave us Ch. *Antoc Daydream*, Ch. *Jefsfire Joyous Jodie* and *Witchcraft of
Rokeby* with her numerous Champion and C.C. winning descendants, particularly
Ch. *Romney of Rokeby*. (It should be noted that, in the 5th edition, Romney's
Family was given, in error, as F.2.)

Ch. Anfield Model
*Born 1902*

Ch. Squire of Tytton
*Born 1904*

*T. Baker*

Ch. Blue Princess Alexandra
*Born 1907*

Ch. Ormskirk Foxall
*Born 1907*

AND HIS SON

*Baskerville*

Parkside Pro Patria
*Born 1910*

# CHAPTER 4

## THE BLUE MERLE

ALTHOUGH of such special interest as to demand a chapter of its own, the blue merle must never be regarded as 'separate' from the other colours. All are Collies, divided only by coat colour, and, in my opinion, it is the greatest possible mistake to offer separate C.C.s for blue merles, separated from tricolours and sables—which are classed together, as happens in France, for instance.

The blue merle is, in fact, one of the commonest original colours of the Sheepdog. In the mid-nineteenth century this colour was very ordinary, and merle Sheepdogs were found in all parts of England.

It is a pity that the original name of the colour—'marled' —ever became changed to the word we know today, for 'marle', a corruption of marbled, so exactly describes the desired markings. A merle, on the other hand, is a blackbird!

The perfect blue merle should be of silvery blue in colour, dappled and splashed with black, nowhere in large spots. The collar, chest, feet, legs and tail tip may be white, and there may or may not be a white blaze. The blue merle should carry the bright tan markings in the places in which we normally expect these in a tricolour. The eyes of a blue merle may be blue, either or both, or part of either or both.

To me the blue merle colour is the most attractive of all, and fascinating, both to the geneticist and to the practical breeder. The blue merle pattern is a modification of black due to the presence of the dilution factor, and to the granules of pigmentation in each hair being less numerous than in the dog of whole colour, and it is also due to the fact that the granules of pigmentation are arranged in a particular pattern in each hair. For this reason the *real* blue merle is a difficult colour to achieve in perfection, and probably because of the difficulty it presents such a fascinating task to undertake.

The blue merle pattern cannot appear unless at least one parent is a blue merle. (It should, however, be stated here that

D

two sables, mated together, when both happen to be carrying the merling or dilution factor recessively, have been known to produce mottled dogs but these cannot be described as *blue* merle as they are usually of very poor colour.) The *blue* merle pattern cannot appear unless the bi-colour (black and tan pattern) is present, for the dilution factor *must* work on the bi-colour to produce the blue merles.

As has already been said, the blue merle colour is one of the very oldest in the Collie breed and blue dogs were frequently seen on farms as companions and workers. Possibly this was the reason—because they were considered 'common' —that merle Collies almost entirely disappeared from the show-ring, puppies of this colour being drowned at birth. Thus the colour became almost extinct, and if it had not been for the efforts of a few stalwarts who, in the latter part of the nineteenth century, set about resuscitating this colour, we should almost certainly have no blue merle Collies today.

We still have a long way to go in establishing the perfect colour—and much can be learned from the famous merle fanciers of the past. The foremost of these was, undoubtedly, Mr. W. Arkwright.

Mr. W. Arkwright's Kennel was dispersed as long ago as 1890, but he had, at that time, the most outstanding strain of the colour known, and it is doubtful if it has since been equalled. His dogs were of exceptional colour, the true silvery blue, with tan and white markings. He bred scientifically, with one end in view—the perpetuation of the clarity of colour, and the improvement of type. He contended that the GOOD blues came from the mating of merles with tricolours, and that the BEST blues were produced from the mating of blue merles with black and tans. Unfortunately this latter mating is denied us, as black and tan Collies are extinct today.

Mr. Arkwright did not like the mating of merle with sable; he found that this gave muddy coloured merles and bad coloured sables, often with blue eyes, but he, and the other breeders of that time, occasionally had to practise such a mating, for the sables were undoubtedly far superior in type, and the majority of blues and a good many tricolours lagged sadly behind.

As we no longer have to admit that the sables are superior

to the merles or tris, it would be to the lasting improvement of the blue merles if the merle x sable mating in our breed was entirely abandoned.

Sable x merle always has produced, and always will, rusty coloured merles and blue-eyed sables, albeit not in the first generation perhaps, but that anathema, the blue-eyed sable, may crop up in succeeding generations. The blue-eyed sable, being genetically a merle, can produce merles when mated to any colour, but it is nevertheless to be abhorred.

The mating of merle x merle is sometimes carried out, and often most successfully indeed, but herein lies a danger—the production of defective white puppies wholly white or in part, puppies born blind or deaf, or both, and, carried to extremes, puppies born with deformed eyes or no eyes at all.

The breeder who mates merle to merle where the resultant litter will have three or more merle grandparents, is taking a risk somewhat beyond the bounds of safety, but it is a mating which frequently produces winners! The defective whites born from such double merle matings usually find their way into the bucket, but the blue-eyed whites could prove most useful, for, mated to tricolours, they frequently produce merles of singular colour excellence.

.    .    .    .    .

The beginnings of the blue merle as a show dog are fairly clear-cut, except that, in the early days, the colour of the dogs used to produce the true blue colour were frequently differently described in different places, though the same dog was being referred to!

For example, the first sire of any note in the production of the blue merles was a dog named *Scott*, the property of Mr. F. B. Brackenburg, of Downham, Norfolk. *Scott* is officially recognized in the K.C.S.B. as being grey, tan and white in colour, with china eyes, yet Mr. Arkwright's description of him is that of the perfect blue merle, 'Silvery blue, beautifully clouded with black, white collar, chest, feet and tail-tip, with one blue eye'. *Scott* was a very typical Collie of his day and did his share of winning. Mr. Arkwright tried to buy him and when he failed he mated his bitch *Russet* to him. Now 'Russet' is described by Mr. Packwood as 'red sable' but in the K.C.S.B. as 'red grizzle' and for myself I am inclined to think that this latter description is probably the true one and that, in reality, she was a sable merle. Be that as it may, the progeny of 'Scott' and 'Russet' virtually laid the foundation of the early blue merles.

*Ch. Blue Ruin* added considerably to blue merle history when, in 1888, at the Kennel Club Show, at the age of four years, she won the Collie Club Trophy for the best of breed, and thus became the first blue merle ever to reach the top in open competition with the other colours.

She is described as being 'a beautiful colour, and in all respects a lovely Collie, so shapely that when out of coat she could have been a Champion Smooth!' Two years after this great feat America claimed her, but she did leave some progeny behind.

Although Mr. Arkwright's was the premier name in blue merles he was not alone, for Mr. J. A. Doyle was a keen supporter of the colour, but he helped more by guaranteeing blue merle classes at the shows than as an exhibitor. Mr. S. Boddington was also a keen merle fan, and whilst Mr. J. Power's name is more often associated with the other colours, he had in *Barwell Lass* a fine example of a merle among his early exhibits.

Unfortunately for this colour, Mr. Arkwright decided to concentrate on his Sporting Dogs and on April 17, 1890, his entire Kennel of Collies was sold at auction and the dogs dispersed all over England.

For a while the blue merles were in the doldrums, and practically none of this colour was ever seen in the ring. However, the Birmingham breeders began a revival and Mr. F. Barlow (Yardley) secured a dog of Mr. Arkwright's breeding, *Blue Devils* (by Blue Sky ex Blue Blazes), to assist in the resurrection of the colour. Bitches, both sables and tris, were mated to him, the blue merles retained and then bred again to the best type dogs in the other colours, and so gradually the colour came back and the type improved.

Mr. A. C. Thompson was among those whose blue merles achieved much success and a bitch of his breeding, *Blue Fancy*, became the foundation bitch of Mr. C. H. White's Kennel, and Mr. White will be remembered as the breeder of *Blue Princess Alice* and *Blue Princess Alexandra*, the latter probably one of the best 'broken-up' merles we have ever seen.

In the early years of this century another who made a great contribution to the blue merle ranks was Mr. H. E. Packwood, whose 'Billesley' prefix became a byword in the colour and whose *Billesley Bluey* is the foundation bitch of today's Family 2.

In 1907 the lovers of the colour got together and established the Rough Blue Merle Collie Club. The Club undoubtedly justified its existence, many new recruits to the merle ranks being enrolled. The Club decided to hold its annual show in conjunction with the Birmingham National and the first of these was held in January, 1910, when the winners were, in dogs, Mr. W. L. Tippett's *Typewriter* and in bitches Mr. H. E. Packwood's *Billesley Blue Blossom*.

The Hon. Secretary of the Club, Mr. H. C. Hill, as was to be expected, was a blue merle enthusiast and he owned, among others, *Southport Gray Charmer* (by Master Merledale ex Edgebaston Ena—by Ch. Squire of Tytton). This bitch was purchased by Mr. Mason for export to America, but before leaving the country Mr. Mason bred a litter from her, by Master Willie, and among the pups was *Southport Blue Star* and this dog established a great step forward in blue merles. Fortunately he remained in this country, for Mrs. Hume-Robertson (Porchester) recognized his attractions and bought him, and in his very first litter he sired the great dog *Ch. Porchester Blue Sol* (ex Porchester Grania). Blue Sol most definitely put the blue merles right on the same plane as the other colours, and most of today's winners can be traced back to him, either directly or indirectly.

Mr. Tait, too, fell victim, and the Wishaw prefix came to be associated with the blues, the best probably being *Ch. Wishaw Blue Lettie*.

The Seedleys also claimed their share of merles, and Mr. Lord's skill as a breeder gained great success. The best known of his winners was *Ch. Seedley Blue Sky*.

This brings us to the outbreak of the First World War, and gradually the Blue Merle cult declined, but in the early years after the war the Rev. T. Salter took great interest and the 'Mountshannons' started to make their mark. Miss Daisy Miller with her Gypsyvilles had a big part to play and her dog *Knight o' Blue Mist* (by Gypsy James ex Gypsy Blue Peggy) sired a number of litters of excellent colour. Knight o' Blue

Mist was a long way removed from being a good Collie, for he had a dense, curly coat, very reminiscent of the old English Sheepdog, and he was short tailed, but whatever we may say about him he was almost entirely responsible for the resurrection of the blue merles after the First World War, and had it not been for him it is extremely doubtful if the breed would know this lovely colour today. Mr. E. C. Pierce, with his Eltham Parks, helped the colour along and Miss I. Jones established a blue merle Treffynon line with the purchase of Eltham Park Blue Blossom.

So the showing and breeding of blue merles crept up again in the early '20s, and the first blue merle to become a Champion after the war was the Rev. T. Salter's *Ch. Mountshannon Blue Splendour* who gained his title in 1925.

In 1927 Mr. and Mrs. Pyle bred *Ch. Glenack Kingfisher* and his name occurs at least once in almost every blue merle pedigree today. Miss Molony's Westcarrs prefix became associated with the colour, and a little later also Mrs. George's Beulah. At the L.K.A. show in 1929 *Westcarrs Blue Moon* won the bitch C.C. To this daughter of Lucas of Sedgemoor and Westcarrs Blue Mascot must go the greatest possible credit, for no fewer than 32 of our post-war C.C. winners, including the present-day Westcarrs and Shiel blue merles, trace their pedigrees direct to Blue Moon.

The first blue merle Beulah Champion in Mrs. George's ownership was *Ch. Beulah's Silver Merienda* (Ch. Backwoods Flutter ex Beulah's Silver Tern by Ch. Glenack Kingfisher) who goes down in history as the dam of that pillar of the breed, and cornerstone of post-war blue merle breeding, Beulah's Nightvictorious by Beulah's Nightshadowing. Merienda's sister, *Beulah's Silver Marina*, also achieved her title in the ownership of Mrs. Pleydell-Bouverie, beating her sister in the race for the honour.

1939 saw the end of Championship shows for another seven years; the Kennel Club did not restrict breeding, as it had done in the earlier conflict, but left the matter to the good sense of the breeders themselves.

When shows started again blue merles were indeed in a sorry state; in fact, once again almost extinct, and probably numerically even less strong than in the early '20s. Mr. and

Mrs. Cliffe had *Ch. Lyncliffe Blue Lady*, but as she was born in 1940 she was already getting on when showing was resumed in 1946, and she was practically the only blue seen in the ring at that time. However, one or two stalwarts, notably Miss Molony, Mrs. George and myself, did their best to re-establish colour. The first months of 1949 were epoch-making for the blues as two 'history-making' litters were born in this period. The one, in my own Kennel, by Westcarrs Black Bisley ex Lilac of Ladypark, produced the first post-war-bred blue merle Champion in my *Ch. Silvaseabear from Shiel*, and her litter-sister, *Lobelia of Ladypark*, who became the foundation bitch of the post-war blue Westcarrs. Three months earlier Mrs. George had bred a litter by Beulah's Silver Don Glorio ex Beulah's Nightvivid which produced *Ch. Beulah's Silver Don Marjo*, *Ch. Beulah's Silver Medialuna*, *Ch. Beulah's Silver Mantilla* and the C.C. winner *Beulah's Silver Don Mero*.

Another bitch to which great credit is due is the unshown *Lilac of Ladypark* by Maroel Blue Mandarin ex Beulah's Night Flare by Beulah's Nightvictorious. As a tiny puppy Lilac was savaged by her mother, and of the whole litter Lilac was the only survivor. But as a result of this attack her beauty was spoilt. She was bumpy in the head where her skull had been cracked, but this glorious coloured blue merle became the dam of two Champions and has a further 15 champion or C.C. winning descendants. Many of her descendants are sable, as one of her Champion daughters, the lovely *Ch. Lena of Ladypark* (by Lucky of Ladypark), was a sable and white.

Miss Molony mated *Lobelia of Ladypark* to Rifflesee Royalist (by Ch. Lad of Ladypark ex Lilac's dam, Beulah's Night Flare) and this very nice piece of line-breeding gave us *Ch. Westcarrs Blue Minoru* and his C.C. winning litter-sister, *Westcarrs Blue Minerva*. There is no doubt that here is a merle line which is breeding on, for my Ch. Silvaseabear mated to Beulah's Silver Don Mero produced the C.C. winner *Silvaseagull from Shiel*, who in her turn when mated to *Ch. Westcarrs Blue Minoru* produced *Ch. Silvasceptre from Shiel*, and when *Ch. Silvaseabear* was mated to Minoru she produced *Silvacymbal from Shiel*, who, after winning a C.C. at the age of eight and a half months, was exported to the U.S.A. while Ch. Silvasceptre's younger sister is great-grand-dam of Moondrift of Dunsinane. *Minerva*, mated to Mywicks Monitor, produced two more illustrious blue merles the litter brother and sister Westcarrs Blue Myboy and Ch. Westcarrs Blue Mygirl. Both these, however, have left these shores, the former for America, the latter for Sweden.

Whilst not wanting to appear to dwell too much on my own stock, I would like to stress very strongly the great influence of the tricolour dog *Beulah's Nightvictorious* on the post-war blue merles. Those of us who were courageous enough to line- and in-breed to him reaped a great reward. I need only state that Nightvictorious was the sire of *Westcarrs Black Bisley* and *Beulah's Nightvivid* and grandsire of *Lilac of Ladypark, Rifflesee Royalist* and *Ch. Sombresextens from Shiel* (to whom Ch. Silvaseabear produced two more C.C. winning daughters), and great grandsire of *Beulah's Silver Don Glorio*, for us to understand the debt owing to this little-shown 'war baby'. Nightvictorious was a most glorious-headed dog, excelling in expression, and coming very close to Mr. Arkwright's ideal black and tan, for his white was not very evident!

As a result of these two 1949 litters the future of the blue merles was assured. Yet another bitch from Mrs. George's litter, *Beulah's Silver Magdala*, mated to *Ch. Dewshill Dynamite*, produced *Ch. Tideswell Blue Prince* and his litter-sister, *Danethorpe Silver Dell*, whilst Mr. Underwood claims another blue merle Champion in *Ch. Danethorpe Silver Dew*.

The blue merle wheel turned full circle when Miss Molony's *Ch. Westcarrs Blue Minoru* captured the British Collie Club Trophy (late the Collie Club Trophy) for best of breed at the British Collie Club Show in March, 1955. Was this the first time since the day of *Ch. Blue Ruin* in 1888 that this trophy had been won by a merle?

# CHAPTER 5

# THE STANDARD AND ITS INTERPRETATION

THE FIRST standard for the Collie was drawn up in 1881 and revised in 1898 and 1910. In 1950, for the first time in the history of British dogdom, the Kennel Club published, officially, the standards for every breed, so, in that year, a further, revised standard came into being.

From that date it was impossible to make any alteration to a standard whatsoever, without permission of the Kennel Club, and this is only granted when there is a strong majority verdict among breed clubs, for some revision or clarification.

In the late 1950s it was felt that the standard for our breed would serve a far better purpose if it was somewhat amplified and clarified, and for the next ten years work on this idea was pursued until in February 1969 the Kennel Club finally approved the revised standard which is set out below.

This is, undoubtedly, the most important thing which has happened to the breed in the last fifty years.

### THE COLLIE STANDARD (COLLIE ROUGH)

*Reproduced by permission of the Kennel Club*

CHARACTERISTICS. To enable the Collie to fulfil a natural bent for sheepdog work, its physical structure should be on the lines of strength and activity, free from clodiness and without any trace of coarseness. Expression, one of the most important points in considering relative values, is obtained by the perfect balance and combination of skull and foreface; size, shape, colour and placement of eye, correct position and carriage of ears.

GENERAL APPEARANCE. The Collie should instantly appeal as a dog of great beauty, standing with impassive dignity, with no part out of proportion to the whole.

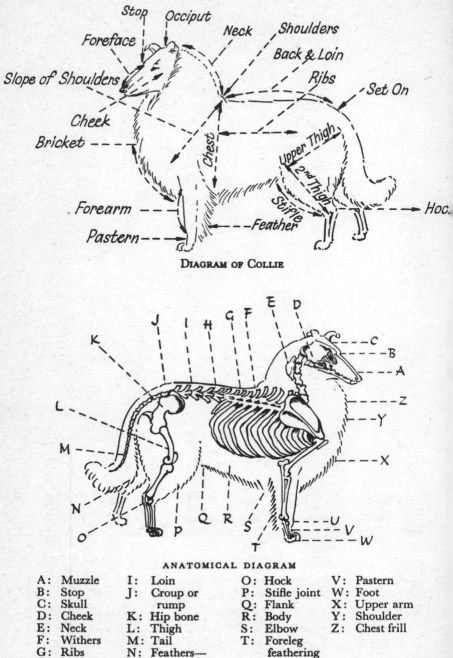

DIAGRAM OF COLLIE

ANATOMICAL DIAGRAM

| | | |
|---|---|---|
| A: Muzzle | I: Loin | O: Hock | V: Pastern |
| B: Stop | J: Croup or rump | P: Stifle joint | W: Foot |
| C: Skull | K: Hip bone | Q: Flank | X: Upper arm |
| D: Cheek | L: Thigh | R: Body | Y: Shoulder |
| E: Neck | M: Tail | S: Elbow | Z: Chest frill |
| F: Withers | N: Feathers— breeching | T: Foreleg feathering | |
| G: Ribs | | U: Knee | |
| H: Back | | | |

HEAD AND SKULL. The head properties are of great importance and must be considered in proportion to the size of the dog. When viewed from both front and profile the head bears a general resemblance to a well-blunted, clean wedge, being smooth in outline. The sides should taper gradually and smoothly from the ears to the end of the black nose, without prominent cheek bones or pinched muzzle. Viewed in profile, the top of the skull and the top of the muzzle lie in two parallel, straight planes of equal length, divided by a slight, but perceptible, 'stop' or break. A mid-point between the inside corners of the eyes (which is the centre of a correctly placed 'stop') is the centre of balance in length of head. The end of the smooth, well-rounded muzzle is blunt, but not square. The underjaw is strong, clean cut and the depth of the skull from the brow to the underpart of the jaw, must never be excessive (deep through). Whatever the colour of the dog, the nose must be black.

FIG. 1.—No stop. Roman nose

FIG. 2.—Pronounced stop. Receding skull

FIG. 3.—Correct head

EYES. These are a very important feature and give a sweet expression to the dog. They should be of medium size, set somewhat obliquely, of almond shape and of dark-brown colour, except in the case of blue merles when the eyes are frequently (one or both, or part of one or both) blue or blue flecked. Expression full of intelligence, with a quick, alert look when listening.

FIG. 4.—Correctly set eyes

FIG. 5.—Eye too light, small and mean    FIG. 6.—Eye too round

EARS. These should be small and not too close together on top of the skull, nor too much to the side of the head. When in repose they should be carried thrown back, but when on the alert brought forward and carried semi-erect, that is, with approximately two-thirds of the ear standing erect, the top third tipping forward naturally, below the horizontal.

FIG. 7.—Correct ears

FIG. 8.—Correct ears

FIG. 9.—Prick ears

FIG. 10.—Low-set ears

MOUTH. The teeth should be of good size, with the lower incisors fitting closely behind the upper incisors; a very slight space not to be regarded as a serious fault.

NECK. The neck should be muscular, powerful, of fair length and well arched.

FORE-QUARTERS. The shoulders should be sloped and well angulated. The fore-legs should be straight and muscular, neither in nor out at elbows, with a moderate amount of bone.

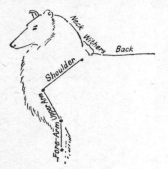

FIG. 11.—Correct lay-back of shoulders

FIG. 12.—Shoulder placement too steep, upper arm too short

BODY. The body should be a trifle long compared to the height, back firm with a slight rise over the loins; ribs well sprung, chest deep and fairly broad behind the shoulders.

FIG. 13.—Correct turn of stifle

FIG. 14.—Straight stifle

HIND-QUARTERS. The hind legs should be muscular at the thighs, clean and sinewy below, with well-bent stifles. Hocks well let-down and powerful.

FIG. 15.—Correct hock and
hindquarters

FIG. 16.—Cow-hocks;
narrow hindquarters

FEET. These should be oval in shape with soles well padded, toes arched and close together. The hind feet slightly less arched.

FIG. 17.—Correct foot          FIG. 18.—Weak, thin foot

GAIT. Movement is a distinct characteristic of this breed. A sound dog is never out at elbow, yet it moves with its front feet comparatively close together. Plaiting, crossing or rolling are highly undesirable. The hind legs, from the hock joint to the ground, when viewed from the rear, should be parallel. The hind legs should be powerful and full of drive. Viewed from the side the action is smooth. A reasonably long stride is desirable and this should be light and appear quite effortless.

TAIL. The tail should be long with the bone reaching at least to the hock joint. To be carried low when the dog is quiet, but with a slight upward swirl at the tip. It may be carried gaily when the dog is excited, but not over the back.

FIG. 19.—Correct tail carriage           FIG. 20.—Gay tail

COAT. The coat should fit the outline of the dog and be very dense. The outer coat straight and harsh to the touch, the undercoat soft, furry and very close; so close as to almost hide the skin. The mane and frill should be very abundant, the mask or face, smooth, also the ears at the tips, but they should carry more hair towards the base; the fore-legs well feathered, the hind legs above the hocks profusely so, but smooth below. Hair on the tail very profuse.

COLOUR. The three recognised colours are sable and white, tricolour and blue merle.

*Sable.* Any shade from light gold to rich mahogany or shaded sable. Light straw or cream colour is highly undesirable.

*Tricolour.* Predominately black with rich tan markings about the legs and head. A rusty tinge in the top coat is highly undesirable.

*Blue Merle.* Predominately clear, silvery blue, splashed and marbled with black. Rich tan markings to be preferred, but their absence should not be counted as a fault. Large black markings, slate colour, or a rusty tinge either of the top or undercoat are highly undesirable.

*White Markings.* All the above may carry the typical white Collie markings to a greater or lesser degree. The following markings are favourable—White collar, full or part; white shirt, legs and feet; white tail tip. A blaze may be carried on muzzle or skull or both.

WEIGHT AND SIZE. Dogs 22–24 in. at shoulder, bitches 20–22 in. Dogs 45–65 lb., bitches 40–55 lb.

FAULTS. Length of head apparently out of proportion to body; receding skull or unbalanced head to be strongly condemned. Weak, snipey muzzle; domed skull; high peaked occiput; prominent cheekbones; dish-faced or Roman nosed; undershot or overshot mouth; missing teeth; round or light coloured and glassy or staring eyes are highly objectionable. Body flat-sided, short or cobby; straight shoulder or stifle; out at elbow; crooked fore-arms; cow-hocks or straight hocks; large, open or hare feet; feet turned in or out; long, weak pasterns; tail short, kinked or twisted to one side or carried over the back; a soft, silky or wavy coat or insufficient undercoat; prick ears, low-set ears; nervousness.

Comparing this revised standard with that of 1950, it will immediately be noted that although most of the old wording has been retained, parts of it have been transposed so that they now fall under different headings. A big attempt was made to describe the head in much greater detail, and this, it will be found, now makes it very much easier to visualise the points of balance in the head, as well as, it is hoped, giving a very much clearer picture of the overall smoothness of the head, and especially stressing that the muzzle should be firm and well rounded and that the jaws should show no sign of weakness, particularly the underjaw, which, in previous standards, was never stressed at all, and which is certainly a very strong factor in giving perfect balance to the head.

E

The paragraph referring to eyes has been changed by the inclusion of one word—but, oh! what an important little word. The old standard read 'Eyes are a very important feature, and give expression to the dog' but it failed totally to say what kind of expression. The addition of the one little word 'sweet' before the word 'expression' has, undoubtedly, produced a very different picture. The only other additions here are a few words dealing with the permitted colour of the eyes of the blue merle.

Any deviation from the accepted shape, placement, size and colour of the eyes, is extremely important. The oblique set of the eyes is essential with a dog who bears a muzzle as long as that of the Collie, for if the eye is set in any other way the dog cannot have the benefit of full vision, and in this respect the almond shape of the eye also has an influence. A Collie with round, square-set eyes, can only see in a forward direction; unless these round eyes happen to be set far apart on the side of the head, which ruins the whole expression. Now, in the list of 'Faults' the word 'round' has been added and instead of the faults regarding eyes being seen as 'objectionable' they are now described as '*highly* objectionable'.

Little has been done with the paragraph relating to ears, except that, by describing the part which should be tipped over at the top as 'the top third tipping forward naturally' a guide line has been set up for judges who, in the past have found it difficult to decide just how much the ear should be tipped when it was described only by the words 'the tips slightly dropping'.

No alteration at all has been made to the paragraph on teeth, but missing teeth have been included in the Faults. In that which describes the neck the words 'and somewhat arched' have now been substituted by 'and well arched' which is surely a rather more definite term.

With reference to the body those rather vague words 'should be rather long' have now been deleted and the wording of 'should be a trifle long compared to the height' give a much clearer picture of the requisite balance required, and now, with the definite knowledge that the back should be 'firm, with a slight rise over the loin, there should no longer be any excuse for a 'sway-back', which has, in the past, sometimes been allowed to pass.

In earlier standards the description of the hind-quarters made no reference to the position of the hock, and the fact that reference to them was made in the description of feet seemed anatomically incorrect. The inclusion of the words 'Hocks well let-down and powerful' at the end of the paragraph on hind-quarters, gives a much better picture. The position of the hock is of extreme importance, for a dog in which the hock is placed too high, cannot get his hind legs sufficiently well under his body to enable him to produce the very strong drive from behind, required by a dog with shepherd work to do.

One very important addition to this new standard is the fact that, for the first time, the action of the Collie has been des-cribed, and I think, described so well, that there is little more which need be said to help clarify the definition.

At last the length of tail has been defined. The words 'moderately long' in the old standard could be interpreted so very differently by different judges, that they were almost useless, but now that we are told that 'The tail should be long with the bone reaching *at least* to the hock joint' there is no longer room for mis-interpretation . . . but some notice must be taken of the position of the hock, for if a dog has a hock placed much too high, then of course he does not need such a long tail to reach it!

In describing the coat the clause has been amplified. The addition of the words 'should fit the outline of the dog' are extremely important, for a coat which is too 'stand-off' makes a dog look short and cobby, when, in fact, he may not be so. The well-fitting coat, running smoothly back, and sweeping down over the loins to join the line of the tail, stresses the flowing lines required in the correct hind-quarters.

The old standard with its words 'Colour and markings are immaterial' were so misleading as to allow for a Collie of any colour whatsoever to be exhibited, had one had such a dog and wished to do so! At last the three colours have been defined, and defined clearly, so that there should now be no argument at all as to what each colour should really look like. The inclusion, under each colour heading of the most objectionable shades of each colour, now leaves no room for discussion. This, plus a clear word picture of the true white markings which are so typical of our breed, shows us exactly what our Collie should look like.

The paragraph on faults has been greatly extended. The

fact that the words 'head of Borzoi type to be strongly condemned' have now been omitted, is surely to be regretted, but
this was demanded by the Kennel Club who now no longer
wish that, in the standard of any breed, comparisons should be
made between one breed and another. Several faults, never
previously listed, though always frowned upon, have now been
included, and this should be a big help to judges who could, in
the past, have been accused of faulting a dog for something
which the standard did not state was a fault in the breed. The
inclusion of 'nervousness' as a fault is of great importance.

It will be most interesting to see what difference this much
clarified standard is going to make, and what influence it will
have on the future of the breed. Well interpreted I can only
think it can do nothing but good.

# CHAPTER 6

# HOW TO BEGIN

Dog breeding is really rather like swimming; there are three ways of going about it—you can be thrown in, fall in, or actually learn the subject properly! For purposes of this chapter I am going to assume that you have not already been thrown, or fallen, in but that you really want to learn the job thoroughly.

Assuming you have already made up your mind that it is Collies you want to breed, then, if you possibly can, spend six months at least as a trainee in a reputable Kennel of the breed, where you will have every opportunity to learn all you can about Collies. I say 'six months at least' for this is barely long enough as it does not give you time to carry through the rearing of even one litter, and the ideal period surely would be a year. Much can be learnt from books, but it is this practical experience which really counts.

It is not always easy in any breed to find the right Kennel, for you want to be sure it is one where the owner is willing to pass on his or her knowledge of the breed. Not only the practical knowledge of management, rearing and grooming, but—and almost more important—the knowledge of the strains and families within the breed, and a clear picture of the past which you, as a newcomer, can gain only by hearsay.

Rather naturally many breeders want to guard their secrets, but you must find one who has the interests of the future of the breed at heart, and whose only aim is not simply to defeat his fellows in the ring. There are breeders who can see far enough ahead and who are anxious that the work they have done shall be carried on when they can no longer do so themselves. It is in a Kennel such as this, and from this kind of breeder, that you want to learn. From someone who will help you to carry on where the present older generation of Collie breeders must, perforce, eventually leave off. Those breeders who want to see the Collie go forward will help you right enough. You will fairly easily discover to which of these groups a breeder belongs if you manage to ask a few questions.

For your part, there must be a great willingness to learn. There are many novices who start out asserting they are keen to learn, but who really only want to 'get there quickly' without putting in any ground work. A 'get there quick' plan is almost never a 'stay at the top' plan, and it is the consistent breeder who, from a small Kennel and a few brood bitches, turns out top-class winners year after year, and who has undoubtedly put the greatest amount of study, brain and common-sense into his breeding plan, who will consistently achieve top honours. Too much real knowledge and good hard spade work are needed in this dog business for anyone to stay at the top the easy way.

Remember, too, that if you are hoping to be able to learn by picking the brains of someone who has spent many years building up a successful strain, you are expecting to gain great assistance and privilege from this and on your side you must be ready to help in every possible way in the general daily routine of the Kennel. No job in the Kennel is too humble to be done well by you in your training. Kennel life is not all feeding and playing with puppies and taking dogs for walks. There are plenty of irksome chores to do and there are long hours; all-night sessions with a sick dog or a bitch giving birth to her puppies; there are late nights and early risings, but there are also new young hopes, and show-ring prizes and great satisfaction in the work. It is a job where one never ceases to learn. Even after years and years of breeding there is always something turning up.

Should you happen to be one of the few who can still afford to pay big prices for top-class winning stock, and should you go out and buy a certificate winning bitch and a Champion dog, it may avail you nothing except a few more prizes in the ring, for unless you have a deep-seated knowledge behind the purchase those two high-priced and beautiful animals will perhaps breed nothing better than pups for the pet market, whilst someone less well blessed with this world's goods, but with a great deal more knowledge of the strains and breeding programmes which have brought success, might produce next year's top dogs from parents hardly fit to grace the ring, and at a fraction of the cost of your big winners.

Your first task must be to read all you can, and especially about the standard of your chosen breed, and to learn to interpret that standard to the best of your ability. The standard is the yard-stick by which any specimen of a breed must be measured. Read it and read it and read it again—then go to a show, taking a copy of the standard with you for reference, and in your own mind line up each Collie you see against the 'mind-dog' you have drawn from the reading of the standard. Go to show after show, and at each of them ask question after question of established breeders. Do remember, though, that there is a time for all things, and don't expect the harassed exhibitor, arriving at the show with three or four Collies and having a bare thirty minutes in which to get them ready before the first class will be called into the ring, to be willing at that moment to answer your queries! No; in the morning, if Collies are first in the ring, wander round the benches if you will, but without interrupting hard work, look at the dogs and then take a seat at the ringside, and with your catalogue in your hand watch the judging intently. At the big Championship shows catalogues are expensive, but they are a 'must' to a would-be seeker after knowledge; you just cannot follow the judging without one.

When the judging is over the exhibitors will have time to help you, and I know they will be willing to do so. The judge, too (provided he is not rushing off to judge some other breed), will probably be only too pleased to explain his placings in a certain class if perhaps they have worried you. But again a word of warning. There are ways and ways of asking questions! The approach, 'I watched your judging; why did you put Mr. A's "Collie Frill" over Mrs. B's "Collie Flower"?' is much less likely to meet with a kind and helpful reply than: 'I am trying my hardest to learn about the breed before starting in Collies myself, and I was watching you judge. I wonder if you would mind telling me what you liked so much about Mr. A's "Collie Frill"?'

There are very few Collie breeders who will not be anxious to help you; most of us remember the days when we were beginners, too, and the questions we used to ask the then top-flight breeders.

Few of us these days have either the time or the money

to start with a lot of dogs, and anyway you are much more likely to achieve success if you start with one or two. Besides, the temptation to keep several puppies from your first litters is almost beyond resisting and so, in no time at all, you no longer have just one or two!

When choosing your stock, here again be prepared to put yourself in the hands of the established winning breeders. Ask to be allowed to visit the Kennels, explain that you haven't yet quite decided what stock you intend starting with, and go from Kennel to Kennel looking at the type and general standard of quality within each Kennel before you part with any of your precious cash. But, at the same time, don't expect us not to try to sell you something whilst you are there—we shouldn't be human if we didn't!

You will note that between the different Kennels and the different strains there is a fairly wide divergence of type. It is up to you to decide which of the types, in your opinion, comes most nearly within the pattern of the standard, then to see which of the Kennels has that type most clearly defined in all the dogs in the Kennel. When you have decided this you will have chosen the Kennel from which you wish to make your initial purchases.

Remember that what paints and canvas are to an artist, the dog and bitch are to the dog breeder. They are the medium with which your beautiful picture, your perfect Collie, will be built. You are the embryo artist when you set out to breed your first litter, but you are working with flesh and blood, and where the painter can erase his errors and horrible mistakes with a few swift strokes of the brush, your errors and mistakes will grow for all to see, and you cannot destroy them without being inhumanly ruthless. If you are planning to breed Collies seriously, then you are taking on a charge which is a great trust; the art of breeding something beautiful is almost a dedication. You must be prepared for heartbreak; you will have to learn the hard way if you are to learn at all, but if you set out with the desire and purpose clearly before you you will surely attain the heights and you will surely also have with you the good wishes and help of all those of us who are already trying to do the same thing.

Almost all dog breeders, no matter what their chosen breed,

will handsomely admit that the Collie is the most beautiful
dog of all. Look to it, then, that we, as creators of this beauty,
maintain it at the highest possible level. Our purpose must be
to build and build on foundations already laid, until we have
produced a Collie nearer perfection than any which we have
yet seen.

The next section deals with the purchase of foundation
stock and the other things you will want to know when you
obtain your first Collie, but here I want to make you realize
just what is so much needed in any dog breeder who is not
merely the owner of a 'puppy-factory'. Each one of us needs
patience, perseverance and practice. Patience to give us endurance to face all our set-backs—and they will be many;
perseverance to start again when all our planned matings
have turned out wrongly; and practice which will come when
we get plenty of these set-backs.

All that I have said already is, of course, the ideal—but
now how about coming down to earth and being rather more
practical! You will already have 'fallen in', I expect, before
having this book in your hands, and your first Collie may
already be yours. (It seems to be becoming a habit recently
to give a Collie as a wedding present!) Doubtless, then, someone will come along with the suggestion that, 'It's a nice kind
of dog; why don't you show it?' Possibly the idea appeals and
you immediately rush off to find details of the shows, and off
you go on the due date with your Collie on the lead and your
hopes high. Back you come at night, but your hopes have been
dashed; your Collie just didn't make the grade. Now you may
belong to one of two groups of people, one group being those
who say: 'Dog shows are silly, anyway. I'm not going to bother
any more.' And if you belong to this group I doubt whether
you would be reading this book, so more certainly you belong
to the other group which says, 'That was rather fun; I'd like
to go again, and I'd like to do some winning and have a shot
at beating the big names.' In short, you have been bitten, and
the disease known as the 'dog game' is a very violent one from
which the patient never recovers—he simply gets worse and
worse! Your desire now is to have a good Collie, or, better
still, to breed a good one, and your question—'How am I to go
about it?'

You must consider carefully the situation in which you are placed. Have you enough room to breed a litter and keep several of the puppies, which you will need to do if you want to find yourself with a good one to show? It takes years of practice to pick out your certain best in the litter as soon as it is born, and in the early days at least you will have to 'run on' several youngsters so that you can be sure you are not parting with a possible champion.

Can you afford to rear a litter really well? There is no chance that you will make a fortune at the dog game, and not much that you will even make it pay its way, at least until you are breeding stock that is able to carry your name to certain heights in the show-ring. A Collie family, as you will learn in later pages, costs a good deal to rear properly, and it is no good at all skimping the early weeks of your puppies' lives. Your future winners are made or marred during the first few months.

Assuming that your answer to these two questions is satisfactory, go ahead and plan for that Kennel you hope to have.

## FOUNDING YOUR KENNEL

Having decided upon the Kennel from which you propose to buy your first dog or dogs, it is nevertheless important, before making your purchase, to be sure you have suitable accommodation for the puppy, or adult, when you bring it home.

A Collie, kept as a house pet, is ideal, but even then the dog wants a place it can call its own, and a corner where, it will readily learn, it can remain undisturbed. Whether puppy or adult, the dog wants a bed which is cosy and out of a draught, and to me the ideal place is a box (24 × 18 × 20 inches), laid on its side, and with a piece of wood about 4 inches wide nailed across the lower part of the box to keep in the bedding, whatever it may be. Many people are astounded when they learn that all my adult Collies sleep in such boxes, more astounded still when they see how a Collie can 'disappear' into one! But the dogs have all, at some time in the past, been given an alternative, either a large box or a bench raised from the ground, and their own choice every time is the small box. This is the actual sleeping accommodation provided whether in house or kennel.

However, if you are planning to breed a litter from your

Collie you will require a place other than a box in the house, and the most convenient, both from the point of view of the dog and of the owner, is a shed at least 6 ft. by 4 ft. and high enough for one to be able to stand up in without braining oneself all the time! The shed should have a run or some kind of enclosure attached to it, and the bigger this is the better, for the adult dog, as well as the puppies, will want to use it, and a Collie litter, to do itself well, needs plenty of playing space.

Assuming, then, that you have the accommodation ready, there are two probable methods of starting your Kennel. First, and most usual, method is to start with a puppy. Now there is a great deal to be said both for and against this method. You are probably longing to have a puppy to bring up yourself, to train in your ways and to watch through all the changing months of its early life. All these are points in favour of having a puppy—and there is one thing better than having a puppy and that is having two puppies! They are less trouble than one, they keep each other out of mischief and each acts as the other's plaything; two puppies together are always occupied. As a general rule, puppies do much better in pairs or more, than does one isolated baby, and you will usually find that the bigger breeder, purchasing a puppy to add to the Kennel, will nearly always buy a second one of the same age to 'run with' the first (unless there is already a puppy the same age at home), and when the pups are older will discard the unwanted one. Against starting with a puppy is the long wait until you can show and breed from it, and also the risk, ever present, that the pup may not turn out as well as was hoped, and you may then have to start all over again, for the breeder who sells you the puppy, no matter how reputable and honest, can only say that he or she thinks that it is likely to make a top show specimen, and then hope for the best! You may be at fault yourself, if it does not turn out right; so much depends on the rearing of a puppy.

Let us assume that you have decided to start with a puppy. You will write to the owner of the Kennel whose dogs pleased you most, asking what stock the owner has for sale, and not forgetting, please, to say exactly what you want—dog or bitch puppy, approximate age, colour, show potential or not, and anything else you can think of; you have no idea of the amount of correspondence wasted when you simply write and say, 'Have you any puppies for sale?' The poor breeder may have four or five litters ready when you write and obviously cannot detail each pup, without having some idea of what you are after. He may even breed more than one kind of dog! Having discovered that the Kennel in question has pups of the desired age, etc., make an appointment to call. I say 'make an appointment' not because the average Kennel owner is afraid to be caught unexpectedly, but because, in these days of staff difficulties, the owner may not always be available, and you may choose a moment when no one is at home. Even if kennelmaids are there, the potential purchaser will usually learn far more if the breeder himself is present.

If you have decided on a puppy of about 8–12 weeks, then you will do best to place yourself completely in the hands of the breeder and say, 'Look, I want a puppy that I will be able to show, and one that will be well worth breeding from.' Most of us are honest and on an approach like this will do our best to help. The potential purchaser who most enrages a breeder is either the one who comes along and says, 'Of course, I only want a pet,' pays a pet price and later blames the breeder when it does not win in the ring; or the complete novice who (and I quote an actual case) comes and says: 'I want the best puppy you have got, but I'm not taking the one you pick for me. I want to pick my own.' In the true story I am telling this happened when there were over twenty puppies—not Collies—from several litters, all in one large run. I removed the two pups I was not prepared to sell at all, and let the prospective buyer spend as much time as she liked with the pups. She asked me the price for the pick of the remaining pups and I told her. Later she came along with one of the very worst puppies of the whole lot, laid the cash on the table and asked for the pedigree. I tried to point out that she picked a pup which would never do any winning and would hardly be worth breeding from, but she knew best, and was certain that my protestations were because she had chosen the best pup! The results were obvious, and needless to say the pup never did any good, but rather to my surprise she bred a winner! Do place yourself in the breeder's hands; you will almost certainly get a square deal.

It is not very easy to tell you what to look for in an eight-week old puppy, for the young stock of different strains tend to look very different strain from strain at this age. But no matter what the strain, there are some essentials in which you cannot go wrong. Look for a well-reared, plump baby, with good, sturdy leg-bone, his shoulder properly placed and laid, good short hocks (it is almost impossible to select movement at this age; all puppies 'waddle', and angulation is not easy to gauge in our breed at this age, either), a really long tail, set on low. It does not matter if the tail is carried in the air when he is tiny; all babies use their tails as a 'rudder' to give balance, if it is set on low it will not be a 'gay' tail later in life. Your puppy should have a thick, plushy, teddy-bear coat, with long hairs standing up through it. The pup to look for is the one which comes up to the gate as you approach, full of curiosity and friendliness; do not choose the one which is inclined to hide rather than be gazed at.

Now we come to the puppy's head, and this is the part which varies most according to the strain, but the puppy to avoid, no matter what the strain, is the one with 'perfect' ears and long, lean head. The perfect ears almost always go prick, and the 'long, lean head' will almost certainly finish up snipy and receding. The placement of the ears and the shape of the eye are the head points which will not change. Choose a puppy whose ears are not placed too far apart, nor on the side of his head, nor almost touching at their base on top of the skull. The inside bottom corner of the ear should be right above the centre of the eye. It doesn't matter in the least, at this age, whether the ears are tipped over, falling over, or both leaning in one direction (as if the puppy had spent days standing in a prevailing wind!), one up, one down, or even turning over backwards or inside out, so long as they are nicely placed on top. It is the low ear which can never become right.

The eye, in shape, should be as 'almondy' as possible, and the placement should be such that the outside corner of the eye should slope upwards towards the ear, so that the whole eye placement is 'slanty'. The eye should be as dark as possible without being black, and if at this age the eye still looks bluish, or faintly hazel, it is almost certain that the puppy will have light eyes, though this is not infallible advice as eye colour can, and does, change with age. The size of the eye changes too as the dog grows older, and with age the eye gets larger. For this reason it is wise to choose a puppy with a small eye, but not so tiny that it gives a 'piggy-eyed' impression, quite foreign to the soft, sweet expression of the Collie. I do not propose to give any indication of what to look for in head shape at this age; this might only be misleading, for, as I have said already and will reiterate, head shape varies so much with the individual strains.

One more point on the question of two puppies. The beginner is well advised not to go in for a dog puppy. So often one is asked for a dog and bitch puppy, 'suitable for mating together later'. This is such a mistake. Either put your money which you planned to spend on two puppies into one really tip-top bitch puppy (it will repay you hands down in the end) or, if you want two, make it two bitch puppies. After all, the very best dogs in the land are available to anyone for a reasonable fee, and you are much more likely to breed a top-class puppy in this way than if you start with a dog and bitch pup. Always remember that it is your duty to your fellow-breeders and your chosen breed to breed only from the VERY BEST; second-rate foundation stock is useless. A bitch with a first-class pedigree, and who in herself is good, but perhaps is useless for the ring as the result of an accident, will so often be just what you want, in that she will most probably 'produce the goods', and her price will be reasonable. You will have read one or two true stories of this sort during your perusal of this volume; to mention two, there was the dog 'Scott' in the late '80s, and 'Lilac of Ladypark' in modern times.

Consider also the possibility of starting with an adult—and here I am certainly writing only in terms of bitches, for an adult dog, if he is really a 'top-notcher', will cost a great deal of money (if he is for sale at all!) and if he is not a top-notcher he is not worth purchasing, for all the use he will be to you.

A good adult bitch is not come by cheaply, either, but she is much more likely to repay her purchase price than is a dog.

There is yet another avenue. The average large Kennel has not enough room to keep all the brood bitches it requires, and very often the owner is willing either to sell a bitch 'on part breeding terms', or to lease a bitch. The latter method is not one I like as I consider it unsatisfactory to both parties, but the 'breeding terms' plan is usually good, and of great benefit to the novice starting out. Naturally actual terms will depend upon the quality of the bitch in question, her age, etc., but frequently you will find that a bitch, soon to be ready for mating, will be let out 'on terms' of, say, half her value in cash, and a certain number of puppies from her first litter, to be selected by her original owner. Generally the agreement goes a little further and covers exactly the arrangements for the payment of the stud fee; it probably states that the stud dog is to be selected by the original owner of the bitch, has a clause covering the loss of the bitch before the terms of the agreement are fulfilled, and a clause stating that, when the terms have been completed, the bitch shall then become the unconditional property of the purchaser. (A specimen agreement will be found in the Appendix.) As a rule, the vendor remains the registered owner of the bitch and appears as the registered breeder of the litter, but this is a matter for mutual agreement. Whatever the arrangement, your share of the litter should be registered with your own Kennel name and not that of the original owner.

To me, this is an ideal way to start as you are reasonably sure of getting a good beginning. The choice of the stud dog usually rests with the original owner, and as a result of this you know that you will have behind you his years of experience, and the choice is likely to be a much wiser one than you, without very much experience as yet, would be able to make for yourself. Further, the vendor will be most anxious that the puppies shall be well reared if some are to come back, and you will receive every possible help in this direction too, and ultimately you will have two real assets, probably the second-best puppy in the litter for your own, and the bitch herself.

Many Champions have been bred from bitches acquired in this way; I'll let you into a secret—my own first Champion was so acquired, though in that particular instance, thanks to the kindness of Miss Grey, I chose the stud dog myself, and I was the actual breeder of the litter.

Weigh up carefully the pros and cons of each method of founding your Kennel, then go ahead and do what seems to you to be best.

CHAPTER 7

## ESTABLISHING A STRAIN

SURELY the ambition of all breeders, large or small, is to
breed a Champion. 'Oh, anyone can breed a Champion,' you
hear people say, and with a certain amount of truth. Anyone
*can* breed a Champion, but how many can do so consistently?
Dogs true to type and bearing a marked resemblance to one
another?

Unfortunately there are too few breeders with the necessary
time, patience and money to be able to carry the task through
to its conclusion. You will notice that I do not list knowledge
as a necessary qualification, and there is reason for this. If
you have time and patience the knowledge can be acquired.
Unless it is acquired all other qualifications are useless. A
strain cannot be established in a few months; it is the work
of years. Years of study, trial, error, disappointment and final
joy when the 'dog of dreams' is evolved.

When definite traits are apparent in all the dogs from a
certain Kennel, then, and only then, has a strain been established. A strain is not a Kennel-name, tacked willy-nilly on
to a collection of dogs bred in that Kennel; it is real live flesh
and blood, a walking advertisement of a certain breeder.

How can the breeder be sure of producing certain characteristics in his own dogs? The result of years of study and research by great scientists is at our disposal. It is up to us to
apply the knowledge they have left us.

Experiments carried out by the Abbé Mendel have undoubtedly been the most useful for our purpose, and they are
simple to understand. It was he who proved that when two
individuals, each pure for a pair of opposite characteristics
(such as tallness and dwarfness in the pea with which he
carried out his experiments), were crossed, the first generation
of the offspring would all look like the tall parent, so determin-
ing the dominant characteristic, but carried the factor for
dwarfness recessively. When two of these hybrids were crossed,
the second generation produced an average of one tall, one

Ch. Magnet
*Born 1912*

AND HIS SON

Ch. Poplar Perfection
*Born 1916*
*A drawing by Prudence Walker from a reproduction of an old print*

Eden Educator (as a puppy)
*Born 1923*

Ch. Laund Lukeo
*Born 1923*

short, breeding pure for the characteristic, and two hybrids like the parents. The two hybrids appeared tall, as did the tall offspring, the fourth appeared short, and this one did not even carry the tall factor recessively. The tall hybrids carried the factor for dwarfness and themselves produced both types of offspring.

So it is with the Collies today, and we are lucky that other breeders, studying along Mendelian lines, have already determined for the most part which traits in our breed are carried as dominants and which are recessives. Every individual carries a pair of factors for the same characteristics, one received by him from each of his parents. An individual in which like characteristics are paired is known as an homozygous individual, and one in which unlike characteristics are paired is known as heterozygous. Recessives are *always* homozygous and always breed true to their own type, which is a test of their purity. Naturally one can determine which type of individual each animal is only by the result of test matings. Remember, too, that one individual can be homozygous for a certain characteristic and heterozygous for others. The breeder's task is to decide what kind of factors his animals carry and how they behave in combination with the factors of other individuals.

We have a harder task than Mendel with his peas! He wished only to establish one thing—height. With our Collies the factors for the various characteristics are carried differently, as has been said, and while we are trying to establish one characteristic we may so easily lose another. For example, you are trying to fix natural ears, and to this end you use dog A and bitch B. Unfortunately dog A has a slightly wavy coat, bitch B a straight coat, but this is only incompletely dominant to the wave, so the resultant litter will have a large proportion of natural ears, but a percentage will also have wavy coats. Your next task, then, will be to breed out that wavy coat and yet retain the natural ears—and so the battle goes on, fixing one characteristic, possibly to lose another, then the fight to regain the second characteristic, hold the first—and all this possibly at the cost of a third! It is this which makes our task so intensely interesting and, incidentally, makes perfection so very difficult to attain.

While we accept the law that like produces like, we must

F

also accept the other which says that no two animals are ever identical. Because no two animals are ever identical, selection is possible, and because like produces like selection is effective.

It is essential, in trying to produce perfection, that one uses not only two dogs as near perfection themselves as is possible, and that in their deficiencies each complements the other; it is also essential that a breeder should learn to 'read' a pedigree correctly. A pedigree is not just a collection of names on paper, with perhaps the Champions written in red. It is, or it should be, a whole volume. It is the dog's family tree, and each name in it should conjure up, for the intelligent breeder, a picture of each of the ancestors in question, his good points and his bad, and all that it is possible to know about him.

The new breeder cannot be expected to do this from his own knowledge, but there are plenty of 'old hands' among us today who can still 'see' the names in the pedigrees, back to many more generations than the customary five, and who are only too willing to pass on what they know if the novice really wants to learn, but there are so many beginners today in our own and every other breed who 'know it all' within six months of buying their first dog.

If the pedigree you are studying contains the name of a certain animal doubled and re-doubled, then you may assume that the animal to whom the pedigree belongs carries in its genetic make-up a large proportion of the genes of that particular ancestor.

It is important to consider not only the pedigree but also the owner of the pedigree itself, for despite the 'doubling' up, or line- or in-breeding as it is called, it is possible that the dog in question may not carry a large proportion of its illustrious progenitors' genes, for despite the doubling of the line this can happen; but if the animal resembles the general type one accepts from this doubled ancestor, then one can assume that he himself carries a large proportion of similar germ-plasms.

The pedigree must not be considered alone, any more than the individual animals for mating should be considered alone. The pedigrees and the dogs must be considered together, and then one should have some idea what to expect in the immediate progeny.

There are three distinct methods of breeding. Out-crossing,

line-breeding and in-breeding. All three methods have their advocates, and certainly the short cut to success, if there is such a thing, is in-breeding or very close line-breeding, but although this is a successful method it demands much care and forethought and a great knowledge of the ancestors to whom one is planning the line- or in-breeding programme. Out-crossing is the mating of two unrelated, or almost unrelated, individuals, and this method is practised exclusively in some Kennels, but personally I do not advocate it, and rarely does a dog or bitch, the progeny of a complete out-cross mating, who may yet be a Champion itself, prove to be a really prepotent breeding specimen. A perusal of the pedigrees of Champions in the Appendix will stress this point. In-breeding, in its true sense, is the mating of brother and sister, father and daughter, mother and son. Except occasionally, to fix some very definite point, such intense breeding is rarely resorted to. Line-breeding is the mating of every relation between half-brother and sister, up to cousins, and it is usually found that very intense line-breeding—half-brother ex half-sister, grandsire ex granddaughter—will prove most effective. Oddly enough, the mating of grandmother to grandson is rarely successful.

However, no plan of intense line-breeding should be embarked upon without a very firm intention to cull, and cull ruthlessly, the resultant litter if this should be necessary.

It must be remembered that no in- or line-breeding can establish things which do not already exist in the two individuals chosen for the mating. Intense line-breeding will intensify all the points the two individuals have in common, or which their common ancestors have, and points both good *and bad* will be intensified equally.

The inexperienced dog owner usually has a deep-rooted idea that every in-bred or line-bred dog, or what the pet owner usually calls 'highly bred'—a meaningless term which always reminds me of a well-risen loaf!—must be either delicate, nervous, mentally deficient or all three!

You cannot breed in any new feature by in-breeding, but can only intensify what is already there, both the good points and the bad. No in-bred dog who comes of sensible, nerve-free stock will be nervous *because* it is in-bred. If it shows any of these tendencies they must have been present in the parents or inherent in the ancestors. This, then, is the vital need, to be absolutely certain that the dogs to which you wish to in- or line-breed, and through which you are planning to in- or line-breed, must be absolutely healthy, both mentally and physically, and also as free from the faults, and as richly endowed as possible with the good points, as the standard of the breed demands.

It is therefore essential to choose, for such a programme, two animals with the least possible number of common faults —and whose common ancestors are likewise as faultless as possible—and then to look at the resultant litter quite ruthlessly, and reject *at once* any progeny which shows the common fault in even the slightest degree. It is quite useless at this stage to be 'to their virtues ever kind, to their faults a little blind; the reverse must be the case. The point that the puppy which shows the fault *even in the slightest degree* should be rejected should be stressed again; it is almost certain that this puppy will be the most prepotent for that fault. The brothers and sisters may carry the fault recessively, and only a test mating can prove that point, so do not ask for trouble by keeping the *apparent* offender when you may find you have an unseen 'nigger in the wood-pile' too!

The appended pedigree of Ch. Silvasceptre from Shiel gives an example of intense line-breeding, and this is the closest line-breeding I have ever carried out. It was my intention to give myself the greatest possible infusion of the blood of Beulah's Nightvictorious I could have. The fact that I was 'playing with fire' in mating two blues was an added risk. Whilst the litter was 'in preparation' I was told lurid tales of what the result would be, and these included 'all mis-marked', 'all mis-shapen heads and roman noses', 'all bent spines'! The risk I *knew* I was taking was the appearance of a large percentage of whites because of the high percentage of the blue-merle dilution factor, and I also knew that I ran a risk of eye trouble.

The litter produced eight puppies. Three were tricolours, four were blue merles, the eighth was almost pure white. There was only one puppy with a visible defect at birth; fortunately it was the white (which had a tail curled round like a bull-dog's!).One blue merle died soon after birth, and the remainder of the litter are all winners either in this country or abroad. No eye trouble appeared at any time in any of the puppies, except in Silvasceptre herself, whose eye was injured in an accident! So much for the gloomy forecasts of the result of intense line-breeding.

At the time of writing Sceptre has just whelped a litter of five, one tricolour and four blue merles, to her tricolour grand-sire, Rifflesee Royalist. A glance again at the pedigree will show you that this gives an even higher co-efficient of the blood of Nightvictorious than was carried by the original litter, and at birth there is no puppy to cull. As they grow on some fault may be apparent, but we shall have gone to press before the final results can be known.

This is set out to show to what lengths such a breeding programme can be carried with safety, and with an almost definite assurance that in the resultant litter there will be a high proportion of really top-class progeny.

.        .        .        .        .        .

Two definite extremes of type are discernible in Collies. The tall, flat-sided type, with a very long, lean head and a long body; the short, chunky type, not long in head and with a broad back and short body. The Collie ideal lies somewhere midway between these two. It is therefore helpful for us to know which of these types is dominant and which is recessive, and from there to see for ourselves which is the easier and which the more difficult to obtain.

As so many genes control the development of even one part of the dog, it is extremely difficult to make positive state-ments, for many of the characteristics are 'incomplete domi-nants' and do not always follow a definite set plan, but the following table should be useful:

Short, chunky type, dominant to long, lean type.
Prominent cheek bones, incompletely dominant to fine cheeks, rounded foreface.
Wide skulls, incompletely dominant to lean, fat skulls.
Level mouth, incompletely dominant to uneven mouths.
Straight front legs, incompletely dominant to crooked front legs, weak pasterns.
Good stifles, incompletely dominant to cow-hocks.

Natural ears, dominant to prick ears.
Large ears, incompletely dominant to small ears.
Small eyes, dominant to large eyes.
Almond eyes, dominant to round eyes.
Dark eyes, dominant to light eyes. Except in blue merles where the
    wall-eye is epistatic to brown.
Sable, dominant to tricolour or blue merle.
Tricolour, dominant to blue merle, but blue merle is not a true
    recessive owing to the presence of the dilution factor.
White face markings, dominant to plain faces.
Straight hair, incompletely dominant to wavy hair.
Coarse, harsh hair, dominant to fine hair.
Short hair (as in the Smooth), incompletely dominant to long hair.
Correct length and carriage of tail dominant to short, gay tail.

A study of this list in relation to one's own dogs makes interesting reading, and also stresses one thing that is most encouraging—that a number of the most desirable traits in the breed can be established fairly easily. Whether the individual breeder decides to attempt to achieve his ideal by in-breeding, line-breeding or by careful selective breeding of unrelated dogs matters not so long as there is a definite plan to produce a certain type; a plan backed up by sound knowledge and the ruthless discarding of any 'doubtful' products of certain matings if they carry even one of the characteristics considered undesirable in the strain.

The scientific breeder tries, with every litter born, to improve his stock in at least one particular point. As a breeder he has an obligation to the breed he has chosen, and to his fellow-breeders—to produce only the best that his brains and knowledge can evolve. The breeder must seek to perpetuate only those characteristics most desirable in the breed. The speed with which he can produce stock superior to that of his earlier generations is the measure of his knowledge and success.

The motto of every breeder trying to establish a strain should be 'Patience, Perseverance, Pups'. Patience to give him calm endurance to all his set-backs; perseverance to start again when all his carefully planned matings have gone wrong; pups, for they are the proof of the rightness or wrongness of his plan. They alone can show whether the desired characteristics are being established. As they are, so the strain will be built up, until that glorious moment when he proudly hears someone unknown to him say, 'Look, that must be a —— Collie; you can tell that strain anywhere!'

## Colour Breeding in Collies

Undoubtedly one of the reasons for the appeal of the breed is the variety of colours in which it is obtainable, and the fascination of waiting to see which colour will turn up in each litter.

In view of the importance of this subject it is surprising that much more attention has not been paid to it and a greater study made. Experienced breeders may find little for them in this short chapter, but it is hoped that it will assist the novice.

Yet even among the experienced breeders one hears a great many most peculiar theories being expounded, and in some cases there is still an appalling lack of knowledge on the subject.

The main groups of colour in our breed are sable, tricolour and blue merle. All these can carry the Collie 'colour pattern' for white. That is to say, white collar, legs, shirt, feet, blaze and tail tip. There are three distinct types of colour pattern: (1) A solid-colour dog with practically no white visible, except perhaps on the toes or a hair or two at the back of the neck. (2) The Collie marked as we know it and expect it to be. (3) The mis-marked dog in which there is more white than colour. Fortunately this third type is extremely rare in the Collie today. This type of white, however, must not be confused with the almost all-white dog resulting from the mating of two blue merles. This latter is a defective white, caused, probably, by a lethal factor. The type (3) dog in the colour pattern is the dog which can, and does, breed the self-white. This colour, though debarred from the show-ring in this country (although the standard does not exclude it!), can turn up from time to time, and is an admitted colour in the United States, where in fact there is a White Collie Club.

Sable is a loosely used word to describe any shade of colour from clear yellow through gold to rich mahogany. The colour is dominant over all other colours, and depending on the type

Ch. Westcarrs Blue Minoru

Rifflesee Royalist
- Ch. Lad of Ladypark
  - Eden Examine
    - Lyncliffe Lancer
      - Am. Ch. Beulah's Silver Don Mario
      - Leyland Lima
      - Masterpiece of Faux
      - Laund Larissa
    - Seagull
      - Ch. Beulah's Golden Future
      - Ch. Beulah's Golden Feather
      - Beulah's Golden Fanfarest
      - Beulah's Night Black and Beautiful
  - Ch. Beulah's Golden Flora
    - Ch. Beulah's Golden Futureson
      - Ch. Glenack Kingfisher
      - Beulah's Nightshadow
      - Ch. Backwoods Flutter
      - Beulah's Silver Tern
    - Beulah's Golden Kiska
      - Beulah's Golden Shade
      - Beulah's Golden Florida
      - Beulah's Night Mail
      - Beulah's Golden Florida
- Beulah's Night Flare
  - Beulah's Nightvictorious
    - Beulah's Nightshadowing
      - Ch. Glenack Kingfisher
      - Beulah's Nightshadow
      - Ch. Backwoods Flutter
      - Beulah's Silver Tern
    - Ch. Beulah's Silver Merienda
      - Beulah's Night Mail
      - Beulah's Golden Florida
      - Ch. Laund Lindrum
      - Winstonian Biddy
  - Beulah's Golden Fantasy
    - Ch. Beulah's Golden Future
      - Ch. Ashtead Aristocrat
      - Delwick Diana
      - Bruce of Waldemar
      - Bluette of Waldemar
    - Ch. Beulah's Golden Feather
      - Beulah's Nightshadowing
      - Ch. Beulah's Silver Merienda
      - Ch. Beulah's Golden Future
      - Ch. Beulah's Golden Feather

Lobelia of Ladypark
- Westcarrs Black Bisley
  - Beulah's Nightvictorious
  - Westcarrs Warning
    - Westcarrs Wallah
    - Everest Susan
- Lilac of Ladypark
  - Maroel Blue Mandarin
    - Ch. Eden Diadem
    - Blue Baroness
  - Beulah's Night Flare
    - Beulah's Nightvictorious
    - Beulah's Golden Fantasy

From Shiel*

**Ch. Silvasc—** (subject of pedigree)

- **Silvaseagull from Shiel**
  - **Beulah's Silver Don Mero**
    - **Beulah's Silver Don Glorio**
      - **Ch. Beulah's Night Glorious**
        - Beulah's Nightblack and Beautiful
          - Ch. Beulah's Silver Merienda
          - Am. Ch. Beulah's Silver Don Mario
          - Leyland Lima
      - **Blue Princess**
        - Lyncliffe Lancer
          - Am. Ch. Beulah's Silver Don Mario
          - Leyland Lima
        - Warbreck Blue Bubble
          - Blue Mischief
          - Redevalley Dinkie
    - **Beulah's Nightvivid**
      - **Beulah's Nightvictorious**
        - Beulah's Nightshadowing
          - Ch. Glenack Kingfisher
          - Beulah's Night Shadow
        - Ch. Beulah's Silver Merienda
          - Ch. Backwoods Flutter
          - Beulah's Silver Tern
      - **Beulah's Golden Fantasy**
        - Ch. Beulah's Golden Future
          - Beulah's Golden Shade
          - Beulah's Golden Florida
        - Ch. Beulah's Golden Feather
          - Beulah's Nightmail
          - Beulah's Golden Florida
  - **Ch. Silvaseabear from Shiel**
    - **Westcarrs Black Bisley**
      - **Westcarrs Warning**
        - Westcarrs Wallah
          - Beulah's Night Mail
          - Beulah's Golden Florida
        - Everest Susan
          - Ch. Laund Lindrum
          - Winstonian Biddy
      - **Beulah's Nightvictorious**
        - Beulah's Nightshadowing
          - Ch. Glenack Kingfisher
          - Beulah's Nightshadow
        - Ch. Beulah's Silver Merienda
          - Ch. Backwoods Flutter
          - Beulah's Silver Tern
    - **Lilac of Ladypark**
      - **Maroel Blue Mandarin**
        - Ch. Eden Diadem
          - Ch. Ashtead Aristocrat
          - Delwick Diana
        - Blue Baroness
          - Bruce of Waldemar
          - Bluette of Waldemar
      - **Beulah's Night Flare**
        - Beulah's Nightvictorious
          - Beulah's Nightshadowing
          - Ch. Beulah's Silver Merienda
        - Beulah's Golden Fantasy
          - Ch. Beulah's Golden Future
          - Ch. Beulah's Golden Feather

\* The intensity of in-breeding in this pedigree can be appreciated to the full only when it is realized that Beulah's Nightvictorious was full brother in blood to Am. Ch. Beulah's Silver Don Mario.

of the individual, an animal can throw either only sables or
both sables and tricolours.

Tricolour is the name given to the black dog with tan
markings on the cheeks, over the eyes, inside the legs, under
the tail, and with the white collar pattern also present. These
dogs are really genetically bi-colours with the white pattern
acting on that bi-colour.

Blue merle is a modification of black, due to a dilution
factor. It is dealt with fully in another chapter.

Sable, in all its shades, is fairly unpredictable, producing
as it does all shades of sable as well as tri. Even two clear
yellow sables mated together can produce tricolours, but a
sable, homozygous for the colour, will produce only its own
colour, and this can easily be proved by making a test mating
or two, with a tricolour mate. If all the pups are sable, then
the animal can be assumed to be homozygous, and will produce
only sables. Such animals are rare, and of recent years I
believe there is only one stud dog which has been proved
homozygous, and that is Ch. Lochinvar of Ladypark.

Tricolours mated together can produce only tricolours.
Tri x sable can produce both tricolours and sables (except in
the case mentioned above) and this is often a most useful mating
if there has been paling of the sable colour due to the continued
crossing of sable x sable, as the introduction of the tri blood
will make an enormous difference to the colour, even in the
first generation, and often gives sables of very rich hue.

# CHAPTER 8

## COLLIE CHARACTER

BECAUSE of its long association with man in its role of Sheep-dog, the Collie, more perhaps than any other breed, needs the companionship of man to bring out all that is best in his character. The natural shepherd dog role of the Collie makes it by nature a dog of purpose, a dog which is happiest with a job to do, a dog whose brain is undoubtedly superior to that of most canines. The herding and keeping of sheep (I use the word 'keeping' in its fullest sense in this context) has made of the Collie a dog with a tremendously deep sense of property, of helpfulness and of loyalty, and today, when the majority of Collies have no opportunity to act in their natural capacity, this inherent instinct must find its outlet somehow; it may be as a companion, a useful dog about the house, a self-appointed 'nannie' to the family—somehow he will surely make his niche and carve out a career for himself.

The Collie has a character all its own. It is perhaps the most faithful of all dogs, gentle, sweet, extremely affectionate, extremely intelligent, with a brain which seems to reason almost in the way ours does; and he has also a very strongly developed telepathic power, stronger than is apparent in most breeds. For these reasons the Collie is ideal as a family dog. He has a strong sense of possession, and a very strong sense of right and wrong, not perhaps so much of right and wrong in his own way of life, but certainly of right and wrong in ours! The factual-fiction story which I shall tell in a moment explains what I mean.

The Collie is not a dog who readily makes friends with strangers; he has a pronounced sense of discrimination and demands time in which to accept or reject a newcomer. His understanding of one's own moods has to be experienced to be believed, and his personality makes a very big mark on his owner's life. As already mentioned, the telepathic sense is very strong indeed in some individuals. For example, an elderly

Collie gentleman of my acquaintance is the constant companion of his owner who has a small Kennel of Collies. He is the only 'house-dog'. If his owner is going out, just for a brief period, he much prefers to wait in the house until her return, hating to be put into a kennel at any time. However, if she is to be away all day he prefers to pal up with the other dogs and spend the day in a kennel. He knows, unerringly, long before his owner goes to change to go out, that she is going, and *for how long she is going*! and if it is for the day he unhesitatingly puts himself into a kennel, with no word having been said, no suggestion having been made. How does he know? Lacking understanding of the canine mind, we can supply no answer; but it is this facet of the Collie's unique character, brought about undoubtedly by his long years of close association with man, which makes him the outstanding member of the canine race.

Undoubtedly the Collie has a great sense of humour, and many members of the race 'smile' in the way we humans do. He does not like being laughed at, but he loves to be laughed with, and he often treats himself as a great joke. He is always thinking up new pranks to play, new games to get up to, either with you or with his canine companions, but because of this fertile mind of his it is, to my way of thinking, one of the saddest sights in the world to see a Collie, bereft of his full measure of human companionship, falling back on himself for his own life and amusement. A dog 'gone to seed' in fact, and I do not think anyone should have a Collie who is not prepared to give him a good deal of time, and if he cannot be a 'constant companion' at least let him spend a large part of his life with human beings, for there is no dog who so much loves to have its job in life and to be a help.

The tale which follows is no tale of fiction; Flash and Colin exist under other names, and Flash has taken upon himself the duties of children's nurse!

The cottage lies back from the road, in a rough garden. No fence protects the garden from the road. In the garden, too, is a pond in which ducks swim. Colin, just three years old, plays alone in the garden. For a while he is content with his bucket and spade, but presently he gets bored, and toddles off towards the road.

'How wicked to let a baby like that play alone where he can run into such danger,' says the passer-by.

But wait! From close to where Colin has been playing, in the shade of the beech tree, a red shadow emerges. Flash, the Collie, himself the colour of the fallen beech leaves, walks forward and watches Colin intently. The little boy walks with uncertain steps nearer and nearer to the dangerous road. Flash circles the child, and before Colin reaches the road Flash is close beside him, leaning his head and shoulders against the child's body and gently nudging him until his steps are turned into a safer route.

Flash lies down again, head between paws. He seems to be asleep, but one watchful eye is always on the boy.

Colin's next desire is not just to watch the ducks on the pond, but to try to catch them if possible! Flash, accompanying Colin to the water, tries his nudging tricks again, but this time Colin refuses to be turned, and if Flash insists he must end by knocking the child over. Flash has never knocked the child down and does not intend to do so now, but Colin seems intent upon a swim! The Collie goes with the boy, right to the water's edge, and then, oh, so very gently, Flash takes the child's arm in his mouth and, despite Colin's protests and attempts to pull away, firmly, but still gently, leads him from the muddy pond, and feeling Colin is becoming rather a handful, decides that it is time mother stepped in, so leads the child to the kitchen door. The mother, recognizing from Flash's behaviour that Colin has gone too far, releases the Collie of his charge. There is no scratch, no redness even, on Colin's arm, and Mother knows full well that as long as Flash is 'on the job' Colin's play-hours are safe.

No, Flash was not trained for the job. He is just one 'of the family' and as such, in the manner of most Collies, he has accepted his responsibilities. He guards and watches over the little ones, and no safer 'nannie' can be found.

Colin has a brother, Robin, aged five. From time to time, in the manner of all small boys, Robin and Colin scrap, coming to grips with each other. Flash won't allow this! He thrusts first his nose, then his whole tawny body, between the contestants, and wriggles until he parts them. No fights allowed in *his* nursery!

The Collie, used on the Continent as a guard dog, for duty with the Army and Police, is less used for this purpose in our country. But his worth is acknowledged in many countries for his ability to act as a guide dog to the blind. However, it is undoubtedly as a day-to-day guard and general house-dog that he is most appreciated and in which his true value lies. His great intelligence, which at times is almost uncanny, makes him adapt himself to our lives more readily than most breeds. It is probable that this is the result of having lived so close to man in the tending of flocks for untold generations. He has all the assets of a 'big dog'—in that he looks one without being *really* big! Put him in a bath and he is only a small-medium-sized dog. He fits into any size of house; he is gentle, clean and kind. His absolute loyalty and trustworthiness make him the perfect companion, and his innate understanding of his owner ensures that he is a joy to possess. He is a gentleman—he is one of the most beautiful members of the canine race—he is, in fact, a COLLIE.

# CHAPTER 9

# THE STUD DOG

Whilst it has already been said that it is not an economic proposition, nor is it really advisable for the small Kennel, nor the beginnner, to keep a stud dog, the time will come nevertheless when that outstanding dog puppy is bred and reared to become a stud dog.

In the early days you should not allow yourself to be tempted either to buy a dog or keep a dog pup, for unless you are in a position to buy a real top-notcher there is nothing whatsoever to be gained by having a male. In fact, even with a top-grade one there is little gain, for it is unlikely that he will be suitable for all your bitches, and if he is he will be suitable only for one generation of your bitches, until such time as you may have grandchildren of his to put back to him. The very best dog in the land, and the most suitable for each of your bitches, can be used for a relatively small fee, 8 gns.–15 gns. being about the scale for Collie fees. Your own dog, even if he mates all your own bitches, will save you nothing over a year if you take his keep into account, unless he is of such outstanding merit that his services are sought after by other breeders, and this is unlikely to happen unless you are in a position to be able to show him fearlessly all over the country, and this is a job demanding plenty of time, energy and cash.

You may consider it more convenient to have your own dog, and there may be the possibility of him bringing you the odd stud fee or two from the local 'pet' type bitches, but if you are going to look upon the mating of your bitch to the dog which is closest at hand instead of to the dog best suited to her, then you will not get very far in the dog game.

Equally, it is not any use to keep a 'chance-bred' one. That is to say, should you happen to breed a really top-class-*looking* dog, worthy maybe of gaining his title, he will in all probability be useless as a stud force, for he will not have the background essential to the ideal stud dog. He will almost certainly not

95

throw his like, for no stud which is not carefully and scientifically bred has the power to do this, and it is for this reason
that a programme of line-breeding is usually so much more
successful than a programme of out-crossing.[1]

There are a great number of really important qualifications to which a dog should conform before he can be considered
as the ideal stud. He must come of a pedigree which is such
that it has been proved to carry bloodlines which have played,
and are still playing, an important part in the improvement of
the breed, and this pedigree should be really strong for many
more generations than those which appear on the conventional
five-generation pedigree form. You should assure yourself that
for at least ten generations there are no weak or unknown spots.
By weak spots I mean that the blood carried does not go back
to a line which is known to have failed, on either the male or
female side, to have produced good stock.

It will probably not be possible for you to 'see' his pedigree
as a visual thing for all these generations, but by careful
questioning of the old hands, and recourse to reading of the
past, it should become possible for you to build up the picture
you must have in your mind. It is not enough for a stud dog to
come of a Champion sire, however prepotent that sire may be;
remember that the son has only half his make-up from his sire
(and you can rest assured that he will not have inherited only
all his father's good points, but some of his bad ones as well!),
the other half of his make-up comes from his dam. It is absolutely essential that she must be a more than typical member
of the breed. If she is not a winner on merit, she must be a bitch
who has already proved herself as being prepotent in passing
on those essential qualities which go to improve the breed.

The potential stud dog must come of stock in which there
is no known inherent tendency to any particular disease or
constitutional weakness, quite apart from his merit on show
points. Needless to say, to be of any real economic value to you
he must also be good in himself, for without some successes in
the show-ring there will not be the demand for his services,
unless he should happen to be a dog of outstanding prepotency
who had his show-ring chances marred by an accident. In such
a case a dog may be sought after, but it will be appreciated

[1] See Chapter 10.

Ch. Seedley Supposition
*Born 1921*

*C. M. Adams*

Westcarrs Blue Moon
*Born 1928*

Ch. Backwoods Fellow
*Born 1930*

Laund Lindrum
*Born 1928*

that the time of waiting until his services are sought after will be a lengthy one, for he will be able to prove himself only through his progeny, and as one swallow does not make a summer nor will one youngster, no matter how good, make his sire's name as a stud. The unshown stud dog must be able to turn out youngster after youngster of excellence, and of similar type, before there will be any great demand for him. The stud should also be a dog of excellent temperament, for the shy dog is the greatest possible detriment to any breed. He must be a 'dog' and have no trace of femininity, and he must be capable, sensible and virile in his stud work.

A Collie, being among the medium-sized breeds, should not be used at stud too young, but on the other hand his first attempt should not be left too late, for it is often difficult to get an older dog started. I consider that the ideal for a Collie is to have his first bitch when he is about ten months old; he should not have a further bitch until he is 16-18 months of age, and from then on, for the next eight to twelve months, he should certainly not have more than one bitch per month, preferably only one in two months, but because of the difficulties of these things being seasonal we often cannot choose.

The young stud should be trained from the very beginning in the way you intend him always to mate his bitches, and you will find it a saving both of your time and the stud dog's energies if he is taught to expect his bitches to be held for him. For the first mating with a young dog it is most important that an experienced brood bitch, known to be flirtatious and easy to mate, should be used. The very worst thing that can happen to a learner stud dog is for him to fail to mate his first bitch; it will make him uneasy, lose condition, and, on a later occasion when he is asked to do the job again, he will have lost confidence in himself. If his first bitch is easy and 'teaches him the job' he will rapidly learn from her how to deal with more awkward ones he may meet later in life. It is often advantageous, too, if the bitch can be one he knows—not his own constant companion, however, for quite often a dog who knows a bitch too well—if they are always kennelled together or are both house-dogs—will refuse to have anything whatever to do with her, and this is another point against the keeping of a stud dog by a small Kennel.

G

It is advisable that, for a first mating at least, there should be two attendants, one to hold the bitch by her collar, the other to assist the dog.

The dog and the bitch should first be introduced to each other on the lead, so that you can be sure she is ready to meet him willingly and to indulge in a little mild flirtation. If the bitch seems happy about it the two dogs should be taken to a small run, or a shed, or to wherever you intend the mating to take place, and released there. Do not allow the play to last too long, for the dog will quickly become hot and his energies be wasted. It is so very important that you assure yourself as nearly as possible that the bitch is not going to snap at the dog; a bite at this stage might put him off for months. As soon as the bitch has shown she is really willing to stand firmly for the dog, she should be held by the collar, and the dog should be allowed to mount.

At this moment the second attendant should hold the bitch by her rear end, from underneath, and without making any fuss, or getting in the dog's way, slightly raise the vulva, to make it easier for the dog to penetrate. The best way to do this is to sit on the ground, on the left-hand side of the bitch, and place the left hand flat under the bitch, from the side, and backwards between her hind legs, with the vulva just lying between the first and second fingers of that hand. In this manner the exact position of the penis can be felt and the dog given every possible assistance. As soon as the dog penetrates and starts to work rapidly, the right arm can be passed behind him and he can then be held firmly and gently until the 'tie' has taken place. Even a bitch which has previously been mated will usually groan or whimper slightly during the swelling of the penis as the 'tie' is being effected, and it is wise at this time to talk reassuringly, not only to the bitch, but to the dog, for he may fear he has done something wrong if the bitch is crying under him. Be sure to tell the young dog he is a clever boy! When the 'tie' is complete the dog will usually indicate that he is ready to get off the bitch and turn. He should be helped in this, for any chance of pulling away must be avoided, as this can cause a rupture to the dog and/or irreparable damage to the bitch. I find that the best way to hold them whilst the dog is getting off and turning is to take the tails of both in the one hand—with the bitch's tail *under* the dog's leg, of course—this leaves your other hand free to assist the dog to get his leg over the bitch if this is necessary.

It might be advantageous here to explain the 'tie', for it is something which is peculiar to the canine and kindred species. In other species of mammal the male is equipped with Cowper's glands, which eject the semen in a swift emission immediately the vagina is penetrated. The dog, unsupplied with these glands, can emit semen only gradually on the drip principle, and therefore the absence of Cowper's glands has been offset by the 'tie'. As soon as the penis enters the vagina it begins gradually to swell until, at about the middle of the penis, there is a very pronounced bulbous swelling which makes it impossible for the dog to retract without doing very grave damage. To make things doubly sure, whilst the penis is swelling the muscles of the bitch contract round it, and hold it firmly, and the duration of the length of the muscular contraction of the bitch controls the length of the 'tie'. It is for this reason that the length of time varies from bitch to bitch and is not always the same with the same dog. The normal length of time for the duration of a tie is about 10-25 minutes, but variation is so great that the tie may last from moments only to as much as an hour or more. During the tie the bitch should be prevented from sitting down, fidgeting, etc., and the dog should be kept under surveillance all the time. If necessary, the bitch should be held gently.

You may find that the young dog, whilst not minding the bitch being held by her collar, resents her being held by her rear. If this is so, then for this first mating he should be allowed to mate her in his own way, but the moment he penetrates he should be helped, as described above, and at the same time the left hand should be placed in the position already described so that he will be more accustomed to it for his next attempt. A great deal of time spent in getting the young dog's confidence in being handled is time well spent in this first mating; so much time will be saved on subsequent occasions, more especially when the time comes when he has a difficult bitch brought to him who resents his attentions and has to be held.

It should be remembered that the young dog, being used

for the first time, will probably emit semen in which the sperm are dead, and therefore a first mating on the dog's side should always be a dual mating. The second ejaculation is likely to be fertile, as the old, wasted sperm will have been passed out, and for this reason it is always wise, if not essential, to give a second service at a first mating. The same remarks apply if the dog has not been used for a long time, and if there has been a long interval between his matings a second service should be given. With these two exceptions, if the first mating was satisfactory there is rarely, if ever, need for a second service.

It may happen that a bitch, particularly a 'maiden', though appearing to be ready and 'standing' willingly to the dog, may yet turn on him when he tries to enter. It is quite possible, in such a case, that if you separate them and let them meet again some hours later, or the next day, all will be well and she will accept him with no trouble at all, provided that she is not later than the fifteenth day in her season. On the other hand, the bitch may have a slight stricture and she should be examined for this. Particularly if it is a case of the bitch being willing and the dog, try though he may, being unable to effect penetration, should a stricture be suspected. Grease a finger (which has a short nail) and slide the finger gently into the vagina; a slight stricture can be broken down easily and almost painlessly in this way, and then the dog will have no trouble. However, if an obstruction is found which cannot be dealt with in this manner, the bitch must be attended to by a veterinary surgeon before she can be mated. If the condition is detected reasonably early in the season the necessary dilation or operation can take place and a service still be obtained in that same season, but if it is not discovered until the bitch is going off, then she will have to wait until the next season. In any instance of the dog having great difficulty in penetrating, although he is attempting this correctly, a stricture should be suspected and the bitch examined at once before the dog wears himself out on a fruitless task.

The stud fee for any dog should be set, and agreed upon, before the service takes place. An established stud dog will stand at his advertised fee, but the dog mating his first bitch always presents a slight problem. Nevertheless, the fee at which you value his services should be clearly stated prior to the service, for the fee to any dog is paid *for the service* and not for the *result* of the service. This is all very well with a proved dog, but with an unproved one it is wise to say either that you will take a puppy in lieu of fee (always very much to your financial advantage) or—and I consider this is the fairer method—the fee, as stated, shall be paid when it is known that the bitch is in whelp. By this arrangement no one stands to lose anything. With this exception, all stud fees are payable at the time of the service, unless the owner of the stud dog has agreed to a different arrangement with the bitch's owner.

Quite often one is requested to take a puppy instead of a fee even to a proved dog, and the bitch's owner should not feel that this denotes any lack of confidence in the merits of the stud dog, nor even in his merits to that particular bitch, if the stud dog owner cannot agree to such a suggestion. There is nothing more awkward for the owner of a Kennel than to have one 'odd' puppy, of an age different from the others in the Kennel, and for this reason and no other it is frequently necessary for the stud dog owner to turn down such a suggestion. Most of us, however, try our best to be helpful and if we cannot accept a puppy in lieu of a fee we shall probably be able to make some other suggestion.

It should be stressed that whilst a 'tie' is desirable it is not necessary for there to be one for the mating to be a success. There are some dogs who never 'tie' a bitch and with whom bitches rarely miss, but naturally both the owner of the stud dog and of the bitch feel that things are more satisfactory if there has been a 'tie', and in a case where there has been no 'tie' it is usually wise, if only to create good feeling, to let the payment of the fee depend upon whether the bitch conceives or not.

Allowing for the exceptions mentioned above, it is not necessary or desirable to give two services to a bitch, but if for any reason it has been agreed that there should be two services, the second should take place as soon as possible after the first, and certainly within twenty-four hours.

Whilst the stud fee is payable for the service and not for the result of the service, most stud dog owners say that, should there be no puppies, there will be a free service to the bitch next time she comes in season, provided the stud dog is still in the same ownership. This is not compulsory in law and is simply a 'gentlemen's agreement'.

If it is agreed to take a puppy instead of a fee, this should be clearly set down at the time of mating. Special points which must be enumerated are whether the pup is to be the first or second pick of the litter, and at what age it is to be selected, and taken away (not always the same thing!).

A dog which is placed at public stud should already have been proved; that is to say, there should be at least one living litter born to him. (It is important to stress that word 'living', for it does happen, in rare and isolated cases, that the dog carries a lethal factor which causes the death of all his puppies at birth.) He should have a stud card which the owner can send out to those who enquire about him, and this card should give all the details that the bitch's owner is likely to want to know. His fee, colour, preferably a photograph, his Stud Book number, if he has one, if not, then his registration number, and a copy of his pedigree, preferably to five generations. It must also carry your address, phone number and name of your railway station. It is a wise precaution to state also that whilst every care is taken of visiting bitches no responsibility can be accepted for them. This little clause can save you a packet of trouble should an accident occur whilst she is in your care.

In conclusion, it is hardly necessary to say that of course your stud dog must be kept always in the pink of condition and free from parasites of any kind.

# CHAPTER 10

# THE GREAT MOMENT: YOUR FIRST LITTER

As you will already have realized, quite the most important part of any Kennel is its female foundation stock. However many bitches or bitch puppies you propose starting with, do make the very most you can of them; much better to have one really good bitch to start with than two mediocre ones, and best of all is one really good bitch which has proved herself as a producer of top-class winning stock—if you can persuade any owner to part with such a gem!

Let us take for granted that you have already followed the advice in the earlier chapters, and that now your first bitch has reached the age when you are expecting her to come into season and are hoping to mate her.

You will not, of course, have left it until now to decide to what stud dog you are going to send her. Provided that you are free to make the choice yourself (by which I mean that you have not obtained your bitch on part-breeding terms), then you should have begun to think out, long ago, what you consider the ideal mate for her. First, study her pedigree most carefully, and find out all you possibly can about her antecedents. Discover whether there is a good dog in her pedigree which has proved himself to be prepotent for those characteristics for which you most admire him. If he is still alive and still producing stock, weigh up the possibilities of putting your bitch back to him. If it is impossible to use him, but you are still anxious to try to establish those good points of his, try to find a descendant of his, a son, or grandson, or better still a double grandson, who also excels in these good points, and who you know, if possible, has proved himself to be a carrier of these good points also.

Now you have chosen the mate. The next thing is to write to the stud dog owner telling him when you expect your bitch to be in season, and making a tentative booking to the stud dog. Then, as soon as she is really in season, write again *at once*, telling him the actual day on which she first came into season, and suggesting what day you propose sending or taking her to be mated. Taking her is the ideal, but this cannot always be managed, and it is far, far better to send your bitch away to be mated to the most suitable dog than to use a less suitable one just because he happens to be handy. But if you expect to have to send her away it is essential that the necessary arrangements should be made well in advance, for you will, of course, have to send her in a box or hamper and it has to be a fair-sized container to house a Collie! You will find that most stud dog owners have a box which they are willing to lend or hire to you provided that you make the request in plenty of time. You may think it is rather mercenary to say 'hire' when the dog's owner will be getting a fee, but remember that these boxes cost a fair amount of money these days and that every journey they make shortens their lives. Often the 'return empty' journey creates the most wear and tear on a box, for the railway has no respect at all for these empties, it seems. Your bitch herself may cause a great deal of damage as she may object to being boxed, and fight a battle with it at some time on the journey, and then the box is returned to its owner very much the worse for wear. I have had them come back with the bottom or sides very nearly scratched and gnawed right through. For this reason it is very much more satisfactory to have your own box so that the bitch can sleep in it at night for several nights and thus get accustomed to it before making the journey. More will be said of travelling boxes, dimensions, etc., in a later chapter.

Do not imagine for one moment that just because your bitch is now nine months old she will come into season, and if she does she will be too young to mate. Most general books on dogs tell us that the bitch usually comes into season at nine months of age and then at six-monthly intervals. There is only one thing wrong with this—no Collie I have ever met seems to have read those books! It is much more likely that a Collie will show no signs of coming into season until she is twelve months old or considerably more.

The first sign that can be looked for is usually a whitish, thick, but slight, discharge from the vagina. If you have a dog he will probably show some interest in her when this first starts. Within a day or two the discharge will gradually colour until it is red. Being a Collie, it is most unlikely that there will be any appreciable swelling of the vulva, which happens in most breeds and which the books always tell you to expect! Frequently I have had bitches booked to my stud dogs, and the date for bringing them arranged, only to be rung the night before and told, 'It's no use coming, she hasn't swollen in the least.' This is something which can be completely discounted in our breed, and a bitch is usually mateable without this sign appearing at all. A bitch herself usually indicates when she is ready to be mated by lifting her tail. This she will do when confronted with a dog, often for another bitch; if she is rubbed gently on the back just above the root of the tail; and also if the vulva is touched gently. When I say 'lifts her tail' perhaps this should be rather more fully explained. She does not fly her tail over her back, as with a 'gay' tail, but she will lift it stiffly from the root and flick it directly over sideways, so that the tail sticks straight out at an angle of 45° before drooping down with its natural weight. When rubbed, or sniffed by a dog or another bitch, she will move her tail, still in the same position, from side to side. This, undoubtedly, is the moment to take her to the dog.

Owners of stud dogs have their own particular method of handling their own dogs, and the method of getting a mating has been dealt with in the chapter on the stud dog. The stud dog owner may offer you a second service, say the day after the first, but in my opinion, unless there has been an unsatisfactory, short service the first time, or unless there has been no 'tie', a second service is quite unnecessary, unless the dog is mating his first bitch or has not been used for a very long time, and it is easy to appreciate that the owner of a top stud dog which is in much demand and used regularly, will not be anxious to give a second service if the first was satisfactory because of the risk of overusing the dog. A popular dog during the 'season' (for these things *are* seasonal) may mate three dogs a week for a short period, sometimes more, and if everyone wanted two services the poor dog would hardly ever have a day off!

It is well to let the bitch rest for a while after the service before starting the return journey, if this is possible, and she must of course be kept just as much under surveillance for the remainder of the season as she was in the first part, for a bitch, once mated, can be mated again by another dog. Then there is no guarantee of the paternity of the puppies.

For the first four weeks after the mating there is no need to give the bitch any different treatment at all. During this period it is well-nigh impossible to know whether she is in whelp or not. The only likely indication will be an erratic appetite, on her food one day, off the next, and possibly (if she is a bitch you know really well) you may notice some slight changes in her character. She may alter her habits and personality very slightly, and this is naturally more easily discernible in a bitch which is a 'house-pet' than in one which leads a kennel life. At approximately 25-28 days from the date of mating, a veterinary surgeon can usually tell you whether the bitch is in whelp or not, and if she is, then from this time on she needs extra attention. Her way of life should not be altered at all; her exercise, provided it was adequate in the first place, should neither be diminished nor increased, but food is the all-important item for the next few weeks when she is carrying sometimes as many as nine or ten puppies, and she must be helped in every possible way to make a good job of it with the minimum amount of strain on herself. Collies, on the whole, are extremely good mothers, both when expectant and nursing, but they are also apt to be very self-sacrificing, and if the bitch is not properly looked after she will almost certainly drain her own body to give to her unborn puppies.

As soon as you know she is in whelp her feeding should be completely altered, and I consider the ideal diet for a pregnant bitch, from the fourth week after mating until she whelps, to be:

Breakfast: Cereals or wholemeal bread, with 1 pint milk, 1 teaspoonful cod liver oil and 1 teaspoonful calcium phosphate. A raw egg, if possible; if not possible daily, then as often as can be managed.
Mid-day: 1–1½ lb. raw meat (lean).
6 p.m.: As mid-day.
10 p.m.: A bowl of biscuit meal soaked in stock or milk.

The bitch will probably not be able immediately to take this complete change from her ordinary diet of two meals a day; she should be accustomed to it by an increase of one meal the first day, then an increase in the size of the meat meal the second day, and the fourth meal offered on the third day. By the end of 4-6 days she should be quite happy in the new routine.

Don't worry unduly if occasionally she refuses a meal, or even all her meals for one day, but don't let it become a habit. If she gets a bit fussy over her food try to vary the diet. Persist with the raw meat unless she absolutely refuses to eat this, which is unlikely, but the meat can be varied. Mutton makes an occasional flavoursome change from beef or horse, or, if she is very difficult, try her with the meat lightly cooked once a day and raw for the other meal. Rabbit will almost always tempt the most difficult feeder, but if you are stuck with a problem it is up to you to use your ingenuity and ring the changes until you find what really tempts her most. It is rare that you get an in-whelp bitch which is a 'bad-doer' but these suggestions are 'just in case'. I have one particular bitch who has a different 'fad' every time she is in whelp! (As she has had six litters I am getting used to her!) For instance, she would not eat at all before her first litter unless everything had cheese sauce on it! For her second she would not look at cheese but wanted everything slightly flavoured with rabbit. Her raw meat was most welcome provided it had lain for a while in cold rabbit stock before being given to her—and so on. Mind you, I am quoting extreme cases; I do not believe in pandering to fads and fancies in any dog except a bitch in whelp, but if you get one of these being 'choosey', then in my opinion she must be pandered to.

Beyond keeping your bitch adequately fed, and supplied with plenty of *fresh* drinking water, there is only her exercise which needs attention. During the early days she should have plenty of unrestricted exercise, but she should never be forced to go for a long walk by being 'dragged'. Almost certainly she will gallop as usual and chase birds or whatever her favourite pastime may be. There should be no need to restrict her in any way, and she will adjust her own exercise as the days advance. Only if she is normally exercised with other dogs which are very boisterous and likely to knock her about should any alteration be made, and if this was her normal way of exercising she should be taken out either alone or with one staid Collie of either sex who will not chase and hustle her. Many people prefer that a bitch in the last two or three weeks of pregnancy should be exercised only on the leash. This I cannot agree with, for several reasons. Firstly, that it is much more tiring for any dog to exercise on the leash than free, because they have to adjust themselves to our pace, which is far from normal to them, and, secondly, a willing, friendly bitch will be much less likely to show that she does not wish to go far by hanging back on the leash than she will if she is free and can quietly but firmly indicate to you that it is 'time to go home'!

It is important to see that the bitch you intend breeding from is free from worms and skin disease. It is advisable to worm the bitch some two to three weeks before you expect her in season, but if she has 'caught you on the hop', as they so often do, do *not* worm her between the time of the onset of her season and the time of mating; neither should you worm her within three weeks of the date of service, but it is usually safe to use a good reliable vermifuge between the third and fifth weeks. However, to avoid accident, it is best to consult your veterinary surgeon in this matter.

One other preparation which is often neglected but which (I speak from experience) if not taken care of can cause the death of a puppy. Be sure to cut the 'petticoats' and long hair from under the tail of your bitch. I have on more than one occasion known of new-born puppies being caught in their mother's hair, and either being strangled or breaking their necks if mother gets up quickly, or at best being carried out of the box and then falling off into the cold. This is a most important point.

Now to the whelping arrangements. The bitch should be allowed to become accustomed to the place where she will be expected to whelp at least two weeks before the date she is due. The best place for the bitch to whelp is in an outside shed; alternatively, an empty room in the house where she will know she will be undisturbed, for, while a Collie as a rule likes to know that her owner is present with her whilst she is whelping, she certainly does not want to have her puppies in the lounge where all the family, as well as the visitors, will be coming and going.

Whether she is to whelp in a shed or in a spare room she

must have a suitable box in which to whelp, and I do not think
that the importance of such a box can possibly be overstressed,
for a great number of the puppies which die, either as soon as
they are born or within a day or two after this event, do so
because the whelping conditions have not been satisfactory.

A large box, approximately 4 ft. wide by 3 ft. deep, is a
good size. It should also be about 2 ft. 6 in. in height and should
have a covered top. It is preferable that the whole of the 4 ft.
side should not be open, but that it should be boarded up,

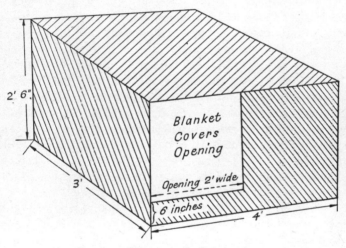

FIG. 21.—Diagram of whelping-box

leaving an entrance of some 2 ft. in width, and there should be
a board along the bottom of the opening at least 6 in. high. A
thick blanket should hang from the top, completely covering
this opening. This then makes the dark, cave-like den to which
the bitch in her natural state would have taken herself, and in
which every particle of heat given off by the bitch and her
puppies is conserved as much as possible, so the babies are
living in a fairly high, even temperature.

However, these precautions for keeping the babies warm I
rarely consider to be adequate. More new-born puppies die
from getting chilled than from any other reason and it is
extremely difficult to resuscitate a tiny mite once it has been

thoroughly chilled. Consider for a moment that the puppies, at birth, are suddenly and rudely shot into this world from the temperature inside their dam of some 100° Fahrenheit, and imagine the shock it must be to their little systems to find themselves, wet and miserable, in, at best, a temperature of 60°, and if in winter most probably down to, or below, freezing.[1]

So into the already snug box I always place, hanging from the roof, a 24-in. tubular electric airing cupboard heater, and this is turned on on any but the very warmest of our heat-wave summer days. If the box is a well-made one, this will keep it at approximately 70°, so long as you do not forget your thick blanket in front. This temperature may seem high for the bitch, and indeed often makes her pant, but if she is given plenty of liquid, both milk and fresh water, I have never known it have any adverse effect on the mother. Naturally when you wish to dispense with the heater this must be done gradually, and the ideal is to have the heater thermostatically controlled. If you are not lucky enough to be able to do this, then the heater must be turned off for short spells at first, and at the warmest moment of the day, lengthening these periods gradually.

Much use has been made recently of infra-red lamps for the rearing of puppies, both over the whelping-box (when the box must be an open one) and later in the kennel when the 'tinies' start to run about. They are excellent, particularly in the latter case. The infra-red lamps need very careful adjustment and care must be taken of their possible effect on the eyes both of the mother and of the litter. Naturally the type of heater I use has no beneficial rays, but as a heat-promoting unit I consider it ideal, and there is no risk to eyes as it gives no light. Some kind of heat is undoubtedly essential, and quite apart from the object of keeping the babies from getting chilled there is also another important point. It is an accepted scientific fact that quite a large proportion of the food consumed is used to keep up the body temperature, and this part of the food is then lost to its purpose of body-building. As tiny puppies can eat only very limited amounts of food the more of it that can be used for

---

[1] It must always be remembered that a new-born puppy has no 'shivering mechanism' and therefore no means of warming itself by muscular contraction for about seven days after birth.

body-building the better, and it can be assumed that if puppies are kept warm less food is needed for use as a 'heater' and more of it can go to promoting growth.

One other point on this same subject. Never feed the in-whelp bitch with really cold food, even her raw meat should just have the chill off it, for every time she consumes stone-cold food her body temperature drops, and for a while the functions of her body are concerned with turning the food into heat-promoting substances, instead of growth-promoting ones, and each intake of cold food therefore halts, temporarily, the growth of the unborn puppies.

I have never found it necessary to have any kind of 'guard rail' inside a Collie whelping-box, although I know that some people consider them absolutely essential, and for this reason I mention them here. If such a rail is thought necessary it should be placed inside each of the three complete sides of the box, about four inches from floor level and about four inches from the sides. The purpose of this rail is to prevent the bitch from crushing a puppy between her back and the wall of the kennel, should a puppy get behind her.

There are various opinions as to what is the best type of bedding to use for a bitch to whelp on, but I am certain there is nothing so satisfactory as several layers of newspaper. The bitch, before whelping, will rip up her bed anyway, and the paper can be changed frequently, and as often as it becomes wet. Straw and hay should *never* be used, for it is easy for the bitch to lose a new-born puppy in such bedding; also, straw, particularly, may prick the eyes of the tiny pups and cause damage and possibly blindness. Whilst wood-wool is 'safe' in regard to eye damage, it is still likely to cover up a new-born puppy whilst the mother is attending to the next addition to the family. Even for older puppies hay should never be used as it carries and breeds lice.

The accepted period of gestation is 63 days, but most Collies, particularly maiden bitches, will have their puppies a day or so earlier, so one may start to expect them by about the 59th day. It is a wise move (because it is a very sure guide and may save the owner some disturbed nights) to start taking the bitch's temperature twice daily, about six days before she is due.

At this stage it will usually be found that the temperature is slightly sub-normal, around 100°, but before the pups are imminent the temperature will fall considerably, at least as a general rule, usually down to about 98°. Once the temperature reaches this low level the puppies can be expected within the next twenty-four hours. Occasionally a bitch's temperature will drop even lower (I had one which always went down to 96°), but they are the exception. Equally exceptional is the bitch whose temperature barely drops at all.

Another indication that whelping time is near is that the bitch, when at exercise, will stop to pass water very frequently. Later still she will begin to be very restless, and when this stage is reached she should be taken to her whelping-box at once. There she will probably begin almost immediately to tear up her newspaper, and she may continue with this pastime for as long as a whole day before the next stage is reached. During this period leave her quiet and look in on her every hour at least so that you may know when she begins to strain.

As the labour pains actually begin she will become more and more restless, pant a great deal and breathe very quickly. She will also turn frequently and look at, and lick, her tail. Sometimes the first puppy is born almost as soon as the pains begin, but equally frequently there is a lapse of as much as one-and-a-half hours between the onset of the pains and the birth of the first puppy. The bitch will not strain constantly during such a long period, but will alternate bouts of vigorous straining with spells of rest to regain her strength. If a period of two hours passes from the time of the onset of the pains without any signs of a puppy being born you should contact your veterinary surgeon at once. One cannot stress this point too strongly, and it is for this reason that you should look in on your bitch frequently after she goes to her whelping-box, so that you may know exactly when she first shows signs of straining.

There is no doubt whatever that almost every bitch likes to have her owner with her at this time, and while they do not like being fussed about they do so much appreciate the fact that you are just sitting quietly by.

From time to time there is the bitch which *must* whelp in the spot she chooses, and this may be your lap, but really you will almost have to put up with it, for if her mind is made up on this you will be quite unable to change it!

Collies, as a rule, are very easy whelpers, and no difficulties need be expected, but if a puppy gets held up, either because it is too large or wrongly presented, or because the pelvic opening is too small, that puppy naturally prevents the birth of the remainder of the litter, and any hold-up may mean death to them.

Without wanting to cast gloom on your preparations for your first whelping, it is always best to be prepared, and here is a list of those things you should have ready to hand when you think the whelping is imminent: Cotton wool, permanganate of potash, sterile scissors, a bowl of hot water and a Turkish towel.

When the labour pains really start, immediately turn on the heater in the box, unless the temperature of the whelping room is above 65° (most unlikely in our English climate!), so that the babies may have a warm home to be born into.

In a normal whelping you will notice first a greenish discharge staining the newspaper and then, soon after this, you will see the membranous water-bag protruding from the bitch's vulva. Each puppy is enclosed in a separate sac. Keep your eyes open but do not attempt to help her at this stage, and if all is normal one of two things will happen: either the bitch will tear the sac as it is protruding, letting the fluid escape, to be followed almost immediately by the whole puppy, or else the puppy will suddenly shoot into the box, still enclosed in the sac. The bitch will then immediately rip the sac open and lick up the fluid. The puppy will still be attached to the placenta, or after-birth, by the umbilical cord, and this the bitch will bite and sever, and then she will eat the afterbirth. This done (it usually takes place in a matter of seconds) she will immediately turn her attentions to the puppy, licking it, often quite roughly, until it breathes and gives its first cry.

Sometimes, with a first litter, the first puppy arrives and mother just doesn't know what to do. If this is the case it is up to you to do it for her, and to do it quickly. You must pick up the puppy, slit the bag which, though tough, can readily be broken with the fingers, and the puppy will fall from the bag. Look quickly to make sure there is no mucus in the mouth or

H

air passages, then give it to the mother, holding it to her muzzle, when she will probably begin to lick it at once. If she still remains 'clueless', take the puppy and rub it briskly with the Turkish towel. The pup will almost certainly cry and mother will equally certainly immediately say, 'Hey, give me that; that's mine!' and your troubles will be over. Once her instinct is aroused she will carry on from there and deal with the remaining pups herself. However, it is always wise to stand by, for if you leave her the worst may happen, and a puppy be suffocated before it can be cleared from the sac. The mother, having claimed the first pup when it cried, will probably take over and bite through the cord and sever the pup from the after-birth, but should she not do so the owner must do it for her. Therefore you will require your sterile scissors with which to sever the cord about 2 in. from the puppy's body. Have ready the permanganate of potash crystals so that, should there be any bleeding from the cord, caused either by the scissors or the bitch's bite, you can apply some, which will stop the bleeding at once.

Quite frequently the puppy will appear in the box, and yet be attached to the after-birth still inside the mother's body. In such a case it is necessary to make sure the after-birth appears; if it is retained after the birth of the last puppy it will certainly cause trouble. Sometimes, too, the mother will sever the cord with the puppy outside and the after-birth still in the passage. Again, make sure the after-birth is passed.

The natural action of the bitch is to eat each after-birth as it is severed from the puppy. My bitches are always allowed to do this, for this was a provision of nature for the nourishment of the bitch when, in her wild state, she had to stay in her lair after whelping and could not go hunting for food for a time. The eating of the after-birth is beneficial to the bitch as it contains many essentials which are good for her, and whilst providing nourishment it also acts as a laxative. There are two schools of thought on this subject, some breeders standing by and taking each after-birth as it is severed and destroying it.

There is no regular interval between the birth of the puppies. Sometimes a matter of minutes only may elapse between the birth of the first and second puppies, sometimes an hour or more, and if it is this long period the bitch will lie quiet and rest and frequently lick the puppies she has, stimulating them to live and eat. It is an ever-recurrent miracle to me to see the new puppy, still wet, blindly struggle to the nipple within a moment or two of being born, and start in on his breakfast!

Almost always, at some time during the labour there is a very long pause between the birth of the pups, and this usually indicates that the 'half-way' mark has been reached. Do not think that by this I mean that if your bitch has already had six puppies she is going to have twelve; the bitch's uterus is made up of two separate horns and the puppies lie in each of these, and when whelping begins, normally all the puppies from one horn are expelled first, then there is generally a fairly long pause whilst the second horn takes over the job and expels its quota of the litter. The horns do not necessarily hold an equal number of pups; in fact it can be very uneven, but there is a definite pause when one horn takes over from the other.

During the whelping the bitch may refuse all drink, but if she will take milk there is no reason why she should not have it, and if it is given it should be given as cold as possible, despite all earlier comments on warm food, for the cold will stimulate the labour pains, whereas warm milk might be conducive to sleep.

When you think she has finished whelping give her a drink of milk (I always leave a bowl in the whelping-box with her) and leave her to sleep for some hours, after having removed all damp bedding and given her fresh, dry newspaper.

A maiden bitch may not appear to have any milk at all when the puppies are born, and she will probably produce milk as soon as the pups start to suckle. Others do not produce milk for about a day, but this is rare. However, a new-born puppy can quite well exist for twenty-four hours without milk, though he should not have to do so, but do remember that he cannot exist for very long at all without warmth.

The first three days in the life of a puppy are vital, and the bitch should be looked at every few hours during this period so that one may spot at once if a puppy is being pushed away by the others and not getting his fair share of food, or if he is pushed away and has become chilled. Immediately on opening the door of the whelping room one should be able to know at once how the litter is doing. There is nothing more delightful than to be met with either complete silence, or delicious sucking noises! One is sometimes met with crying pups; however, this need not always give you cause for alarm, for the pups may be only giving hungry cries if you have arrived at feeding time. There is one sound which I never like to hear. This is the cry which sounds like a young kitten mewling, for this is the very distinctive cry which denotes a hungry puppy which is weak and sickly and for which it is difficult to do very much. However, should you find a puppy pushed away and cold, despite your heating precautions, pick him up at once and take him away, wrap him in a blanket and pop him in a cool oven (with the door open of course) or under the griller of an electric cooker for a while. A puppy, apparently dead, has often been revived in this way and gone back to its mother an hour or so later and never again looked back. Just one word on taking the puppy away. Mother will almost certainly resent this, so try not to let her see. Take out two puppies together, both in the one hand if possible, slip the weak one into your pocket or down your neck, and quickly put the other one back. Collies are clever but they can't count yet![1]

Always watch most carefully to see that one weakly baby is not constantly being pushed out; if it is, make sure that it gets its fair share of the milk-bar by holding it on to the nipple for a definite period (ten–twenty minutes) every two hours for the first day or so. It will probably pick up, thanks to this attention, and after a couple of days be able to take its own place and keep up with its hardier brothers and sisters. Many a really good puppy has been saved in this way and the trouble entailed is more than worth while.

If, because the mother cannot care for them, or if only because the litter is very large, you have to hand-rear a puppy, it is something which can be accomplished. The complete hand-rearing of a litter is a most wearisome task, for the puppies must be fed with the greatest regularity, every two hours, day and night, for the first week at least.[2]

I find that Lactol, which is specially prepared for puppies and is therefore equivalent, in essentials, to bitch's milk, is the best to use. You can do no better than to follow exactly the

[1] See note on page 123.     [2] See Appendix 6.

directions given with the food. There is on the market a most excellent bottle, John Bell & Croydon's Premature Baby Feeder. This is marked off in teaspoonsful, and has a small teat, just about the size of a Collie's own. Further, the milk can be very gently pressed into the puppy's mouth, until it gets the idea of sucking.

If you want to help a bitch with a big litter by supplementary feeding always select the weakest puppies in the litter and try always to feed the same puppies.

If only supplementary feeding, then the mother will look after the puppies, cleaning them and keeping them warm. However, if you are rearing a litter which has no mother, then it is essential to keep them very warm, and you must also do something to simulate the motion of the mother's tongue on them. After feeding, their tummies should be gently rubbed in a circular motion with a small piece of cotton wool dipped in olive oil, and this motion continued until the bowels act. The puppies must be kept clean, by wiping with cotton wool dipped in mild antiseptic, and care must be taken to dry the puppies afterwards. They can be dusted with a plain talcum powder or boracic powder if desired.

Hand-feeding should continue, with the spaces between meals getting longer, until the puppies are three weeks old, when raw meat can be added to the diet and the usual method of weaning gradually introduced.

Everything used for these babies must be kept just as clean as if you were feeding a human baby, and all their bowls, bottles, etc., sterilized, and the bottle and teats kept immersed in cold water.

The bitch will be most reluctant to leave her litter for the first day or so after whelping, and I never make a bitch leave the nest for the first twenty-four hours if she does not wish to do so, but after this period has elapsed she should be encouraged to take a short spell away, just long enough to relieve her bladder twice daily. Gradually she will increase these spells of her own accord, but in my opinion no bitch should be allowed to take normal exercise until such time as she has completely finished with her litter, for too much excitement and exercise will cause drying up of the milk, and possible collapse from calcium derangement. The ideal, to my way of thinking, is for the whelping kennel to be in a run to which the bitch can have access at all times if she so wishes. A good mother will not be seen in the run very often, and then only for a few minutes at a time, whilst a naughty mother can be shut in with her pups if necessary.

For at least twenty-four hours after the last puppy has been born the bitch should have no solid food at all, being kept on milk (preferably goat's milk), Lactol and gruel. If at the end of this time she appears perfectly normal, a little solid food may be introduced in the shape of fresh raw meat, but it is preferable to keep the bitch on fluids for two days, and I feed meat during this period only if the bitch turns against milky foods, which she may sometimes do. Fluids, however, can include raw eggs beaten up in milk, and if she has had rather a trying time it is always advantageous to add glucose to her liquid foods for a day or two. A dessertspoonful twice a day is sufficient.

Continue to keep the puppies bedded on newspaper; using a blanket even after whelping is concluded may be risky for the bitch may push it up into folds, and a puppy become lost in it. Frequently you will find that a bitch refuses to have any bedding at all in her box, and will either push it right out or into the corners. Undoubtedly the bitch knows best what she wants and if she insists on this all bedding should be removed. You may find that the babies, because of the strength of the pushing with the back legs to hold themselves against the teats, will develop sore pads on their back feet if they are directly on wood, but I have never known this have any lasting ill-effects and I have had a number of bitches who refused all bedding.

Once the first two days are passed, the bitch must be given all the food she will eat. I always put my bitches back at once on to the five meals a day they have been accustomed to during the pre-natal period, and in addition the bitch has a bowl of milk constantly in her box with her. I am not in favour of encouraging any bitch to leave her puppies and for the first few days at least they are fed actually in the whelping-box. By leaving the milk in the box there is, of course, the risk of it being spilt, but I have very rarely found this happen, and as a result of this leaving of the milk you will find that your bitch will drink between 4–5 pints a day in addition to her usual feeds, and if she has a big litter this is a great advantage. Should the unlikely occur and your Collie produce only one or two pups, instead of the average 6–9, she will need much less food, and, anyway, unless she is a real glutton will probably adjust things herself. But with a litter of six or more do remember that she needs a really adequate quantity of meat, at least 2 lb., preferably 3 lb., daily. There is no food which 'makes milk' as does raw meat.

With a very big litter, or in the event of your suspecting that the quality of the milk is not very good—which you will soon detect by squeaking, discontented puppies—the addition of Lactagol to the bitch's food is a great help. This is obtainable from any chemist and a Collie should be given the full human dose advised on the packet.

All puppies are born with dew-claws on their front legs. Very few Collies are born with back dew-claws as well. Should they be, then these MUST be removed. There is not a hard and fast rule in our breed about the removal of front dew-claws, so you can do exactly as you like in this matter. For myself, I never remove them, for I cannot see the point of putting pups to unnecessary suffering. Back dew-claws are another matter, and if you find these are present call your veterinary surgeon and have them removed when the puppies are 3–4 days old. It is an easy job to do, but not a nice one, and one which you really cannot do yourself unless you have previously seen it done properly.

When the puppies are three weeks old (with a large litter, especially if the bitch is young, even a little earlier) you can begin to wean them, and their first meal should be one of raw scraped meat, about one dessertspoonful per puppy. Of course you will need to feed each puppy separately, with your fingers, until after a day or two they become accustomed to the meat. At three weeks and two or three days they can have two meat meals daily, each of one heaped dessertspoonful, and a day or so later yet a third meal can be offered, but this should be one of milk, thickened with Farex. By the time they are four weeks old the babies should be having 3 oz. of raw meat daily, in two meals, and a third meal of Farex and milk. At the beginning of the fifth week the babies can be introduced to a fourth meal, this time a starchy meal, preferably of one of the well-known brands of puppy biscuit meal, such as Saval No. 1 or Weetmeet No. 1, *very thoroughly* soaked in milk or stock. To soak meal thoroughly it should be measured out and at least twice its volume of liquid, almost at boiling point, poured over it, and it should then be covered and left to soak at least four hours before feeding to the babies. Towards the end of this fifth week their final meal can also be introduced. This can either be another meal of biscuit or (and I prefer this) a meal of barley kernels soaked in cold milk overnight. If I am giving this, then the biscuit meal is soaked in stock, so that at this age the puppies are getting two meat meals, two milk meals and one meal of biscuit and stock daily, as follows:

   7 a.m.  Barley kernels soaked overnight in milk. Add half teaspoonful cod liver oil and quarter teaspoonful calcium phosphate per puppy.

11 a.m.  3–4 oz. raw meat.

  2 p.m.  Farex and milk.

  5 p.m.  3–4 oz. raw meat.

  9 p.m.  Biscuit meal soaked in stock.

As soon as you begin feeding the babies the mother will be taken away from them for increasingly long periods, until at five weeks old she is with them only at night, if at all, except for a playtime morning and evening.

I am not a believer in vegetables for dogs, whether adult or puppy, as the stomach and digestive juices of the dog are not equipped to deal with these fibrous matters, but at the same time a whole carrot makes a lovely toy, and there is some advantage to be gained from nibbling this!

It is absolutely essential that all meals should be given to an exact time-table, whether to pups or nursing mothers, and too much attention cannot be paid to this detail.

Except for the meat meals, I have made no attempt to give a guide as to the size of the meals, as it does vary so much from puppy to puppy, and it is a question of adapting to each pup; but as a rough guide a Collie baby at five weeks should get about a quarter-pint of milk in its Farex meal; the same with the barley kernels, of which it will need two tablespoonsful unsoaked. Its biscuit meal, after soaking, should be about half a breakfast cupful, but I stress that this is no definite amount; one pup varies so very much from the next. Only your own judgment can guide you.

Daily the size of the meal should be slightly increased but the number will never go above five. This number remains until the puppies are 10–12 weeks old, when the meals should be decreased to four in number, but the size of these four increased to offset the loss of a meal.

When eight weeks of age the babies will be taking 4 oz. of meat at each meal, and charts for feeding at various ages are set out elsewhere. Naturally, after the first few days of meat feeding it is no longer necessary to scrape the meat, and by the time they are four weeks old the meat should be given chopped into small pieces and as the puppies get older so the size of the pieces will become larger. Some breeders, and I am one, believe in feeding the meat meal in one lump for the puppy or adult dog to chew and tear for itself, so at six weeks of age my puppies get their meat in a lump, and the size of the lump is increased as the puppy grows.

As soon as the puppy is on to a breakfast meal this should have added to it half a teaspoonful of cod liver oil and a quarter teaspoonful of calcium phosphate per puppy. The calcium should be continued until the puppy has finished teething at eight months of age, but in the early days it should be increased gradually until at four months of age he is receiving the adult dose of one teaspoonful. The cod liver oil should be increased gradually also up to one teaspoonful and this dose continued more or less throughout his life, except that it is advisable to cut it out for a while should we happen to get a very hot summer!

It sometimes happens that when puppies are first put on to mixed food, as opposed to their mother's milk, they will have diarrhoea. This is nothing to become too worried about, but nevertheless it must not be allowed to persist. A meal of gruel made from arrowroot and milk, with a little glucose added, is helpful, as is a meal or two of Allbran, and the addition of half a teaspoonful per pup of McLean's stomach powder to each non-meat meal will also prove beneficial. I do not suggest that you use all of these remedies, but here are three to choose from!

Almost every puppy has worms. No, that is not a sweeping

statement, but the absolute truth. Puppies, whether they show marked symptoms of round worms or not, should *always* be wormed at six weeks of age, but puppies which show marked symptoms should be wormed two weeks earlier at least. The signs of worms are great distension of the tummy after a meal; discharging eyes; very loose, pale-coloured motions; passing of worms in the motions and vomiting worms. If puppies show any or all of these signs they should be wormed early, at, say, four weeks of age. Whether they show signs or not they should always be wormed at six weeks, anyway. There are a number of excellent vermifuges on the market, but it is preferable to consult your veterinary surgeon on the matter. Worm your puppies on a dry day, free from cold winds if possible, and try to avoid any chance of the puppies catching a chill for 48 hours after worming.

For no reason that I can discover, it will almost always be found that a litter from a maiden bitch is far 'wormier' than subsequent litters from the same bitch, and it is therefore specially important to watch for signs of infestation in a maiden bitch litter.

Many bitches, when their puppies are about four weeks old, will begin to regurgitate their own part-digested food for their babies, whether you are already weaning them or not. This is a perfectly natural instinct for the bitch and should not revolt you in any way, but at the same time it is not the best thing for mother or pups. So, if she starts this habit, make sure always to feed her out of sight and sound of the puppies, and do not let her return to them for about two hours after being fed. Even this does not always suffice. I once had a bitch who, when her puppies were almost four months of age, would go out as much as four hours after being fed, jump a five-foot wire fence and present her now large babies with an extra meal! Don't worry about this habit; it is always the best mothers who have this regurgitating instinct.

It is most important, from the time the puppies are one week old, to pay great attention to their toe-nails, which should be cut, on their front paws at least, at regular weekly intervals, for the baby nails are cruel, and with their regular pounding of mother when seeking for their milk will very rapidly tear and scratch her and make her very sore. Often one is rung up or written to for advice on various points, but an ever-recurring question is: 'My puppies are now two weeks old, but my bitch is being horrid to them and does not seem to want them. What can I do?' My answer is always a question, 'Have you cut your puppies' toe-nails?', and the reply, nine times out of ten, is a surprised 'No'. Here, then, is the answer: cut those toe-nails, look at the poor mother's breasts and apply a soothing cream to those scratches, and you will have no more trouble.

Now your first step has been made, your bitch, if you have fed her well and treated her as you should, will have played her part, and now it is up to you to rear those pups to the best of your ability, in the hope that in this, your first litter, you have a winner if not a Champion.

*Note* (see page 116):

Fairly frequently one finds—especially with a largish litter—that some of the puppies are born with a 'kink' in the spine. Before I knew better I never allowed such a puppy to live, but I now find that these puppies do very well, and, as a rule, by the time they are six to eight weeks old their spines are perfectly normal.

# CHAPTER II

# BUILDING A CHAMPION.
## PUPPY REARING

By the time that the babies are five weeks old the whole of their future is your responsibility, and it is up to you to rear them to the very best of your ability. It may be that there is a potential Champion in this, your first litter—you would not be the first person who has produced a Champion first time of trying—and now you can make or mar it. First difficulty, of course, is to pick the most 'likely-looking' pup, and this comes only with years of experience. But if you have amicable relations with the owner of the stud dog or, better still, if you have your bitch on breeding terms, the owner of either the stud dog or the bitch will give you every help in picking the litter over and helping you to keep the best. If the breeding terms agreement asks you to give up the pick, then the second-best will be clearly indicated to you. For myself, I like to pick a litter as soon as possible after it is born, while the pups are still wet if I can, and after that I don't like having to pick again until the babies are at least six months old. No matter what happens in between, barring accidents, your 'pick of litter' while it is still wet, however ungainly it may become at the age of 4–5 months, will always end up the best of the litter. I do not pretend that at this tender age of an hour or two it is possible to say such and such a pup will be a Champion, only which is the best of the lot; anyone who tries to tell you that a four-hour-old puppy is a potential Champion is just asking for trouble!

Puppies are almost always born with pink noses, and usually these turn black within a few days. However, in a sable or tricolour, with a blaze, particularly where the white hair touches the end of the nose, this part of the nose will frequently take much longer to go black. This need not give any cause for alarm, as very rarely does the nose, in these two colours, fail to change. With the blue merle, very often a much larger area of the nose is pink, and often remains so until the puppy is almost a year old. Sometimes a patch will remain pink all its life—this is so in dogs suffering from poor pigmentation—and there is not very much that can be done for it, but in a blue merle it is not a disqualifying fault, nor will it be found to be strongly hereditary.

The puppies' eyes should open about the 10th–14th day. That is with puppies born at approximately the right time, on the 60th–63rd day. It will usually be found that puppies born well ahead of time, say a week early, rarely open their eyes before the 18th–20th day, whilst puppies born late may have their eyes open by the time they are a week old. This would seem to give credence to the theory that the determination of time of the opening of the eyes is not 10 days after birth but 73 days after conception. If, after the expected time for the eyes to open has elapsed without anything happening, or if only one eye has opened, the eye area should be very gently massaged all round with either butter or olive oil. This is really to make the bitch lick the spot and the use of her tongue in massage will help the eye to open. One word of warning about eyes. Should a foster-mother be necessary, and should you have used a cat for this purpose, it is most essential to take care that the puppies are kept well within their darkened box, for the extreme roughness of a cat's tongue, compared with that of a bitch, tends to cause the eyes to open too early and then danger from light-rays is greatly increased. Special precautions are necessary if rearing on a cat under an infra-red lamp.

Eyes are always blue when first opened, and to the experienced observer there is a great difference between the blue eye which will turn brown eventually and the blue eye (of the merle) which will remain blue. When eyes start to change colour, at 4–6 weeks, is the time when you can assess what shade the eye will eventually be, for the eye which is the last to start changing colour will almost always be the lightest eye in the litter.

Until the puppies are at least six weeks old you will have to do your best for all of them, not just for your pick, until the litter is ready to sell. The diet already set out can be followed, with the increases already noted incorporated, and further diet sheets for various ages will be found in the Appendix. In addition, the puppies must have constant access to plenty of fresh, clear water from the time they are four weeks old. The puppies must either be fed separately or, if feeding several from the same dish, they must always be watched all the time, otherwise there will never be fair play. Some puppies will get too little, the greedy ones will always have more than their share.

Once the puppies are away from their dam their box can be supplied with straw or wood-wool for their bedding, preferably the latter, and the floor of the kennel should be freely sprinkled with sawdust. Collie babies are very clean, and by the time they are three weeks old are usually keeping their bed clean, and this will continue. Sawdust is not the very best of things for puppies to eat, and so, if it is fine weather, it is best to feed the babies in their run, and if it is not, and they have to be fed on the sawdusty floor, spread sheets of newspaper as 'tablecloths' under the feeding dishes.

Puppies, though they love playing with each other, should also have toys to play with, and those recommended are a rubber deck-tennis ring and an old stocking folded in half and knotted—this makes a delightful tug-of-war toy. Never give balls to puppies lest they cause an accident by being swallowed and choking the babies.

Once the puppies have reached the age of eight weeks any that are going to their new homes should do so as soon as possible, and it is advisable to give a feeding chart with each puppy, so that the same diet may be continued. The five meals should be continued until the puppies are three months, and then reduced to four meals, but the size of each meal should be increased, particularly the meat meal, and the three-month puppy will be eating 6–8 oz. of meat at each of his two meat meals. The four meals should be continued as long as the puppy will co-operate, especially during the winter months, and then, when they are cut to three, which should not be before six months of age, they should be:

7 a.m.   Wholemeal bread or barley kernels or cereals, with milk, cod liver oil and calcium. One teaspoonful of each.

5 p.m.   12–16 oz. raw meat.

10 p.m.   Bowl biscuit meal with stock.

Three meals should be continued until teething is over at about eight months of age, and then the puppy can be put on to its adult diet of two meals:

7 a.m.    Breakfast as above, but calcium can now be omitted.

6 p.m.    1-1½ lb. raw meat or paunch, which can be varied with cooked meat and biscuit meal, or cooked fish and biscuit meal, but remember raw meat is the natural diet.

During all puppyhood the babies can frequently be given big, raw bones to chew; they may well cause occasional fights, but none will prove fatal!

In addition to feeding your puppy well during the formative months, great attention must also be paid to its periods of sleep and exercise. In the early months the former is probably even more important than the latter, and so often when a puppy is sold at eight weeks of age its life becomes a misery because it is not realized that he needs just as much sleep as a human baby, and often a wee pup will be taken off to be house-pet to children, who when they are awake expect the puppy to be awake, and this is a point which should be very clearly stressed to your clients.

Correct ear carriage is a very essential part of any show Collie's make-up; if his ear carriage is wrong his whole expression will be marred, and now is the time when you should be watching those ears and training them. (*See* Figs. 7 and 8.)

Until a puppy is about eight weeks of age his ears are generally down on the side of his head, but soon after this age they assume the 'semi-erect' position we expect. Assume it, yes; keep it, no! Ear carriage may vary from day to day, even from hour to hur, but ao puppy which, for the greater part of the time, carries his ears correctly need not give much cause for alarm. However, if at, say, 10 weeks of age a puppy has given little indication that his ears are likely to go up at all, it is best to shave them, but there is always a risk in this, for the low-eared puppy may turn into a prick-eared one after being shaved and it is a point on which I would advise the novice to be very, very careful, taking the advice of an experienced breeder before doing anything drastic! Equally, a puppy who, at this age, has ears which stand erect should be taken in hand *at once*, for once erect ears are allowed to have their way they become hard and unmanageable and the battle is as good as lost. Almost always a Collie puppy will fly one or both ears at some time during the teething period of 4–8 months, and a little advice on this subject when one is selling a puppy is a very useful piece of knowledge to the new owner. The prick ear should NEVER have weights put on the tip. In my opinion this only tends to strengthen the muscle, which fights constantly against the weight, struggling to raise itself again and thereby

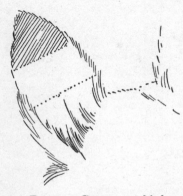

FIG. 22.—Grease one-third inside of ear

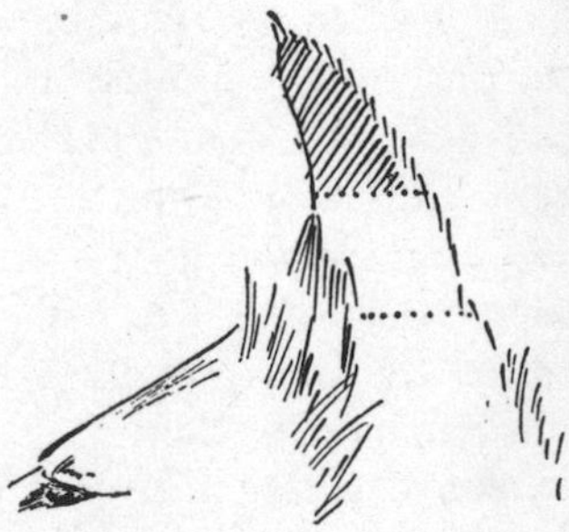

FIG. 23.—Grease one-third outside of ear

strengthening itself, and the struggle ends in a permanently erect ear, which may possibly turn over long enough to see you through a class in a show but which will be up again in no time. The most satisfactory method, in my experience, is to keep the tip of the ear, both inside and out, well greased. I do this by applying a lump of Cuticura ointment, or of wool fat (messier but less expensive), to both faces of the ear flap and for about one-third of its length (*see* diagrams). This should be a thick dollop of ointment and should not be rubbed in. The greased part of the ear may then be dipped into fine ash from the fire, or into bird sand, to stop the grease getting on your clothes and furniture, and at the same time giving just a little weight, which will not strengthen the muscle as the grease

Ch. Helengowan Starboy
*Born 1949*

AND HIS BROTHER

Ch. Helengowan Superior
*Born 1949*

Ch. Danvis Deborah
*Born 1948*

Ch. Silvaseabear from Shiel
*Born 1949*

below will keep the ear malleable. The grease will stay on the
ear for long periods, especially if the dog is kept out of doors,
and can easily be renewed whenever necessary. To remove it
when required it is best to soak the ear in surgical spirit and
then to comb out the grease very gently with a very fine-
toothed comb. Vaseline may be used instead of Cuticura but
I do not find it so satisfactory as it is less sticky and melts off
more quickly. An ear may also go up later in life: when a bitch
comes into season, when she is in whelp, when an adult casts
his coat and frequently for no reason at all! In all cases the
treatment is exactly the same as for the youngster whose ears
are being trained.

At this stage of weaning, and just after, remember that the
puppy has a great deal to do physically. In a very few months
he has to grow from a fat ball of fluff to an elegant, graceful
adult, a show dog we hope. He should be allowed to do this
undisturbed. By this I mean that at the time he is passing
through this period of intensive growth do not try to 'cram'
him with too many other things. He will have to be house-
trained, he will need to be lead-trained, and if you have a car
the earlier he becomes accustomed to travelling in it the better,
for if he is car-sick he is much more likely to grow out of it if he
starts early. Beyond this, do nothing which will demand too much
from him. Let him romp, gallop, eat and, almost most important
of all, SLEEP. Many, many puppies are ruined and stunted in
growth because owners do not seem to realize that the little
Collie needs just as much sleep as a tiny human being. He
cannot use his growing powers to their full extent unless he gets
this sleep.

There are various views on the question of grooming, as
you will note elsewhere, and it is up to you to decide whether
or not your puppy is groomed daily at this time. If you belong
to the 'no grooming' school of thought the daily handling of the
puppy which would occur if he were groomed should be made
up to him in some other way, for this handling is a very important part of his education. If he is not being groomed, see
that he has a daily game with you; a rough and tumble is good
for him, especially if he is an only puppy with no kennel-mates
to tease and play with him. Some breeders make the mistake of
always creeping about in their puppy houses, never crashing

I

a feeding bowl, etc. This is all wrong. The more noise a puppy becomes accustomed to the better, and if he associates noise with the happy event of the arrival of his food, noise will soon lose its fear for him. Again, a bit of noise will help you to spot the shy puppy in the litter if there is one.

Fortunately in our breed the puppies are not scrappers and several growing youngsters can be housed together, provided the accommodation is big enough, so that if you are 'running on' two or three pups from one litter the question of an extra house does not arise, provided the first was large enough.

Although a well-reared Collie puppy should remain plump from the time of its birth until maturity, it will nevertheless go through a stage when it will be 'all legs and wings' and when you will despair that it will ever be fit to show! Provided he is well covered nothing else matters, and the condition of the puppy is solely your responsibility. It is almost impossible to over-feed a Collie between 3 and 9 months old, so give him all he will take. Collies are rarely greedy; he is most unlikely to over-eat. If he has been well supplied with bone- and body-making foods, given plenty of fresh water to drink, a warm, dry house to sleep in, plenty of exercise, fresh air without draughts, and daily human companionship, you can rest assured that his deficiencies as a show specimen, if any, are not your fault, but were inherent in him.

So often it happens that one sells a puppy as a most promising show prospect, and then, when the time comes for the pup to make its show debut, it fails to win. The purchaser is disgusted with the breeder for having sold him a dud, when 99 times out of 100 the fault lies entirely with the owner who failed to rear the puppy correctly, despite any guidance on the subject given by the breeder.

Puppy rearing, whilst a most engrossing occupation, is nevertheless a scientific one, and should never be treated lightly. It is a very great responsibility. The serious breeder with a litter to rear must be always on the alert, with a ready eye to spot any sign of things going wrong; he should anticipate all those things which could happen, and always be one jump ahead of the puppy. This is more important than I can say. Time and time again an accident has happened because the person responsible has been unable to foresee a contingency:

the board standing against the kennel wall, which will fall if a puppy bounces on it; the toy which is getting worn and which may, at any moment, start coming away in pieces and choke the puppy; these, and a hundred other things which can so easily be foreseen if one keep's one's eyes open, are all part and parcel of successfully rearing a puppy.

Rearing *one* puppy is the most difficult thing of all. Always try to make it two at least! They exercise each other, keep one another out of mischief and provide a healthful competition at feeding time. The ideal, always, even if you are sure there is only one 'certain champion' in the litter, is to keep a second puppy to 'run with' the first. You can always sell the second puppy when they are no longer in need of one another, and even if you 'sell it for a song' it will owe you nothing, for it will have saved you lots of trouble and helped you to turn out a very much better puppy, by playing companion, than if you had kept only one baby in the first place.

Puppy rearing is an exacting occupation, but it is also of the very greatest interest, and it is an occupation in which the breeder, no matter how many years of experience there may be behind him or her, can always, with every litter, find something new to learn. Every bitch, every puppy, is an individualist, and for this reason the whelping of a bitch and the rearing of a litter are the most absorbing tasks I know.

# CHAPTER 12

# FROM DAY TO DAY. MANAGEMENT

No MATTER how many dogs one keeps, be it just the single house Collie or a Kennel full of them, there are certain general rules which must be obeyed. They concern:

> *H*ousing.
> *E*xercise.
> *A*limentation.
> *L*ove.
> *T*raining.
> *H*appiness.

These rules, all kept, add up to the happiness and the health of the dog.

HOUSING.

Even if the dog is the only one and will be in your house all the time it is essential that he should have a bed of his own, to which he can retire at any time he chooses and to which, on occasion, he can be sent, if you wish him away from you for any reason. As has already been said, a tea-chest is loved by most Collies, but a canvas bed of the stretcher variety raised from the floor on short legs and about 3 ft. long by 2 ft. 6 in. broad is also adequate. The tea-chest, because of its sides, and the raised bed will automatically be free from draughts, and even the best constructed of dwellings usually has a draught at floor level. The house dog which has no bed of its own cannot be blamed for sitting on the sofa out of the draught.

The bed can be provided with a mattress made of a sack filled with wood-wool if desired; this keeps the bedding from straying and also is easily washed and renewed. His bed *must* be kept clean.

I do not consider that a stretcher-type bed is suitable for

outdoor kennels, and here the tea-chest or similar box is practically a necessity. The box should be laid on its side so that only one end is open, and this end should have a board across it, at least four inches high, to keep the bedding in place. To my mind, there is no bedding so suitable as wood-wool, and unless you are in the happy position of growing your own straw you will not find wood-wool any more expensive than buying straw. It is cleaner and looks nicer, and there is considerably less risk of a bale of wood-wool being infected by rats with some disease, such as mange or leptospirosa, than there is with a bale of straw. The tea-chest should not be placed directly on the floor of the kennel but be raised on a wooden platform at least four inches high.

The ideal kennel for a Collie is a wooden shed, well lined and free from draughts, about 6 ft. × 8 ft. in size, and of a height in which you can comfortably stand. Such a kennel, with two sleeping boxes, can house two adult Collies, and as a rule our breed is very much happier kennelled in pairs at least. Small 'loose-boxes' set in rows inside a larger building are also very useful and give added warmth.

It is not usually considered necessary to heat the kennels for a Collie, and except for warmth for babies I consider it unhealthful to do so. Provided the dog has a good deep bed, free from draughts, he will be contented. Should the weather be excessively cold added warmth can be given by attaching a sack to the top of each sleeping box and letting it hang down the front.

The flooring of all kennels should be of wood, and if, as often happens, you are converting an existing building which has a concrete floor, sections of this should be boarded over, or at least supplied with close-slatted duck-boards, so that the dogs cannot lie on the concrete.

All wooden boxes, benches, etc., should be easily removable for cleaning, and the kennels themselves must be kept scrupulously clean. All woodwork should be creosoted annually, but be careful not to let the dog back until all the creosote is dry.

Kennels should be cleaned daily and thoroughly scrubbed with disinfectant at least once a week. This applies to adults; naturally baby puppy kennels require daily disinfecting and scrubbing. Not too much water should be used at any time because of the difficulty of getting the floor dry again, but if a good stiff scrubber is used and the floor mopped afterwards with an almost dry mop, any remaining surplus water can be got rid of by sprinkling the floor with a fine coating of sawdust, leaving it a few minutes, then sweeping it up and putting down a fresh supply of sawdust. Every kennel or run in which the dog is spending a large part of his time must be supplied with a large bowl of fresh, clean water, and these water bowls must be refilled at least twice a day.

In a largish or medium-sized Kennel it is necessary to have a certain number of runs. Though our breed is not quarrelsome and can readily be housed and exercised in fairly large numbers, one cannot have the entire Kennel running around all day. Concrete, brick or paving is ideal for the surface of runs, but obviously, because of the expense entailed, no very large runs can be so surfaced. For large runs or all-day 'play-pens' grass is best. Collies left in such runs are happy and play well— a Collie alone in a run of any size is usually miserable or, at best, bored.

If possible, every run should have a tree in it to provide shade, and if there is no natural shade then some must be provided. If the run is not attached to the dog's sleeping quarters some kind of shed or covered protection must also be provided, especially in the case of young puppies.

EXERCISE.

All exercise should be regular. Collies do not need hours of 'road work' on a lead, and I have never found any to benefit from such exercise, though in some breeds it is essential. But the exercise must be daily, and a house dog which is never free in a run should be exercised twice daily. The best exercise for a Collie is free running and playing in fields, and this is something which is simple if you have several dogs, for they exercise each other. The one dog can best be given free exercise by being taken out with a bicycle if the conditions permit, or taken to the park or similar open space and there be allowed to play ball; the dog gets lots of galloping after a ball well thrown, and galloping is essential to our breed.

Naturally the town dog has less opportunity for free galloping but things must be arranged so that he gets some.

No dog, however well trained in either town or country, should be allowed on the road off a lead. With the traffic such as it is today it is not fair either to the dog or to the driver. Too many dogs are still allowed to roam about alone, and we all know what a toll dogs take in road accidents, both to themselves and to others.[1]

The Collie should be exercised whatever the weather. In hot weather the exercise should be done in the early morning and evening. The Collie will not come to harm if exercised in the rain; the coat protects the dog from the elements and on returning home he can either be given a place to roll on a big bed of straw or wood-wool, or, if a house dog, be wiped down, preferably with a chamois leather as this absorbs the damp and mud so well and is quickly wrung out and used again. Snow is the dog's delight, and this does present some small problem because the snow balls-up on their leg feathering and between their toes, and this must be combed off before the dog is put back in his kennel, otherwise it will melt gradually and make the bedding wet. No dog in a damp state should be put into his bed; he should be allowed to dry off first, in a rolling place of straw or in a deep box of sawdust, before being put back into his kennel.

ALIMENTATION. (FEEDING.)

This, too, must be regular, and the adult Collie usually does best on two meals a day: a light breakfast, and the main meal in the evening. The feeding of puppies was dealt with in the previous chapter, and diet sheets for various ages are set out in the Appendix.

The ideal diet for all dogs is raw meat, this, after all, being their natural food. The main meal should consist of raw, lean meat on at least five days out of seven. This can be alternated, or the other two days can be made up by giving paunches, or raw herrings.

Additions which can be made to the ordinary feeding plan, and which are very valuable in certain cases, are raw eggs and changes of food in the meat line, such as rabbit, sheeps' heads, tongue, heart, etc. However, all these meat extras should be

---

[1] See note on page 141.

cooked; I never risk feeding offal raw (except human-consumption liver), and they are mainly of value for their broth, or because they bring a change of flavour to a difficult feeder. Another item which is of great value is pigs' trotters, for these, boiled down, make wonderfully rich stock, especially good for puppies.

The average Collie requires 1 – 1½ lb. of raw meat per day, and in addition a breakfast meal of wholemeal bread, and either milk or stock. Unfortunately the price of bread today makes things difficult in a large Kennel and it is probably more economical to feed wholemeal biscuit meal than bread. There are a number of such meals on the market and these may be fed either dry or soaked according to your or your dog's preference. It is always better not to feed the meat and cereal meals mixed together. Far better to give the carbohydrate in the morning, and the protein, or meat meal, alone at night.

Paunches can be fed raw or cooked, but raw is to be preferred, and if the paunches are from a human-consumption slaughter house they are best fed not only raw but unwashed, for the value to the dog of the minerals contained in the half-digested grass found in the paunches is very great.

Herrings should be fed raw and whole. The bones will not harm a dog. However, it may be found that herrings, unless they are fed regularly so that the dog becomes accustomed to them, may prove rather rich and make the dog sick. This must be a question of trial and error. If the herring is cooked it must also be boned. It is usually found that cooked herring will not upset a dog, even if fed only rarely.

Bones must always be given raw. Cooked bones splinter and are dangerous, and all bones given should be large shin bones. The country Kennel owner will often be fortunate enough to obtain animals which have proved unsuitable to send to the slaughter house (still-born calves, for instance), and these can be fed cut up, just as they are, for even the smallest bones of a young calf, or a new-born lamb, will not injure the dog.

Whilst raw food is the ideal it is sometimes not always possible to live up to this ideal, and on such occasions cooked meat, or simply the broth from the cooking, must be relied upon. If the main meal has to be one of biscuit meal this should never be fed in a sloppy state. The meal should be soaked well in advance, by pouring boiling stock over it, covering it and leaving it to cool. The different meals on the market absorb different quantities of liquid and it is up to you to work out proportions, but always make certain that you add only enough liquid to make a dry, crumbly meal. However, be sure there is enough liquid, for a biscuit meal which is only half soaked is dangerous, in that it usually causes indigestion.

Every dog, puppy or adult, should have the regular daily addition of cod liver oil, one teaspoonful for an adult, on one of his meals each day. Except for this, no other regular addition is necessary and the money wasted on synthetic foods which are unnecessary must be very considerable. Additions to the food of the puppy, the pregnant bitch, the mcuh stud-used dog, and the dog which is not in tip-top condition are different matters, but for the ordinary fit dog no such additions are necessary.

However, all dogs benefit from at least an occasional, if not a regular, course of one of the yeast preparations, such as Vetzyme, and these are loved by most dogs.

If you feed natural foods, feed regularly and feed dry, you have the foundation of a fit, healthy Kennel.

LOVE.

This goes almost without saying, but the Collie, because of his history of close association with man, needs extra human companionship. By love I do not mean sloppiness with your dog, but simply the knowledge to him that he is of use to you, and that he is appreciated.

TRAINING.

This almost grows out of the last requirement, for a Collie lives to serve and in his desire to serve he trains himself to a certain degree. The untrained Collie is a nuisance to everyone, his owner and his friends. Every dog, as every child, needs discipline, and is the better for it. Every puppy must be taught certain elementary things. He must learn his name, of course, and this is a lesson which needs little teaching; the constant use of his name when you are with him in the Kennel, the call of his name before putting down his food bowl, will teach it to him in no time at all. From this point he can be taught all you wish him to know. He must learn, knowing his name, that when he is called he must come, and the best way to teach him this is to reward him every time he comes up as you call him. A pocket with bits of biscuit or a Vetzyme tablet or two in it is practically a 'must' when you have puppies on the place. However, so much of his training depends on the way you go about it. Never call the puppy unless you mean him to come, and having called him insist that he *does* come. Never allow a puppy, or an older dog, to get away with anything. Even if it takes you ten minutes that puppy, once called, has got to come, and no matter how long he takes he is still a 'good dog' when he comes, and must still be rewarded. Maddening I know, but if you once scold him or beat him *after he has come*, then you have destroyed his faith in you. To his mind he was called and he came; he will associate the punishment with the fact that he arrived—he cannot reason that he is being scolded for the time he took getting there. If once you scold your puppy when he comes, then you have only yourself to blame if he never comes again.

Next he must be taught to walk on a lead. This is best taught when the puppy is quite young, 8–10 weeks, and the best method is to use a slip lead for the purpose. I do not mean a chain choke collar, for a chain should never be used on any Collie's neck; it will spoil his hair. The ideal is a fine leather, or thin cord, lead of good length with a ring on one end. The free end is passed through the ring. The loop then goes over the puppy's head. The moment the puppy pulls back the lead tightens round his neck; when he is free with you he does not feel restraint at all. It is essential when giving a puppy his first lessons on the lead to have him alone, somewhere where there are no distractions, where he can give you all his attention and you can give him all yours. In the very first lesson it should not matter at all in which direction the puppy goes. Don't try to make him go with you; once the lead is on and he is moving with it on, go with him! This is the simplest method of teaching him that things are not nearly as bad as they seem, and after a short period of the puppy leading he will be ready to come with you as you call his name. Do remember to talk to him reassuringly all the time, and to praise him unceasingly in this early lesson.

By the use of the slip lead and the method described I have never found a puppy who would not co-operate after a lesson of 15 minutes. And 15 minutes, for ordinary lessons, is too long, but the first time you decide to lead-break your puppy you must not give in until at least he is walking *his* way with the lead on. The puppy who throws himself in the air, screams and yells and generally behaves like a maniac is much simpler to break than the little mule who sits down, looks solemn and says, 'If you want me, pull!'

With this exception of the lead lesson, no lesson should be longer than five or, at the outside, ten minutes in duration for a young puppy.

Having taught him to come when he is called and to walk on the lead, his other lessons will follow simply. He will have to learn to sit and to lie down when he is told, but beyond this, for the ordinary companion dog, or dog in a Kennel, he needs to learn little else. He will teach himself the rest as he becomes 'educated.'

The golden rules for any kind of training are to get your dog's interest and trust, to be consistent, never to lose your temper, and to keep your words of command clear and simple. Don't use the word 'Down' today and 'Lie down' tomorrow; you will only confuse the dog.

Collies have been making their mark in no small way in the show obedience tests lately and they are particularly suitable for such training because of their delight in service. If you are seriously considering training your Collie to such heights it is almost essential that you attend a training class. There are many good ones today in almost every part of the country.

The young puppy should become accustomed to seeing strangers and to being handled by strangers from quite an early age; in this way his faith in human nature will be developed. He must also be educated to traffic and other strange noises, and this is dealt with in the next chapter. With one dog in the house this sort of thing is easy, it all comes as a matter of course, but if you have several dogs in a Kennel do make sure that they get their turn at being educated to the big wide world, particularly if you live in the country. Take them to the main road once in a while, always on a lead, of course, to let them see the world go by!

There remains only the question of house-training. This is very simple with a Collie, a naturally very clean breed. Common sense on your part is what is most necessary. Be sure that the puppy is always taken to the same place when he is put out, so that he may learn more quickly what is required of him. He will want to relieve himself immediately after a meal, so watch him whilst he is feeding and the moment he finishes put him on the chosen spot. In the same way he must be put out immediately he wakes up. If he does make a mistake in the house never do any more than scold him very gently, and take him, at once, to his proper place, praising him when you get there. Smacking is useless for such a crime.

All puppies, and a great many adults, delight in a chewing game. If you do not want the puppy to chew your shoes, stockings, etc., be sure to give him his own toys and make him realize that they are his. An old stocking knotted up is a favourite toy, and an old slipper, too, but be sure that he knows the difference between it and your best ones! His toys should be kept in a special place, so that he may know where to find them when he wants to play. Dogs, like children, can be taught to put their toys away when they have finished playing, too.

To recapitulate: keep commands concise and consistent; be patient; be firm; keep lessons short; never try to teach a puppy anything when it has just been fed; be generous with your praise and tit-bits.

HAPPINESS.

The other five requirements will by now have developed that happy, healthy dog which we all love and need to have about us. Keep your dog happy by companionship, love, a job to do, good food and exercise, and he will reward you many times over.

GROOMING.

There are at least two schools of thought on this subject in our breed. The 'groom daily' school, and the 'almost never groom' school. Both have their advocates and it appears that both are successful, as Collies treated in both ways win the highest awards.

If you are going to groom your dog daily this should be done with a good brush only; too much combing spoils and breaks the coat, and a comb need be used only when the dog is casting his coat. The Collie should be groomed right down to the skin, and the best type of brush for this seems to be one of the radial nylon brushes now available. The power of penetration of these bristles is great.

If you belong to the other school, and hardly ever groom your dog, it is essential to go over the dog once a week for any signs of fleas, for a long-haired dog is fairly prone to these, particularly in warm weather. This second method of managing a Collie is really only practicable with a country-kept dog where he has plenty of opportunity to run in long grass, and the town dog must certainly be groomed regularly to keep him clean.

When the Collie casts his coat every grooming tool you possess must be brought into action and the dog groomed daily, twice daily if possible, until not a loose hair remains. The quicker you get rid of the dead hair the sooner the new coat will come. If your dog's coat is just 'on the blow' and you want to help it out with all speed, give the dog a bath; the unwanted hairs will soon drop out after that.

Bathing a Collie, however, is unnecessary, and beyond perhaps washing the white parts before a show, should never be required if the dog is kept clean by grooming.

Collies are somewhat prone to mattery eyes and, if this condition is apparent, these should be wiped daily either with a solution of boracic or with cold tea. I much prefer the tea remedy.

Beyond this there is little to do for your dog, so it is by no means hard work to keep a Collie.

*Note* (see page 135):

Too many people, unfortunately, consider that the only type of lead which exists is one attached to a chain choke collar. This, in my opinion, is the worst possible type of collar for a Collie. Not only does it break the hair, as the lovely coat catches in the links of the chain, but also, I am convinced that it is specially cruel to a shepherd breed. Not because it chokes (properly used it is no more cruel in that respect than any other kind of collar), but because I am certain that Collies, and kindred breeds, have specially sensitive hearing, and the chain 'clanking' so close to the ears does, I feel sure, cause unnecessary suffering. If you want to use a choke collar—and I advise them—then use a leather choke, made from rounded leather, about fourteen inches long, and with a ring at each end. The result is exactly the same as if you were using a chain, and it has not the two drawbacks attributable to a chain choke.

# CHAPTER 13

# YOUR FIRST SHOW

UNLESS you are breeding solely for the pet market (and if you are you would hardly have bought this book), your ultimate aim will be to show stock of your own breeding, and there is nothing that enhances a Kennel's reputation, and at the same time its sales, more than consistent winning with home-bred stock.

Having bred your litter, reared your selected puppy and got it to the age of about eight months, your thoughts will surely be turning to the idea of taking it to a show or two.

However, it will be almost useless, unless you happen to have an exceptional dog, to take it to a show unless the animal has had some preliminary training for the ring. Provided you have carried out the suggestions in the chapter on puppy-rearing, you will be more than half-way there already, but long before the age of eight months is reached the potential show prospect should have started his additional show training. He must have become accustomed to people, strange places, strange noises. Stores like the local Woolworths, and places such as a biggish railway station, are ideal training grounds. Teach him, too, to go up and down stairs, for you may find that at almost any show there may be stairs either at the approach to the hall or when you get inside, and a dog unaccustomed to stairs hates them. If you live in a house as opposed to a bun-galow, this will present no problem, but if your home is a bungalow make use of the railway station for this lesson too.

Now he must be taught to make the most of himself in the ring. First he will be expected to walk on a loose lead. This point cannot be stressed too much : it is impossible for the judge to assess the dog's movement if he is either strung up so tightly that he is being hanged and his feet are barely reaching the floor, or if he is pulling away on a tight lead and doing the oddest things with his legs. If the dog is being shown on a tight lead any judge worth his salt will ask you to walk the dog again, this time on a loose lead, and if you cannot do this your chances are practically nil. More often than not the dog being shown strung up is a shy, cringing Collie which cannot stand on its legs of its own accord; the loose lead will show this up at once and repeatedly. So give your puppy confidence and get him to walk beside you under all conditions happily and on a loose lead. Incidentally, you need confidence yourself. Any nerves from which you may be suffering will be transmitted at once to your dog, so if he does not show very well at his first show be sure to realize that the blame is probably as much yours as his. As your confidence increases so will his showmanship.

Besides walking confidently on a loose lead the dog will be expected to stand up and show himself. He must stand four-square, and he must be taught to take up this position as a natural thing. When standing he must use his ears, for a Collie is only half a dog and his expression is lost if his ears are not at the semi-alert when the judge is looking his way. You will quickly find the best way to make him do this. He may like a certain noise you can make, he may be entranced by a bouncing ball, he may show best for a tit-bit which you should hold low down or, better still, secrete in your pocket, giving him a tiny piece only now and again to keep his attention.

He should have a daily lesson in ring behaviour by the time he is six months old, but no lesson should last more than five minutes. It is far better to give him five minutes twice daily than one ten-minute session when he is this age, otherwise he will quickly become bored and your work will be useless.

Having taught him to walk on the lead, it is now necessary to accustom him to walk on your left and neither ahead of you nor dragging behind. This is best done by talking to him to keep his attention, which will almost certainly stop him from lagging, and, if he pulls ahead, by giving him a sharp jerk on the lead (never a long, steady pull) accompanied by the word 'heel' or whatever word you choose to use, but do please always use the same word; better a dog which responds to a small vocabulary than a dog which gets lost over a big one. Directly he falls into the correct position he should be praised, and given a tit-bit as well if you wish. As soon as he forges ahead he must be given the sharp jerk again and the word 'heel'. Having achieved your object of getting him to walk happily beside you on a slack lead in a straight line, the same thing must be achieved walking in a circle, and with the dog always on your left. You will be walking in an anti-clockwise direction with your Collie always on the inside of the circle. Once he is walking well in this circle he must be taught to go in an absolutely straight line down the centre, and to turn and come back in exactly the same straight line, always on a slack lead. Reward him with praise and tit-bits when he does this. Now, having got him going straight, teach him to stand and show himself as you come to a halt; he will readily learn to stand at a word of command and it is up to you to see that he does this in the correct position, neither with his feet too close together nor too far apart, with his head held high, his ears up, and the whole of him alert and waiting for the next word of praise. Never let him get away with sitting down when you want him to stand, and if you watch him carefully for any tendency to do this you will soon be able to check it and keep him on the alert. Another tendency will be to 'settle down', by which I mean that although he is still standing he becomes slack, his neck sinking into his shoulders, his elbows spreading out, and his whole body 'settling' on to his feet rather as though he were a jelly on a hot day! This, too, must be checked. If the dog tries to sit, or if you want to alter his position in any way, don't make a big fuss over it by putting your hands on or under the dog; just take half a pace into a different position and he will soon set himself up again. If it is just the position of a front foot that you wish to alter, do so by just touching one paw with your toe. All these things should be done unobtrusively, for the last thing you want to do in the ring is to draw the judge's attention to a possible fault.

Fortunately Collies require little or no stripping as show preparation, and the amount of work put in on their coats depends on your own school of thought on the matter. Provided the coat has been kept free of knots and foreign bodies, live or otherwise, there should be little extra work to do except to give him a good final grooming the day before the show. It is not considered necessary or advisable to bath a Collie; this destroys the natural bloom on the coat and glossiness is completely lost after a bath. However, particularly with a town dog, it is often necessary to wash the white parts at least. This, too, should be done the day before the show, and a good soapless shampoo used. The dog should be partially dried and then the white parts of the coat filled up with one of the cleaning powders. This can be one of the advertised cleaning agents or it can be precipitated chalk, a mixture of chalk, starch and whitening, or powdered magnesia either plain or mixed with one of the other remedies mentioned. If any of these preparations are put into the damp coat they will stay there, and should be left until after the journey to the show has been made the next day, then any fresh dirt picked up *en route* will brush out with the cleaning powder, all of which must be removed before the dog is taken into the ring. This is a ruling of the Kennel Club.

Other than grooming, which we shall discuss elsewhere, the only preparation necessary is a bit of attention to the feet and legs. The feet should be trimmed all round with scissors so that the hair is cut level with the foot itself and gives a clear-cut outline. Further, the hair under the foot between the pads should be removed; this area should, in fact, be kept free of hair at all times, for too much hair between the pads tends to spread the foot and make it look big. The only other hair which needs removing is that from the neck joint to the back of the foot on the hind legs. This part of the leg should be clear of long hair. Some people like to trim a Collie's ears, but I am of the opinion that more ears are made prick by over-trimming by the uninitiated than one would credit, and for this reason they are best left alone. Also, ears which are too trimmed look hard and tend to spoil the soft expression which is part and parcel of the Collie. However, if your dog is one of those which has very long, soft, curly hair growing from the base of his ears at the back of the ear, these should be removed, and this job is best done with finger and thumb.

Doubtless you will be a subscriber to either *Our Dogs* or *Dog World*, or both, and in these journals you will find advertised the dates and places of the various shows.

It is not usually advisable to show a Collie before it is 8–9 months old, for it is rarely in sufficient coat to do itself justice before it is this age, but once it is eight months you can start looking for an opportunity to make your show debut. Whilst, obviously, you will probably want to start at a local show to make things easier all round, it is much wiser, unless you are

K

looking upon the outing simply as one for 'ring experience' for you and your dog, to choose a show where there are classes for the breed, for in Variety classes—classes open to many breeds —you may find that the judge is not very knowledgeable about Collies and you will not profit greatly by the outing. Far better to wait for a show where there are at least two or three classes for the breed, and where, if possible, the judge is an acknowledged Collie expert. Then you will reap much reward from such a show even if you do not win.

Before your dog can be entered for a show he must be registered with the Kennel Club, and if this has not been done already you must apply to them for a form for registration. You must fill up the form, select the name you want for the dog and return the form to the Kennel Club together with the fee. (If you have bought the dog and he is already registered, make sure that you have sent off the transfer application form which you should have received with the dog, together with 7s. 6d., before the date of the show.) If a dog is to be entered, and his registration certificate has not yet been returned to you, he must be entered with the name for which you have applied and the initials N.A.F. (name applied for) after it. So long as the name has been applied for before the date of the show you are in order, but a name *must* be given on the entry form.

Then, having decided upon the show you wish to attend, send to the secretary of that show for a copy of the schedule. Remember that there are three different types of shows, and whilst your local shows will be either Sanction or Limited affairs[1] they will be the best kind to start with, except that these shows will be 'unbenched' ones and the dog will have no place to call his own. Therefore it is wise to take with you a rug or something to which he is accustomed so that he may rest happily while waiting his turn to go into the ring.

Having obtained a copy of the schedule, read it carefully, for there are different types of classes, governed either by breed or number of wins, or both, and maybe governed also by age. The definitions of these classes vary with the type of show, so read them carefully before making your entries; this will prevent the disappointment that is a consequence of entering in

[1] See *The Kennel Club and You*, Chapter 15.

the wrong class—and the poor unfortunate secretary a great deal of work as well!

With a young dog it is always best not to enter in too many classes as the pup will probably become bored and tired if he is asked to keep up a sustained effort of showmanship throughout, say, ten classes, often a possible number in a Variety classification. On the other hand, don't enter him in just one class. He may be somewhat overwhelmed in the beginning and may need a class or two before settling down, and any judge who is really on the job will, if he finds a dog that he could not place in an earlier class because it would not show has suddenly become accustomed to its surroundings and shows in the later class, alter his earlier decision and put the dog higher than it originally was if he considers that the circumstances merit the decision. So give your Collie a fair run; three or four classes are ideal.

The day of the show has arrived. If it is an 'unbenched' show it is almost more important to arrive early than at a 'benched' one, as then you will be able to find a corner in which to bed-down your dog before the crush of exhibitors arrives. Even at a benched show it is wise to be in plenty of time; there are always last-minute 'titivations' to make, the last grooming to do, and you do not want to rush your dog into the ring but to give him time, after his toilet is concluded, to get accustomed to his surroundings. Even the dog which is a seasoned campaigner should have this chance, for although he may have attended many shows the surroundings of each are different and need a bit of getting used to. Remember, too, that at the entrance to the show your dog may have to pass the veterinary surgeon, and if you leave your arrival until late you will almost certainly find yourself waiting in a queue for this gentleman's attention.[1] This queue is the very best place in which to pick up infection, if there is any around; the dogs have not yet been inspected and signs of possible danger not yet noted and the suspect dogs excluded.

By Kennel Club rule the exhibitor is required to bench his dog on a collar and *chain*—not a lead. Like most Kennel Club rules, this one has a very good reason behind it. It is all too easy for a dog to bite through a lead and escape from its bench. Be

[1] Most shows have now abolished this, but don't count on it!

sure to observe this rule; you make yourself liable to a fine if you flaunt it, and you will most certainly cause yourself a lot of worry and heartburn, and the show executive a great deal of unnecessary trouble, if your dog escapes from its bench.

You have arrived, settled down, done the necessary last-minute grooming and now you are ready for your first class. If it is a large show with a multiplicity of breeds, and therefore a number of judging rings, find out as soon as possible where the Collies will be judged and whether they are 'first in the ring'— that is, first on the judging programme. Every ring, in addition to a judge, has one or more stewards. These are men or women who, in a purely voluntary capacity and for the sheer love of the game, give their services to assist with the organization of the show. For this reason it makes me even angrier when I see an exhibitor being rude to a steward than when I see an exhibitor being rude to a judge. It is the custom for one of the stewards to go round the benches before the judging of each breed begins and notify exhibitors that judging is about to start, but the onus for being in the judging ring at the right moment is on the exhibitor entirely, and it is up to you to keep a weather-eye open and see exactly what is happening so that you do not miss your class.

When you go into the ring for your first class the steward who is marshalling the exhibits in the ring will give you your 'ring number'. This corresponds to your number in the catalogue and, if it is a benched show, is the same number as that on your bench. It is a help if you know your number when the steward comes to you; it saves a search through his catalogue after learning your name. All these little points do not appear important but they save so much time.

When all the exhibits for the first class have arrived in the ring the judging will begin, and it is usual for the judge to ask that all the exhibits be 'taken round' the ring, for a start. This enables him to get a good general picture of the dogs as a whole, and usually a sound judge can have a good idea from this initial parade which dogs will be in the first three places when he has finished judging. For this first parade the exhibitors will always go round the ring in an anti-clockwise direction—that is 12, 11, 10, 9 o'clock, etc.—and with the dogs on the *inside*. Remember always that it is the *dog* the judge wants to see, not your legs or your trousers, so always place the dog between you and the judge. The judge will tell the exhibitors when to stop this parade, then he will start his individual judging. Usually the judge likes each dog to be taken into the middle of the ring in turn, and at his signal, and there he will examine each dog. Generally it is expected that you will stand the dog first of all, and make him use his ears whilst the judge gets a general impression. This is where your training at home comes in; the dog should be ready to stand and show himself on your word or signal of command. Then the judge will inspect the exhibit part by part. Most judges, when they wish to look at the dog's teeth, will ask you to open the dog's mouth yourself. This is not because the judge is afraid your dog will bite him; it is to reduce chances of spreading infectious disease should any dog in the ring be in the early stages of such a disease. If you are asked to open his mouth the judge will probably only say: 'Mouth, please,' and it is important to do this correctly, and to have accustomed your dog to having it done. The diagram will show what is required. Do remember it is the teeth or bite the judge wants to see, not the tonsils or what he had for breakfast! The diagrams (on page 150) show you the right and wrong way of carrying out this simple operation.

A judge usually does his best to be helpful to the novice exhibitor, but it must be realized that he has a big day's work to do and he cannot spend five minutes waiting whilst you wrestle with a recalcitrant hound who has never been taught to have his mouth opened.

An exhibitor should not speak to the judge whilst the examination is going on, except to answer questions. These are likely to be only on such points as the age of the exhibit, and the judge most certainly does not want to be told the dog's parentage, nor what prizes he has won, if this is not his first show. The least said in the ring the better, for even the best-intentioned remarks will be bound to cause unfavourable comment.

Having gone all over your exhibit, the judge will then ask you to move him away and back again. Now there are right and wrong ways of doing everything and it can be extremely tiring for a judge with a big entry if every exhibitor moves the dog in the wrong direction and the poor judge has to go hopping from one corner of the ring to the other to see what he wants to see. A good judge will almost invariably indicate the direction in which you are to go. It may be the full length, it may be diagonally across the ring; whatever the direction the procedure is always the same—there and back again, away from and back to the judge in as nearly a straight line as possible. Some judges also like to see the dog from the side. When he asks you to move so that he can see the dog from the side

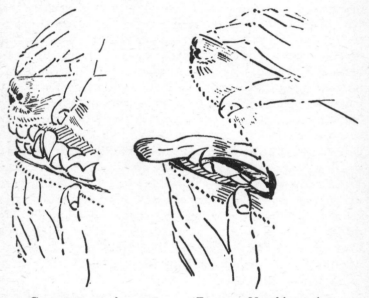

FIG. 24.—Correct way to show          FIG. 25.—Not this way!
dog's mouth to judge

remember that because you have trained the dog to walk on the left-hand side he will be on the *wrong* side for one length of the ring, and it is necessary for the dog to walk on your right for one length. Always remember to keep the dog between yourself and the judge and you can't go wrong.

When he has seen all he wants to see the judge will indicate, probably by a wave of the hand, that he has finished with you, and you will return to your original place unless the indication has been that you are to go to the opposite side of the ring. It is up to you to watch this. But if, before you start in your first class, you tell the steward that you are a beginner, and ask him to help you, you will have done a wise thing, and you will, as a result, feel less lost and learn more quickly. The judge will then proceed in a like manner with every dog in the class, and while he is doing so let your dog rest. It does not matter if he lies down (unless there is a lot of sawdust on the floor), or sits or just lazes on his feet, but sitting or lying down are to be preferred, for the judge may turn round quickly when your dog is standing really badly (and even the best can do this) and then the mental picture he has made may be marred! Keep your eye on the judge, however, and when he reaches the penultimate exhibit in the class make your dog alert again, standing and showing for all he is worth when the judge looks back down the line. He will surely do this, and then, if it has been a big class, he will begin to pick the sheep from the goats, the sheep being sent to one side of the ring, the goats retained on the other. Some judges, having pulled out half a dozen promising ones, will tell the other exhibitors that they may go, but if you have not been given such a word of dismissal do not leave the ring until the prize cards have been handed out.

Let us assume that your first class was Puppy, and that you were placed third—not at all bad for your first show!—and that you have also entered in Maiden and Novice. It is possible there will be three or four new dogs, and also that the dogs which were first and second in the Puppy class are not entered in Maiden—probably they are no longer eligible. The steward will tell you to remain in the ring and automatically place you at the top on one side. The other exhibits which you beat in the Puppy class will be ranged below you, and the 'new' exhibits will come in on the opposite side of the ring. With these new exhibits the procedure will be exactly the same as that outlined for your own first class, and whilst the judge is examining these new dogs give your own exhibit a breather. As he comes to his last new exhibit alert your dog again, have him looking his very best, for although you were beaten in an earlier class here is the moment when the cherished red, First Prize, card may be yours. The judge will compare your dog—his best left from the earlier class—with his best of the new ones, and then slip the new one into place. It may be First, it may be well down the line, and for this reason it is always up to you to be on the alert, but without over-taxing or tiring your dog. You are never beaten till you are out of the ring.

In the last paragraph it was assumed that you had gained only a yellow, Third Prize, card (the Second is blue), and later a red one—rather more than you should hope for at your first show!—but in case you have had real 'beginner's luck' and gained Best-of-Breed, which means the best Collie in the show, there is yet a further step to be taken. In my opinion the winner of the Best-of-Breed award at any show, and particularly at a big show, should feel it is his bounden duty to take the winning exhibit into the 'Big Ring'. This is the main ring into which all the Best-of-Breed winners are called later in the day to compete for Best-in-Show All Breeds. Even if you feel you have not a ghost of a chance your dog should be there, because of the great publicity value to the breed, and if you have had the honour and glory of being placed Best-of-Breed it is up to you to play your part and see that the Collie is represented in the main ring, before what is bound to be the biggest audience of the day, even if it means waiting for a later train and being put to a bit of inconvenience yourself.

If your exhibit is a puppy and has won the Puppy class in its breed and was only subsequently beaten by an adult exhibit of the same breed, then you have the right, and again I think the duty, to appear in the big ring if there is an award for Best Puppy in Show.

At most big shows, in addition to the breed classes there are usually Any Variety classes and/or Stakes classes. These are one and the same thing, except that the Stakes classes usually carry increased prize money or extra prizes in kind. A Variety class is one in which dogs of many breeds may be exhibited, and these are usually judged by a different judge from your own breed judge, and for this reason, if for no other, it is a good plan to enter in one or more, because then you will have the opportunity of more than one judge's opinion on your dog on the same day.

On returning from a show it is always wise, unless your exhibit is the only dog you own, to disinfect him and yourself. This is best done by wiping his mouth and muzzle with a solution of T.C.P. and water and by dipping his paws in a bowl of this, as well as giving your own shoes the same treatment. Most germs of canine disease are passed through the dog's urine and excreta, so those parts which come in contact with the floor are by far the most important. Needless to say, it is asking for trouble to take your dog to a show unless he has been immunized against hard pad and distemper. In these days of 'egg-adapted' vaccines this is a simple and extremely safe procedure, costing a relatively small sum for its great 'insurance' value, and it is only kind to your dog to give him this protection. There are today several of these egg-adapted vaccines on the market and choice will entirely depend on which of them your veterinary surgeon stocks and prefers, so it is useless to enumerate them here. Be guided by him. Although your dog does not become contagious after the injection, it is best to have him treated at least 14 days before a show because it takes about this time for the vaccine to act and to give the optimum of protection. Best of all, of course, is to have your dog treated at 12 weeks of age, as I have already stated.

### THE SHOW FROM THE JUDGE'S POINT OF VIEW

The best way to make an exhibitor see what is most required in the ring is to let him see a class through the eyes of a judge.

The class is assembled, the steward tells the judge that exhibits are ready, and the judge takes the centre of the ring. A quick look round and then 'Round you go'. During this time he can sum up the qualities of most of the exhibits and only if he discovers that your dog has missing teeth, an overshot mouth, a light eye, or some other 'hidden' fault, which cannot be seen without individual handling, will he find it necessary to alter drastically a first impression. During this time it is the *dog* he will be looking at, so keep him always on your left, in the centre of the circle, for you will be walking anti-clockwise, and don't get between your dog and the judge. One other point: please don't bring anything into the ring except your dog on a lead. You cannot handle your dog properly and let him be seen well if you are carrying a handbag in your other hand, or tucked under your arm, nor does a judge want to be hit in the eye with a swinging bag as he bends to examine your dog's head! See that you don't wear a flapping coat, either, for it is impossible to see your dog if he is continually dragging back trying to get away from your coat which is swinging out and hitting him in the face. Circular skirts are just as bad if they are full.

When the judge has seen the dogs going round long enough —and this is no marathon—he will stop the exhibitors and will want to see each exhibit separately. He will want to know the age of your dog, so be sure to know it exactly.

Be ready to co-operate as in carrying out instructions about moving your dog, etc., and if you are one of the late ones to be examined in a class you will help a very great deal if you watch the routine other exhibitors have followed, for any judge worth his salt judges each dog in exactly the same way, and if you are later than the third to be examined you should be able to fall into this routine with no difficulty and so help judge and stewards and save valuable time. If a judge has a big entry and a heavy day's work a few seconds saved by every exhibitor count up into a quite appreciable number of minutes.

Your motto at a show should be, 'Keep my wits about me!'

Do not get in the way of other dogs as they are judged and don't allow your dog to be a nuisance by darting out, even in play, at other exhibits as they go past him. Concentrate on your dog, don't try to push in front of other exhibitors, don't crowd them in the ring. Even if someone else gets in front of you don't worry overmuch; a good judge won't forget a good dog just because, for the moment, he cannot see it.

Don't forget that not all judges judge to the same plan, so if you fall into one routine today don't expect it to be the same when Mr. A. judges next week; his method of controlling his ring is bound to be different. This doesn't mean that one method is better than another; we are creatures of habit and we each get into habits in the ring as much as anywhere else.

There are two places where I think Collie exhibitors, even experienced ones, sometimes fail. It is much easier for the judge to see the dog if that dog is standing on a loose lead *away* from, and looking up at, his handler. Often a judge will step back in order to view the dog from a different angle, and here the handler frequently makes the mistake of allowing, or even encouraging, the dog to come too and then it becomes just a procession down the ring! The judge trying to get away for a distant view and you following at every step! Another great point is that more often than not the dog is presented with his hindquarters to the judge, because your dog is looking up at you and you have turned yourself square to the judge. This can quickly be overcome: turn your own back on the judge, he won't mind; it's only the dog he cares about, anyway. He won't at all mind seeing your back if he can see your Collie's face. Then, if the time comes that he wants to walk round the dog and see him from the other end, don't follow in a circle, too, for all will end up exactly where they started and the judge will have seen nothing new! Also, if the judge is trying to attract your dog's attention it is almost certainly because he wants it to look directly at him, so that he may better assess its expression, and it is maddening if whilst he is trying to do this you still persist with pieces of liver, noises, etc., to keep the dog looking your way.

The judge is in the ring to assess the relative values of the dogs brought before him. I, as a judge, shall be enjoying myself, for I love judging, and I shall hope you are enjoying yourself too. I am not a dragon, but whilst judging is actually going on the ring is mine and I do not like being interrupted. To judge honestly and to the best of one's ability demands a good deal of concentration and it is concentration which should not be allowed to relax. I shall be delighted to give you a reason for placing your dog where I did *after* I have finished judging all the classes, but don't come to me, please, *without* your dog and say: 'What did you think of my dog?', for it is the dog which is in my mind's eye, *not* the exhibitor, and I may be at a loss for an answer through not being able to connect you with the dog you were handling. Bring the dog back to the ring with you.

Most judges are just as anxious as anyone to see you get on, whether you be a novice or an experienced exhibitor, and we are almost all eager to help, but remember there are ways of approaching your judge! Don't rush up and say 'Why was my dog only sixth?' when what you really mean is, 'Please can you tell me what you liked better about the other five dogs who went over him?' There are ways of saying all these things, and judges, particularly after a long and tiring day's judging, can be a bit prickly, you know. Further, I don't advise you to ask a judge's opinion unless you really want the truth! If you are seeking knowledge by which you can then improve your stock and your own knowledge of your breed, well and good. It is almost always possible to find something good to say about even the most lowly placed exhibit, but not all judges have the time to temper the wind, so if you are really lowly placed, and still want an opinion, be prepared to 'take it'!

A dog show is fun, a training ground and a meeting place; let it remain so.

# CHAPTER 14

## SELLING YOUR STOCK.
## FREIGHT AND EXPORT

SOONER or later the problem of how to dispose of your stock will arise. In every litter there must be puppies you will not want to keep, and in order to save unnecessary expense, the sooner they are sold, after they are properly weaned, the better.

There are various mediums in which to advertise, and it is up to you to select the one most likely to suit the stock you have for sale. *Our Dogs* and *Dog World* are both admirable, but less suited to the pet market, for these papers rarely reach those people who are just looking for a pet, and it will be found that the two periodicals are best for promising show stock. The columns of your local paper are, more often than not, the best medium for the sale of pet puppies.

Pricing the stock you have for sale is always difficult, even for the experienced breeder, and it is well for you to get down to the matter seriously and try to figure out just what the litter has cost you to rear. First, take into consideration the stud fee, probably 8–10 gns. Next, consider what the bitch cost you in extra food during the time she was in whelp and the time she was rearing the puppies. An additional £10 here is not out of the way. Then let us imagine that there are six puppies in the litter; they will have cost not less than £30 to rear well to eight weeks of age, and your puppies must sell at not less than 8 gns. each, which leaves you no profit, and should certainly not be sold for less than 10 gns. These prices are fair for a novice breeder to ask, for it must be remembered that the unknown breeder cannot expect to receive the price which a well-known Kennel can demand for its stock. It is very much more satisfactory to be able to sell off your unwanted puppies at an early age, even if for a slightly lower price than you had hoped, than to have them still running around at six months, when the feeding bill will have risen to astronomical proportions and the poorer quality puppies will no longer be fat and cuddly and easy to sell, but looking their very worst, with all their faults exaggerated, and so most probably only bring the same, or a lower, price than you had hoped for at eight weeks.

The show-ring, naturally, is your shop window, and the value of your stock will rise gradually as your name becomes associated with winning stock, and your Kennel name begins to carry real weight. It is absolutely essential to exhibit, and to do so regularly and frequently, if you ever hope to achieve a place where your Kennel name will strike a chord in the minds of other breeders in the Collie world.

It stands to reason that the breeder who has built up a reputation for fair dealing and good stock will be the one who will gain the repeat orders. Such a reputation must take a few years to acquire, and the only way to achieve it is by showing and advertising so that your name becomes known, and then by backing those advertisements with really honest business.

Advertising must be clear and concise. Never advertise a dog by praising it to heaven, and forgetting entirely that it has any faults. You most likely will not receive any reply at all to such advertisements, for all of us are suspicious of the perfect anything! Far better to state clearly what the breeding is of the particular dog or puppy, its show wins if any, and the price at which it is offered for sale, with a line intimating that the fullest details of the dog will be given on request. In replying to any advertisement yourself, be sure to ask the questions you really want to know about, and do remember that it is a great help if you enclose a stamped and addressed envelope. It will only be a few pence to you, but a big Kennel may get a dozen or more enquiries such as yours in one day!

Whilst appreciating to the full the mass of correspondence which pours into a well-known Kennel, it should be the aim of every breeder to try, in each instance, to reply to all enquiries by return of post. This at least gives the would-be purchaser the impression that he will receive further courteous and good service.

If the enquiry comes 'out of the blue' and not in direct reply to a specific advertisement, do describe minutely the dog you are able to offer which you consider may fill the bill. Every dog has its faults, potential Champion though he may be, and it is essential that when extolling his good points those faults should also be mentioned. It is wise, when offering stock, to state 'subject to being unsold' and also to quote the price plus freight, for in these days of high rail charges the vendor is frequently out of pocket in no small way if the freight costs are not added to the purchase price. Many purchasers are unable to call to collect the dog of their choice.

It is essential, when you know you are going to have a litter for sale, to be prepared to despatch the puppies in suitable hampers. At least 50 per cent. of the average Kennel's business is done by despatching stock by rail. For a Collie puppy of eight weeks a hamper measuring 20 in. by 12 in. by 15 in. high is ideal. Such a hamper costs about £4 and will last a long time. Naturally your client will be asked to return the hamper immediately. The advent of fibre-glass boxes is welcome. They are easy to clean, long-lasting and attractive. They are certainly preferable to hampers.

More information on this question of sending dogs by rail will be found later in this chapter.

You will find that you will receive enquiries from time to time from some of the bigger Kennels unable to fill orders from their own stock, especially if you have used their stud dogs or happen to have some of their bitches. When you receive such an enquiry do, in pricing your stock, take into consideration that the intermediate Kennel must be allowed a reasonable margin of profit; state the lowest price you are willing to accept (and if by this means you can sell two or three puppies in one go you are saving yourself a great deal of trouble) and make no complaint if, at a later date, you should learn the price for which the puppy was re-sold. You got what you asked and should be content. It has happened to me that I have quoted a certain price and learned later that the intermediate breeder or seller has gained at least 100 per cent., sometimes more, but this is something which, though it may be irritating, must be suffered in silence!

When a client calls on you for a dog, always ask where he got your name; if from an advertisement, or from a previous satisfied client, well and good, but if you are told that another breeder was responsible for the introduction, then remember it is all a matter of business, and that it is only courteous to send a commission to the person who made the introduction. The usual commission on any such sale is 10 per cent.

It is usually the well-known Kennel which receives export enquiries, but the day will surely come when a novice, building up a certain prestige, will also receive such enquiries. It is even more important to describe with the greatest accuracy any stock available for export, for whilst your disappointed client in this country has some redress, your overseas buyer has none, for our quarantine regulations do not allow a dog to be returned.

There are some people in all breeds who seem to consider that the foreigner's purse is bottomless, and who, as soon as an overseas enquiry comes to hand, double the price of the stock they have for sale. What a short-sighted policy this is, for it must be remembered that the overseas buyer has all the freight costs to pay as well, and that, by the time a dog the size of a Collie reaches such distant places as India or Australia, a further £50–£80 may well be added to the bill. For myself, I would very much rather drop my price a little for an overseas order, knowing full well that a satisfied customer, with a dog bearing my affix, which will win in the country of his adoption, is worth far more to me than the extra £10 I originally wanted for him!

Nothing is more satisfactory than to learn that the stock you sent out to a certain country has helped considerably in the improvement of the breed abroad.

The fact that puppies must be railed in a small hamper has already been mentioned, but a puppy of over four months of age is probably best sent in a travelling box. These boxes can be purchased in a variety of styles from the firms catering for the dog industry. For an adult Collie, or a bitch going to be mated, a box is essential. I find that a sturdy plywood box measuring 24 in. by 36 in. by 34 in. high will take a full-sized Collie comfortably. The box should be fastened with a padlock, and whether the key accompanies the dog or is sent in advance is a matter of personal feeling. I usually use a combination padlock, advising in advance the person who is to receive the dog, of the combination.

If you are one of those who travel by train to shows, then, if the journey is at all long, much the most satisfactory method is

Ch. Westcarrs Blue Minoru
*Born 1951*

AND HIS DAUGHTER

Ch. Silvasceptre from Shiel
*Born 1953*
Granddaughter of Ch. Silvaseabear from Shiel

Ch. Wythenshawe Windhover
*Born 1953*

THE SHETLAND SHEEPDOG

Ch. Riverhill Rescuer
*Born 1951*

to box your dogs during such a journey. Over a long distance the freight will probably be less than the cost of a dog ticket, but far more important is that the dog sleeps in the box and arrives at the show both clean and alert. Quite a point, too, is that dogs are not allowed in the sleeping compartments on railways, and with the dogs boxed the owner can have a sleeper and also arrive alert, but possibly not so clean!

Unfortunately British Railways are far from adequate in their method of handling livestock in transit, and, despite the fact that the dog may be despatched with his selected route clearly marked on his box, it is wise also to advise the station-master at each inter-change station that the dog will be on a particular train, for change to such and such a train. This should not be necessary, but it is, and it saves many heart-burnings about the dog not arriving at his destination at the correct time. However, with a 'rush order' it is not always possible to forewarn the station staff, and a risk must be taken. It is best to consign the stock at Company's risk, but even this does not give adequate protection, and although the term 'Company's risk' might be construed as 'accepting risk to the value of the dog', this is not so, for the most that will be paid on a claim under Company's risk is, for one dog, a maximum of £2. It is therefore advisable to despatch livestock at a 'declared higher value'. It is not necessary to declare at full value if you do not wish, for the mere fact that even £5 has been declared, which entails only a small premium, ensures that 'declared higher value' labels are placed on the container and that a great deal more care and attention is paid to such consignments; the guard of each train having to sign for the package is just one example.

Exporting a dog is a rather more complicated matter and it is certainly best, at any rate on the first occasion, to leave the arrangements in the hands of one of the well-known agents who handle such things, for in certain countries there are complications and until you have gained experience it is well-nigh impossible to cope by yourself.

For every country it is essential to have a veterinary certificate of health for the dog and, if the dog is for showing or breeding, the Kennel Club Export pedigree. Further, if the dog is male, the Kennel Club will not issue this export pedigree

L

without the certificate of cryptorchidism or monorchidism duly signed.[1] For certain countries blood-tests may be necessary, and for some Consular papers will be required. Details of what is necessary can be obtained from the Kennel Club, but if the matter is put into the hands of an agent all should be plain sailing.

Wherever possible, it is most satisfactory to freight a dog abroad by air, and enquiries should be made in every case from the client as to whether shipment may be effected by this means. Naturally it is more expensive, but it is an expense which is well worth while. You will find that the majority of the independent airlines are most excellent in their handling of dogs, and considerably cheaper than the regular air lines. The only countries which will not accept dogs by air are Australia and New Zealand. These countries, because of their great fear of importing rabies, will not allow dogs to enter the country by air, for it would have been necessary for the aeroplane in which the dog was travelling to have touched down in countries which are not rabies-free.

Australia and New Zealand also demand that dogs, even from Great Britain, shall go through a period of quarantine, though it is considerably shorter than our own six-months period. Very few other countries demand a quarantine period for our dogs.

Dogs being shipped abroad by sea must be provided with a shipping kennel, and if by air, with an air-freight shipping box. The selected agent will supply these, but if you are arranging the shipment yourself then it is possible to purchase boxes of suitable dimensions. For sending a Collie puppy by air there is nothing better than a tea-chest. I have used these many a time. I half cover the open end with a piece of plywood and then, with a cheap fire-guard purchased from a chain stores, I make a quite adequate hinged front for the other half, so that the puppy may easily be let out, fed, etc.

Often the question of the cost of shipment makes the chances of your overseas sale coming off a doubtful one, not because the client cannot afford the freight charges as well as the cost of the dog, but because he cannot always get sufficient currency

[1] See *The Kennel Club and You*, Chapter 15.

released to cover the cost of both dog and freight in sterling. This can often be overcome as some, at least, of the agents are willing to accept a dog and collect freight and other charges on its arrival.

All these small points help to lighten the burden to the seller and to the purchaser's pocket!

# THE KENNEL CLUB AND YOU

## A Chapter for the Real Beginner

THERE is so much to learn about dog breeding and showing that the novice is always coming up against terms he does not understand. Sometimes the 'old hands' are not as clear on the subject as they might be, but if they wish to they can skip this chapter!

No one who owns a pedigree-registered dog can possibly have failed to have heard the words the 'Kennel Club', but this club has much more behind it than just the registration of your dog. Its offices are situated at 1–4 Clarges Street, Piccadilly, London, and there, under one roof, everything you can possibly imagine connected with dogs and dog shows is arranged, settled and recorded.

The Committee of the Kennel Club is the governing body of the exhibition of dogs throughout the United Kingdom. The Committee is elected, not from all those of us who have dogs registered with the Kennel Club but from the comparative few who form its own membership, and this membership is confined exclusively to men. The Kennel Club is, in fact, an autocracy. But none of us will quarrel with this set-up, for the Committee does a very arduous and thankless job, and does it right well, *and* in a voluntary capacity. Despite the fact that well over 75 per cent. of the dog-showing community are women, and therefore, presumably, over 75 per cent. of the Kennel Club's income is derived from women, they still have no place on the General Committee, but although from time to time there is an outcry about this, affairs which relate to dogs proceed happily and calmly enough and are certainly more than adequately handled by the band of men in whose hands they rest. Full membership of the Kennel Club, then, is confined to men, but a woman may become a member of the Kennel Club Ladies' Branch, purely a social club, and both men and women are eligible as Associates of the Kennel Club.

The governing body is entirely responsible for the registration and transfer of all dogs; for all shows, working and field trials; for the allocation of Championship status and of Challenge Certificates to the various shows and trials; for the licensing of all shows, including matches, for the recording of all registered societies (and demand an annual, up-to-date statement on the financial affairs of each club registered with them); for the formation of rules covering every possible side of the dog show game, and finally for the punishment of those who infringe those rules. They are responsible for their own monthly publication, *The Kennel Gazette*, and annually the invaluable *Kennel Club Stud Book*. Both of these publications are available to everyone, not, of course, just Kennel Club members.

So you see that at any point in the dog-showing and breeding game you must come in direct contact with the Kennel Club, and a very good thing too, for without this control the dog game would be chaotic.

Occasionally, in various parts of the country, dog shows are held which are unlicensed and outside the control of the governing body. These shows are taboo and beware of them, for if it is proved that you have exhibited or officiated in any capacity at an unauthorized show you are liable to be 'warned off' for life by the Kennel Club itself, and as this 'warning off' means that you are forbidden to attend any dog activity licensed by the Kennel Club, that the stock you breed cannot be registered, that the progeny of your stud dogs likewise cannot be registered, it results in the end of all your doggy activities, and should you happen to be one of those who tries to make a living out of dogs your livelihood is gone. These unauthorized shows are few and far between, but do make sure that the words 'Under K.C. Rules and Regulations' appear on the schedule of any show at which you propose exhibiting. Then you know you are safe.

THE KENNEL CLUB LIAISON COUNCIL.

The Kennel Club Liaison Council, or K.C.L.C. as it is familiarly known, is, as its name denotes, the body which links the Kennel Club with us, the exhibiting public. The members of the K.C.L.C. are elected by nomination of the committees of the registered societies, and then by a ballot from these societies from the various nominees, who become 'Area Representatives' on election, and these, together with representatives of the General Championship Societies and of one representative for each group of dog (e.g. Sporting, Non-Sporting, etc.), form the Council. To these representatives may be passed any suggestions or complaints from the clubs throughout the country, and these items may then be placed on the agenda of the K.C.L.C. for discussion by that body. According to the results of the Council's discussions, the items are either passed or rejected by them, and if passed are then forwarded as recommendations to the Kennel Club, who, as in everything, have the final say. A delegate from the K.C.L.C. has a seat on the Committee of the Kennel Club so that the deliberations of the Council go to the Kennel Club not only as a written document but also with the backing of the delegate. Further, the Secretary of the Kennel Club is also Secretary of the K.C.L.C., providing yet another link.

REGISTRATION.

As has already been said, the first thing to do on acquiring your dog is to register it with the Kennel Club, unless the dog has already been registered. To *register* a dog it is necessary to obtain the appropriate form from the K.C. (this is free), and when the required details have been filled in, to return it, together with a fee of 50p, to the Kennel Club. If your dog has not already been registered before you purchased it (and more likely than not it will have been), the breeder or vendor should give you the necessary form, I–A, already completed as far as he is able, so that you may finish the particulars yourself.[1] If the dog has been registered before purchase you must see that at the time of the sale you are given a 'Form for the transfer of a registered dog'; this, too, you then complete and forward, with £1, so that the dog may be officially recorded as your property. If you are purchasing a dog which has already been registered, his registration certificate should be handed to you with his pedigree.

ENDORSEMENT OF REGISTRATIONS.

It does not seem to be as widely known as it should that a person who registers a dog with the Kennel Club, and who then decides that for some reason he does not wish the dog

---

[1] The registration fee for a dog registered by someone other than the breeder is £1.50 but £2 if breeder's declaration is not signed.

either to be exhibited or bred from, one or the other, can restrict the dog by having the original registration certificate endorsed. This arrangement is an ideal one, and would, if breeders would make more use of it, guard against a puppy, sold very cheaply as a pet, appearing in the ring, or, if it is one with a fault, being bred from and passing that fault to its progeny. It is a particularly useful safeguard in a breed such as ours where a puppy may appear over-shot at, say, three months of age, and is sold cheaply because of that. We know that quite often in our breed an over-shot puppy may grow into a level-mouthed adult, and it is a most excellent safeguard to endorse the registration, on either one or both counts, and then make the proviso with your purchaser that, should the fault correct itself, you will have the endorsement lifted; for this you may do, but only the person who made the registration and endorsement can apply for the lifting of the endorsement. The procedure is simple; you send the registration certificate to the Kennel Club telling them what you want done, and the card comes back marked 'Cannot be exhibited', 'Progeny not eligible for registration', or both, according to your request. Furthermore, this service costs nothing. Since May 1969 we are also allowed a further endorsement: 'Not for export'.

PREFIXES AND AFFIXES.

If you are planning to breed, even in the smallest way, then you should decide, right from the outset, that all dogs of your breeding shall be known by a common prefix or affix—a trade mark in fact. This is valuable to you even if you plan only a 'yearly litter'. It is necessary to apply to the Kennel Club for a special form and to make application on this form for the name you wish to use. When you realize that between 18,000 and 20,000 words are on the records of the Kennel Club as names which have already been granted you will appreciate that the allocation of fresh names is not a simple task, for not only must there be no duplication but also there must be no new name granted which is too close to an existing one. Every name that the Kennel Club is considering granting is published, and the owner of an existing prefix is given the right to object to any new one suggested. Therefore it is wise to start asking for your Kennel name almost as soon as you decide to buy a puppy from which to breed a litter—sometimes the application will be returned a number of times before a final choice is made, and months can easily elapse. The registration of a Kennel name costs £3, with an annual maintenance fee of £1.

It has been the practice of the Kennel Club to re-issue certain names, even in the same breed, after a lapse of a number of years. This seems a great pity, but is something no one seems able to do much about. However, the Kennel Club itself has taken some steps in the matter in the last few years; they now issue a list of names which not only cannot be used as a Kennel name but which cannot be used when registering any dog. At the time of writing only two of the well-known Collie Kennel names are thus protected, Sonnenburgh and Backwoods, and one wonders why certain others (Ormskirk and Wishaw spring particularly to mind) are not so protected, but in actual fact Ormskirk, spelt just the same way, and Wishawe, this time with the additional 'e', are names in the current Kennel Club list of prefixes and affixes. Fortunately, at the moment at least, neither is being used for registering Collies.

## Export Pedigree, Etc.

If you are exporting a dog to any part of the world as either a show or breeding proposition, it will require to have the Kennel Club's official 'export pedigree' as without this the dog cannot be recorded in the stud book of the country of its adoption. This export pedigree costs £2.50 for all countries, and should be applied for when sending for the transfer for the dog. When exporting a mated bitch some countries demand a 'vendor's certificate'; this is an official document, issued free by the Kennel Club, on which the vendor must give details of the mating. Other countries demand a certified pedigree of the stud dog (£2) issued over the seal of the Kennel Club, and it is wise, if exporting a mated female, to enquire from the Kennel Club just which of these documents is required for the country to which the bitch is being sent.[1] For every country in the world it is now necessary, under the rule of our own governing body, if you are exporting a male (of no matter what age), to obtain from the Kennel Club a form known as a Certificate re Monor-

[1] For exports to Sweden it is further necessary to provide documentary evidence that the sire is entire.

chidism and Cryptorchidism. This form must be completed and returned to the Kennel Club when you are applying for the export pedigree for the dog in question. Without this certificate the Kennel Club will not issue the export pedigree.

Because of the importance of this certificate, and the fact that the regulation is new, a reproduction is printed on page 170.

As this question of monorchidism is a veterinary one it is compulsory to have the certificate signed by your veterinary surgeon. This veterinary assistance can be obtained as a rule at no extra cost to yourself, for the form can be signed at the same time as the veterinary surgeon issues the health certificate for the animal. Except for export to the U.S.A. the export pedigree need not accompany the dog, but can be sent by mail afterwards.

CHALLENGE CERTIFICATES.

These, the highest award a dog can obtain, are on offer at Championship shows only, and not always every breed that is scheduled is being granted Challenge Certificates at a particular show, so read your schedule carefully. These certificates are awarded at the discretion of the judge, who is specially requested by the Kennel Club to withhold the award for want of merit. In fact, a judge has always the right to withhold any prize at any show if he does not think that the quality of the exhibits merits an award. With the Challenge Certificate, however, the matter is most serious, for every certificate issued bears the signature of the judge to the declaration that such and such an exhibit 'is of such outstanding merit as to be worthy of the title of Champion'. That is a declaration which no judge should sign lightly, for on the making of champions depends the future quality of the breed. Three such certificates must be won under three *different* judges before the dog can bear the proud title of Champion. The Challenge Certificate, the big green and white card which one is awarded in the ring, is not the official certificate; this follows at a later date, by post, when the win has been ratified and the eligibility of the winning exhibit is declared to be in order. When a dog has won his third certificate the Kennel Club will also forward the Champion's certificate to the owner. This certificate also comes to one automatically and should not be applied for.

BLOCK LETTERS PLEASE

Signature of applicant ...........................................................................................................

Full name and address of applicant ..........................................................................................

..........................................................................................................................................

..........................................................................................................................................

Full name and address of prospective owner ...............................................................................

..........................................................................................................................................

..........................................................................................................................................

Pedigree will be posted to applicant unless otherwise requested (below)

..........................................................................................................................................

..........................................................................................................................................

## NOTES

In the case of an application for an Export Pedigree for a male dog, the certificate A or B must be completed.

An export pedigree cannot be issued unless the dog is registered in the name of the consignee. The application to register or transfer the dog must be completed by the time of application for the pedigree.

If the application is for a bitch in whelp the applicant should also apply for a pedigree certificate in respect of the dog to which the bitch was mated. The fee for a pedigree certificate for this purpose is £2.00.

### CANADIAN EXPORTS

In the case of two or more dogs (or bitches) of the same breed exported in the same consignment to Canada, each dog must be tattooed before despatch with a mark supplied by the Canadian Kennel Club to the importer. This mark must also appear on the Export Pedigree.

If such a mark has been allocated by the Canadian Kennel Club in respect of this dog give exact details for reproduction (by the Kennel Club) on the pedigree.

---

Certificate "A"

To be signed by veterinary surgeon or veterinary practitioner.

---

I certify that I have today examined the dog identified to me as over and that both testicles are fully descended in the scrotum and apparently normal.

Date ......................................................        Signature ..............................................

Address ..................................................        Qualification .........................................

..........................................................................................

---

Certificate "B"

To be signed by the vendor when the dog has not both testicles descended in the scrotum and/or are not apparently normal.

---

I certify that the prospective owner of the dog has been informed
(a)   that both testicles are not fully descended in the scrotum and/or
(b)   are not apparently normal and that with this knowledge he still instructs me to export the dog.
I enclose a letter from the consignee (or some other evidence) to this effect.

Date ......................................................        Signature ..............................................

When certificate "B" is completed the Export Pedigree will be endorsed to that effect.

| TYPED | CHECKED | POSTED | NUMBER |
|-------|---------|--------|--------|
|       |         |        |        |

# APPLICATION FOR AN EXPORT PEDIGREE – £2.50

## Form to be completed with fee and returned to:

### The Kennel Club, 1 Clarges Street, Piccadilly, London W1Y 8AB

*(On the reverse of this form is space for applicant to fill in a three-generation pedigree)*

## BREEDER'S DIPLOMA.

There is yet another award, the granting of a Breeder's Diploma to the breeder of a Champion, whether the breeder is the owner or not, and it is a very nice addition, of fairly recent origin, to the Kennel Club awards as it acknowledges the achievement of the 'stay-at-home' breeder who may be unable to exhibit, and who always sells his best stock to others to show. This diploma, however, is not awarded automatically; it must be applied for in a letter stating the shows at which the dog concerned has won its C.C.s. No special application form is necessary.

## JUNIOR WARRANT.

This award was introduced just before the Second World War, as recognition for an outstanding young dog who may be too immature to gain his title but who is nevertheless above the average in quality. The Warrant is gained when a dog has won 25 points whilst between the ages of 6 and 18 months, and points are allocated thus: 1st at a Championship Show, 3 points; 1st at an Open Show, 1 point. These points are counted only if won in breed classes, and wins in classes for Collies, Rough or Smooth, do not count as these are considered by the Kennel Club to be Variety classes. A great deal of acclaim is often given to the Junior Warrant winner, but I do not consider this award is all it is reputed to be. It is very much easier to win in some breeds than in others. For instance, in Cockers, Boxers, Miniature Poodles, to mention only three breeds, where there is usually a multiplicity of classes for the breed, it is much easier to tot up the necessary number of points than in a breed where there are only a few classes at each show. Further, in the short-coated breeds, and in the smaller breeds, a puppy can often start his show career at six months of age. In our breed it is generally hopeless to start your puppy before it has had a chance to grow its coat, and he may be nine months of age before he sees a ring. The short-coated breed can probably spend all its time between 6 and 18 months being shown. With a dog that starts at nine months it may be that he must be temporarily retired from the ring at 12–13 months, when his coat drops, and he will be well over 18 months of age before he is again fit to show. Another point: a forward, good-coated puppy who happens to hit a string of shows may qualify easily, but that same youngster may go off early and never be heard of again after winning its Junior Warrant. Also, in my opinion, a puppy of a medium or big breed may be ruined by being dragged around the country in search of those elusive points, for too many shows during the growing period are undoubtedly a mistake; an occasional outing if you like, to give the youngster a taste of what is to come, but not a general grind, when he should be at home eating, playing, sleeping and growing.

Beware of that Junior Warrant!

## BREEDING TERMS AGREEMENTS.

These form yet another aspect of the game in which the Kennel Club plays an official part. By no means all bitches who are parted with on breeding, or part-breeding, terms have this loan officially recorded at the Kennel Club; in fact it is a very definite minority, but it is well to know that the Kennel Club does issue a form of contract for the 'Loan or Use of Bitch', which costs £1, and which, if used, covers both parties should any dispute arise, for the Kennel Club then becomes the adjudicator and final court of appeal. This document does not cover all the ways in which one can lend out a bitch on terms, and for that reason many breeders prefer to make their own agreements.[1]

## STUD BOOK ENTRY.

This is the official allocation to any dog or bitch of a *K.C. Stud Book* number, which then supersedes its original registration number. There are two major ways in which a dog can be admitted to the *Stud Book*—by qualification or by nomination. If a dog is entered by qualification he is entitled to free entry, and such entry is automatic. He is granted free entry if he (*a*) wins a C.C. or Reserve best-of-sex award at a Championship show, or if he is awarded 1st, 2nd or 3rd prize in an Open or Limit Class at a Championship show, where Challenge Certificates were on offer for his breed, and provided that such classes were not restricted by weight, colour, etc.; (*b*) wins a prize, Certificate of Honour or Certificate of Merit at Field Trials held under K.C. Rules; (*c*) wins a prize or Certificate of

[1] See Appendix 3.

Merit in Stakes at a Championship Working Trials; (*d*) is awarded an Obedience Certificate in Test C at a Championship show.

## SHOWS.

As has already been stated, there are four types of show: Championship, Open and Limited, and Sanction.

Championship Shows are shows where anyone may exhibit, provided the dog is registered with the Kennel Club, and where Challenge Certificates are offered. These may be multiple-breed shows, or specialist club, one breed, Championship Shows. It is only at these shows that a dog can make his way towards the coveted title of Champion.

Open Shows. Similar to Championship Shows, but Challenge Certificates not offered.

Limited Shows. Shows where the entry is confined to members of the promoting club or society, and restricted to a minimum number of classes.

Sanctions Shows. An even smaller off-shoot of the Limited Show, restricted to not more than 20 classes, to medium grade dogs and to members only.

There is one more type of show, the Exemption Show. These are usually run in connection with fêtes, etc. The Kennel Club gives permission for the holding of a show of not more than four classes. Proceeds usually go to charity. Dogs need not be K.C. registered and entry for these shows is usually made on the day.

## MATCHES.

Matches are competitions between two dogs, the property of members of the promoting club, or between members of two different clubs, when the match is of an invitation variety and another club has been invited to compete. These are not shows. No prize cards may be awarded, but they are a pleasant way of spending an evening and a very good training ground for a youngster before making his debut.

This sets out then all the main parts the Kennel Club plays, and where it is most likely to affect you as an exhibitor.

It should not be forgotten that today the Kennel Club runs the world's greatest dog show, Crufts, in London, in February of each year.

# CHAPTER 16

# FIRST AID AND COMMON AILMENTS

*(I am indebted to Miss Copithorne, M.R.C.V.S., for checking this
chapter and for making suggestions)*

FORTUNATELY the Collie is not subject to many of the complaints, such as eczema, canker, etc., which beset so many
breeds, and for that we have much to be thankful. However, it
is every bit as necessary when dealing with a canine family to
be prepared for accident, and to have the medicine chest always
suitably equipped, as it is for a human family. Most of the
necessary items for inclusion will be found in the household
medicine chest.

TAKING THE TEMPERATURE.

Every dog owner must have a clinical thermometer at hand,
and must know how to use and read it. An ordinary clinical
thermometer is perfectly suitable, but it should be a 'stumpy'
one—that is, one in which the end which contains the mercury
is thick and rounded, not thin and brittle.

The dogs normal temperature is 101.5°.

Dogs which are well fed, exercised and housed have a great
natural resistance to disease, but it is a wise precaution to have
a golden rule in your kennel: If the dog doesn't eat, take his
temperature *at once*. Don't wait until tomorrow to see if he eats
then; there are diseases in which 'tomorrow' may prove too
late. To take the temperature it is useful to have an assistant
who will hold the dog. Make sure the thermometer is shaken
down to 96° or less. Insert the thermometer, which may
have been previously smeared with vaseline, into the rectum
for about half to two-thirds of the length of the thermometer.
Do not use any force, and if there is difficulty in getting the
thermometer inserted alter the position just a little, either up or
down. Leave the thermometer in place for one minute, even with
a half-minute thermometer, and keep hold of the end all the
time. If the temperature is above normal, keep the dog quiet

and under observation until further symptoms show themselves or until his temperature is back to normal and has been that way for 24 hours. Never take a dog's temperature immediately after exercise or excitement of any kind, such as a journey, for this may have raised the temperature several degrees. At least an hour should elapse after exercise before a true temperature can be determined. If it is over 102° when taken one hour after exercise wait another hour and take it again; some dogs take much longer to settle down than others. This is especially true of puppies from six to ten months old.

The old story that a healthy dog has a cold wet nose and that the dog with a dry hot nose is a sick dog is not true, and the state of a dog's nose is no guide at all to his condition, except, of course, when it is in a state of discharging mucus.

A young puppy may run a slight temperature for little or no reason at all, and a puppy during teething may quite often have a slight rise of temperature, but it is still wise, if the temperature persists for more than 12 hours, to call in your veterinary surgeon.

FITS.

Running through the everyday ailments and accidents which your dog may run into is perhaps done most easily by starting with the baby pup and following it through its life, for there are complaints which may be contracted more readily, or only, at certain periods of life. The baby puppy is most likely to be troubled with fits caused either by the presence of worms or by teething. The former kind should never appear, for a puppy so obviously 'wormy' should have been attended to before the irritation brought about the condition which culminates in fits. If, however, the puppy has arrived at the stage where it is having fits caused by worms it is essential to seek the advice of your veterinary surgeon, and not to handle the situation yourself unless you are very experienced, because the subsequent worm treatment might prove too much for the already harmed system.

Collie puppies seem to have a fair amount of trouble in cutting their teeth, the gums often becoming very swollen and inflamed, and it is in these cases that teething fits may occur, though on the whole the condition is rare. A puppy suffering from fits must be kept quiet, and in a cool, darkened room, until such time as veterinary advice can be obtained. In fact, the best thing is to give the puppy or adult a mild sedative such as aspirin (one for a puppy, 2–3 for an adult) and to shut him in a box and leave him in a dark place until the veterinary surgeon arrives. Quiet is essential. There is always the chance that fits are not caused by worms or teething, but may be a symptom of something much more serious, so be sure to get advice. Remember that fits are never a disease in themselves; they are only a symptom of some definite trouble.

Puppies or adults suffering from fits must be kept completely isolated, puppies even from their litter-mates, because all dogs, puppy or adult, tend to attack the abnormal one, and serious injury might be done before the sufferer could be rescued.

STRAINS AND BRUISES.

Puppies will frequently hurt themselves, twisting a leg, etc., when playing, and on rushing up in answer to a frightful scream of pain one will often find a puppy apparently dead lame—so seriously in trouble that he will tell you his leg is broken and he will surely never walk again! Take this baby away from his companions and leave him on a non-slippery floor (lino is not good) until, of his own accord, he finds his feet again. He will often be all right in as little as 30 minutes! However, if the strain or bruise is of a more serious nature, then further action must be taken, and here I swear by a homeopathic remedy. Saturate a pad of cotton wool in cold water and then squeeze it as dry as you possibly can. Now soak this pad in Tincture of Arnica Flowers, apply it to the injured part (but only when there is no break in the skin), and bandage lightly. It is almost certain that the patient will try to remove the bandage, so paint the outside with mustard, which, in most cases, is highly discouraging! The same treatment is equally good for adults. Further, dose the patient twice daily with a dessertspoonful of water to which two drops of Tincture Arnica have been added.

If a dog attempts to chew and tear at his bandages make sure that these are not causing pain. They may have been put on rather too tightly or the injured part may have swollen later, causing the bandage to become tight, which could be a source of great discomfort. Only when satisfied on this point should mustard, or other repellent such as bitter aloes or tincture of ginger, be applied.

*Alternative Treatment for Bruises*, which can be used if the skin is broken. As soon as possible after the injury bathe well with cold water; this helps to reduce bleeding in the bruised tissue and so reduces the swelling. A few hours after the injury bathe with *hot* water, to stimulate the circulation and so help to disperse the results of the damage from the bruise. Use water as hot as you can comfortably bear on the inside of your forearm.

### DIARRHOEA.

This, again, is frequently a 'puppy' complaint and may be caused by a variety of reasons.

Most usually in puppies it is caused by a sudden change of food, or by a chill. In cases of diarrhoea, whether in puppies or in adults, castor oil should *never* be administered. Liquid paraffin, however, is good, and may remove the irritation causing the condition. Liquid paraffin is a soothing mixture as well as an aperient. Castor oil is an irritant and should *never* be used except under veterinary instruction. A puppy with persistent diarrhoea should be placed on a diet of egg white and arrowroot gruel, plus a little glucose. Further treatment may consist of dosing with Boot's chlorodyne, the dose for an eight-week old puppy being 10 drops in half a teaspoonful of water every four hours.

Diarrhoea in adults is more often the symptom of the onset of some specific virus or bacterial disease and is usually accompanied by a rise of temperature. The treatment is the same as that for puppies, but it must be realized that diarrhoea is a condition which must be viewed seriously and if at all persistent veterinary advice should always be sought.

### ECLAMPSIA (PUERPERAL ECLAMPSIA).

This is a condition affecting the nursing bitch and is an illness in which it is absolutely imperative that immediate action, in the shape of sending for your veterinary surgeon, should be taken. The cause is the excessive drain of calcium

M

from the blood at the time when a bitch is nursing her puppies. Good food and the administration of calcium as set out in the chapter on the whelping bitch all help to ward off this condition, but all the calcium in the world will be no use if the bitch has not got enough vitamin D to enable her to utilize the calcium. But even the best-cared-for brood bitches may develop eclampsia and it is more common in the excessively good mother who gives all of herself to her babies. Frequently the only symptom will be the total collapse of the bitch, without any previous warning; she may retain or lose consciousness, and in the former case she will probably get up in a few minutes. It is essential to have your veterinary surgeon on the spot with the least possible delay, for an injection of calcium will put the bitch right in as brief a space as half an hour, but neglect of this collapsed condition will lead to a worsening of the condition and death will rapidly result. Occasionally the bitch will show slight symptoms before the collapse stage. She may appear stiff in movement, pant a great deal and have a temperature. As has already been said, the presence of a temperature will demand that you seek immediate professional advice, and then all will be well, but I cannot stress too strongly the absolute necessity for *immediate* action in a suspected case of Puerperal Eclampsia.

ECZEMA.

Fortunately the Collie rarely develops eczema, this disease being more frequently associated with other breeds. It is non-contagious and is frequently a 'seasonal' condition. There are two forms of eczema, the moist and the dry, and neither form confines itself to any special area of the body, being found anywhere. Moist eczema can appear overnight, or in less time than that. It is quite a common occurrence to put a dog into its kennel overnight in a perfectly fit and healthy condition and to take it out in the morning with an area the size of a saucer which is red, glistening, damp and quite hairless. This sudden appearance, and the fact that these areas are very sensitive to touch, are clearly symptomatic of this condition. This type of eczema cannot possibly be confused with mange in either of its forms. Moist eczema will frequently respond to treatment with calomine lotion, and this may well be tried before taking the patient to the veterinary surgeon. The dog should be placed solely on a raw meat diet, and the addition of the juice of raw tomatoes to the food is also a great help, for the presence of wet eczema indicates a deficiency of vitamin C which is found in tomatoes, oranges and fresh green vegetables.

Dry eczema is also non-contagious and non-parasitic, but it is very difficult to differentiate between the lesions of eczema and of sarcoptic and follicular mange, both of which are highly contagious. It is wise to take immediate professional advice if your dog is suffering from dry, scaly patches on the body, and if the surface of these bald patches is wrinkly. A condition of similar appearance can be caused by the presence of fleas and lice, but a close examination of the coat will soon reveal these. However, only a microscopic examination of deep scrapings will reveal whether the sarcopt or demodect is present, and as this is the main distinguishing feature between dry eczema and mange the advice to take your dog to the veterinary surgeon if dry eczema is suspected cannot be over-emphasized.

Many dogs will take finely chopped lettuce mixed with their food, when this is available. Vitamin C can also be given in tablet form and is exceedingly helpful in treating both skin diseases and septic wounds.

ENTERITIS (Inflammation of the bowel).

Again a serious condition. Its symptoms are loss of appetite, vomiting and thirst, accompanied sometimes by a very high temperature, but more normally by a temperature of no more than 102–104°. Enteritis usually accompanies a specific disease but it can also be caused by worms, chills, decomposed foodstuffs, poisoning of the irritant kind, and by the swallowing of foreign bodies. The treatment is warmth and rest, and purgatives should *never* be given—and above all, *never give castor oil*. The dog should not be given food in the early stages but he may be allowed liquids such as milk, egg and milk, barley water, glucose and water, Benger's Food, groats and arrowroot gruel. If vomiting is a prominent symptom he should be given barley water only. A dose of liquid paraffin may be administered (but, again, *never* castor oil), and if the condition does not improve the veterinary surgeon must be sent for.

EYE INJURIES (*see* Appendix 5, p.233).

It is very easy for a dog to injure an eye, whether the injury is to a puppy by a puppy, or to an adult out at exercise or work. Immediately an injury is noticed the cause should be sought. It may be a foreign body, such as a grass seed, in the eye, and this should be removed at once and the eye bathed with a solution of boracic, or with cold tea (without milk!). I prefer the latter. An eye can often be scratched and in such a case it is well to put penicillin eye ointment into the injured eye, for should it prove to be a more severe injury than was at first suspected this medicament does not preclude any further treatment of any kind. However, if it is intended to use penicillin and it is also considered desirable to wash the eye out first, then the eye should be bathed only with plain warm water, as use of any chemical (e.g. boracic) might inhibit the action of the penicillin.

*Foreign Body in the Eye.* When attempting to wash out a foreign body from an eye it is necessary to hold the dog's head slightly on one side, raise the lower eyelid a little so that it makes a tiny cup, flood this with lukewarm water, then let the dog's head go so that he can blink and wash the liquid round the eyeball. This will often wash out a grass seed or a bit of grit. If you cannot wash a foreign body out of the eye, do not probe for it. Put a few drops of liquid paraffin into the eye, and arrange to take the dog to your veterinary surgeon as soon as possible.

GASTRITIS (Inflammation of the stomach).

The principal symptom of gastritis is excessive thirst accompanied by vomiting, mainly of a white or yellow frothy gastric mucus. The dog is restless, seeks cold places to lie in, yet rarely does the temperature exceed 102°. The condition calls for skilled treatment, but pending the arrival of this the dog should be given nothing but barley water to drink, access to fresh water being definitely forbidden, and a dose of chlorotone (5 gr.) may be administered. The dog may be given ice to lick or small pieces may be forcibly administered. If this is done the barley water need not be given, but he must be compensated in some way for the loss of fluid which occurs through continuous vomiting. The dog must be kept warm, and hot water-bottles (well covered) may be placed at the pit of the stomach to relieve pain and sickness. (You are referred to the next section, Home Nursing of Dogs.) Rest the stomach by withholding all food, and keep the dog warm and dry indoors.

FLEAS AND LICE.

Most dogs, however well cared for, get fleas at some time in their lives, and it is necessary to keep these well under control if only because the flea is the host of the tapeworm egg. Anyway, it does not improve a long-coated dog if he is constantly scratching!

Prevention and treatment are the same: dusting with one of the gammexane powders until the whole dog is covered. All kennels and bedding should be dusted with the powder also, including the cracks between floor-boards and corners of sleeping boxes, for it must be remembered that a flea does not breed on the dog but in cracks and chinks of wood.

*Lice* are small bluish-grey insects which attach themselves to the skin and suck the blood of the dog. An effective remedy is to bathe the dog in Izal shampoo, but it is essential to see that the coat is soaked right down to the skin—not at all easy in our breed—and the shampoo should be left in contact with the skin for about 15 minutes before being rinsed off. During this time the shampooing must continue, and friction be kept up on the skin in order to keep the dog warm. After that time has expired the coat can be rinsed and allowed to dry in the usual way.

An alternative method for lice is to dust gammexane powder thoroughly into the coat, making sure that it reaches right down to the skin. This dusting should be repeated every fourth day until the dog has been treated five or six times. The first thorough dusting will kill all the lice, but as it does not kill the nits it has to be repeated several times to catch them as they hatch.

A most effective method of getting any kind of powder well into the coat is the use of a plastic 'puffer' similar to those used for certain kinds of talcum powder. By this means the powder can be blown right down to the roots, and the consequent saving of powder which would otherwise be wasted is quite important.

*Harvest Mites* or *Harvesters* are tiny little orange-coloured insects with the same habits as lice. As their name denotes, they are usually found during summer and autumn, and it is not often that they are found except between the toes and, in puppies, possibly on the head and round the eyes. These respond to Izal shampoo, but if it is preferred not to bathe the dog a dusting with gammexane powder blown directly on to the clump of mites will kill them at once, though the bodies may not drop off for a day or two.

*Ticks.* Dogs running in the country, and all who are bedded on straw, are liable to pick up a cattle tick at some time or other. If so, do not pull it off; if you do the head will remain and may cause a nasty sore. Put a drop of methylated spirit round the head of the tick and after a few seconds try to ease it out gently (with forceps or tweezers for preference). If you cannot get it off in this way, leave it alone; it will do less harm if it drops off naturally in its own time than if you pull it off. If a tick fixes on to a dog's eyelid or lip, or if the dog is very upset about it, you had better ask for veterinary help. In some countries ticks can carry disease which may be serious to dogs, such as the tick causing paralysis, but fortunately these diseases are not prevalent in this country.

JAUNDICE.

Ordinary jaundice is usually the result of some other disease and can often arise as the result of a chill. There is, however, another type, known as *Leptospiral Jaundice*, and this is the type contracted from the urine of infected rats and mice. It is often thought that this disease is likely to be found only in rat-infested kennels. This is not so. The presence of one infected rat, even if he only passes by *en route* for somewhere else, or the introduction into the kennel of a bale of straw over which an infected rat has urinated, are all that is necessary to introduce the virus to the dog. This is a most invidious disease as the early symptoms are often not noticed at all; the first sign the owner has is that the dog is somewhat lethargic. Temperature is usually normal or sub-normal, and thirst accompanies this condition. In the later stages the dog will vomit, but more often than not by the time the symptoms are such that a veterinary surgeon is called, even by the most careful and conscientious of owners, the spirochaetes (the microscopic organs which invade the blood-stream in this disease) have already set themselves up in the kidneys, where the nephritis they cause has already done so much damage that a cure is well nigh impossible.

However, it is now possible to have one's dogs immunized against this disease. This immunization is not an expensive one, and it is therefore recommended that this precaution be taken if there is any chance of dogs being in a rat-contact area.

Yet another type exists—*Leptospira Canicola*, or canicola jaundice. This is thought to be the cause of a lot of the kidney trouble in older dogs. The infection takes place in young dogs, often with no obvious symptoms, and the consequent damage to the kidney tissue frequently does not show until the dog arrives at middle age and develops 'chronic nephritis'. Immunization against this type of jaundice is also possible and gives a good measure of protection.

### HARD PAD AND KINDRED DISEASES.

It is not considered that this is the right place for a discussion of the symptoms or treatment of these diseases, which are essentially a matter for the professional to deal with. Symptoms are so varied in the same disease that it is almost useless to list them, and beyond saying that a cough should make one suspicious of something, and a cough plus rise of temperature certain, there can be no better advice than to tell you to call your veterinary surgeon if the dog appears off-colour, refuses food, has a slight rise of temperature or coughs. Best of all, be certain to have your dog immunized against hard pad with one of the several 'egg-adapted' vaccines on the market, whichever one is favoured by your owh veterinary surgeon.

### MANGE.

There are two kinds of mange, sarcoptic and follicular. The former is caused by a mite, a microscopic parasite, the sarcopt, which burrows under the skin, and there the female lays her eggs, which, taking only about a week to hatch, rapidly produce the condition of sarcoptic mange. Follicular mange is also caused by a mite, demodex folliculorim. Streptococci and other bacteria often invade the skin damaged by the demodex and cause the boils and pus often associated with this disease.

This type of mange may cause serious illness and even death from toxemia and exhaustion.

If mange is suspected it is essential to obtain laboratory confirmation, by the microscopal examination of deep skin scrapings, and the treatment, which in all cases must be very thorough indeed, must be left to your veterinary surgeon.

STINGS.

Dogs being ready at almost all times to chase and play are frequently stung by the bees and wasps which they consider fair game. Remember that a bee leaves his sting in the skin; wasps rarely do so. You will probably not have seen the actual stinging, so if your dog comes to you with a swollen face or other part of his body (during the 'wasp season') and a sting is suspected, it is wise, first of all, to look for the centre of the swelling and if the sting can be seen there to remove this with a pair of tweezers. Half an onion or a blue bag can then be applied to the seat of the sting—except that if the sting is in the mouth, do not apply blue bag there. A piece of onion can be rubbed gently on the inside of the mouth or, alternatively, the pain can be relieved by the application of a little bicarbonate of soda. It is not necessary to make a solution of this; a little rubbed gently on to the spot with the fingers works wonders. Watch the dog carefully until you are satisfied that the swelling is not increasing, for it is possible, though not common, for a dog to be suffocated by the pressure of the swelling from a sting in the throat. If in doubt, take the dog to a veterinary surgeon, as an injection can be given which will reduce the swelling.

WOUNDS.

Dogs are very liable to get minor cuts, scratches or bites from another dog. A laceration which bleeds freely is usually 'safe' in that it will heal quickly and cleanly. A wound which is more in the nature of a puncture, which is deep-seated and which bleeds little or not at all, is the kind which requires greater care, for this type of wound will often heal from the surface, instead of from the bottom outwards, and therefore will have imprisoned in it bacteria and pus which cause trouble later. Treatment of any type of wound is first to stop the bleeding, which may, in the case of a deep cut, necessitate the application of a tourniquet. Next comes the extraction of any foreign body there may be in the wound. Then the wound must be cleansed with a weak solution of T.C.P., Dettol or similar antiseptic. Lysol and carbolic must *never* be used. It is almost certain that it will be necessary to cut the hair from the area round the wound, and this is particularly necessary with a long-coated dog such as ours. The wound should be kept dressed with penicillin ointment and a punctured wound kept open so that it may heal cleanly from the bottom up. When the time is reached where it is desired to 'dry up' an open wound, to accelerate the healing it is advisable to apply sulphathyzamide powder. Both this and penicillin ointment can be obtained only from your veterinary surgeon or on his prescription, but they are wonderful things to have in your medicine chest at all times.

Urticaria (Nettle Rash).

This is frequently met with and may at first be confused with a sting, for the dog will appear swollen. The raised patches on the skin are, however, flat, and vary in size from a pea to a 5s. piece. There are no scabs and no irritation, and with our breed (unless the condition is seen on the face and legs) it is difficult to notice, but on these short-haired areas the hairs stand straight out. Urticaria is usually caused by an internal toxic condition and the best remedy is a sharp purgative, and in the case of an adult Collie the administration of a good half-teaspoonful of Epsom salts usually has a satisfactory effect. One dose is generally sufficient. The dog should be kept on a laxative diet for a few days. This condition is rarely as serious as it looks, but if it recurs in the Kennel, or in the same dog, a cause must be sought. Very often it is some particular food to which the dog is sensitive—bacon rinds and bloaters (neither the ideal dog food) have been known to cause it. One repeated case was traced to a gravy salt used in boiling up bones to make a tasty soup for the dog's biscuit meal.

Choking.

Choking may occur if a dog tries to swallow too large an object; for instance, any dog is apt to bolt whatever he has in his mouth if approached by a strange dog while he is eating, and many dogs, unless properly trained, will try to swallow any 'find' they may have made rather than give it up to their owner when asked to do so.

If the obstruction is in the upper part of the throat the dog may suffocate in a very few minutes, so *action* must be the word! Open his mouth—even if he tries to bite it's worth the risk—try to catch hold of the object and if you cannot get a hold and pull it up try to push it down gently. If the object goes to the lower part of the gullet the immediate risk of death is over. The foreign body might have to be removed surgically afterwards, but that is a matter for your veterinary surgeon to decide, and at least your dog is alive to swallow something else!

SHOCK.

Any injury is followed by a certain amount of shock. The dog will appear dazed and stupid; he may be shaky and weak or even become unconscious. His breathing will be shallow and rapid, his mucous membranes, as seen in his gums and inside his eyelids, pale, and he will feel cold to the touch. As a rule animals will not take hot drinks, but offer all drinks warm. Give glucose or sugar if possible. Wrap the patient up in a coat or blanket and try to get him warm. Do not, of course, try to force any liquids down the throat of an unconscious dog.

BURNS AND SCALDS.

Shock always follows these two accidents and it is frequently severe. Unless the damage is very slight, never attempt home treatment. Cover the injured area by bandaging very lightly or, if necessary, wrap the dog entirely in a blanket, leaving only the tip of his nose exposed, and get him to a veterinary surgeon as soon as you possibly can. Your main object must be to exclude air from all the burnt areas and to treat the dog for severe shock. Do not put oil or grease on a burn.

Scalds are more difficult to treat than burns, because with a Collie the dog's thick coat holds the hot liquid on to the skin; therefore the best method is to douche the area with lukewarm water as a first measure. Never use *cold* water; this might increase the shock.

Burns and scalds which cover only a very small area can be treated by covering with a paste made of soda bicarbonate (baking soda) and water. Spread this thickly over the injured area and don't let the dog lick it off.

### COLLAPSE.

If an old dog should collapse suddenly, perhaps on a very hot day, move him to the coolest place you can find, make sure he has plenty of fresh air, open his mouth and pull his tongue out and to one side so that his 'air passage' is clear. Rest him on his right side, with his head a little lower than his body.

If collapse occurs in cold weather it is essential that the dog should be wrapped up warmly (although he must still be allowed plenty of fresh air) whilst you await the arrival of your veterinary surgeon.

### FOUL BREATH.

So long as there is no possibility of it being attributed to a specific disease such as hard pad or jaundice, bad breath is almost always due to bad teeth, or to tartar on the teeth. Teeth can be cleaned with hydrogen peroxide solution, or with an ordinary toothpaste, but it is best to let your veterinary surgeon look at them as some may need to be removed.

## HOME NURSING OF DOGS
### (*Kindly contributed by a Veterinary Surgeon*)

All animals, and especially dogs, are creatures of habit, and many of them are seriously disturbed when their normal routine is upset. Because of this, almost all animal patients do best when nursed at home in their own familiar surroundings. Of course this is not always possible; infectious cases must be separated from other dogs, and some, particularly surgical cases, may have to become in-patients in a veterinary hospital for a time.

Whether your veterinary surgeon will agree that your Collie can be satisfactorily nursed at home depends largely on you. Collies are very sensitive dogs, very much one-man dogs, and I think that most of you would prefer to keep your Collie at home, so let us look into the question of canine home nursing.

The essential needs of any sick animal are quietness,

warmth, suitable bed, suitable food and drink, correct veterinary treatment . . . and last, but by no means least, the love,
care and encouragement of a sensible owner. All of us who have
ever loved and been loved by a Collie know the queer telepathy
(I can call it nothing else) that exists between a much-loved
Collie and the owner, so be careful—don't think defeatism, be
as cheerful and hopeful with your sick Collie as you would with
a sick child.

Speaking from a veterinary surgeon's point of view, I find
that Collies, on the whole, are very good patients. They make
a great fight for life, however injured or ill, and are sensible
patients, allowing themselves to be helped. But if separated for
too long from the person to whom they have become attached
they tend to lose interest in life.

Nurse a sick dog in a room in the house or in a kennel close
to the house, or an outbuilding nearby—somewhere where you
can easily get at him day or night, and where you can hear any
cries or barks from the patient. The kennel needs to be weather-
proof and the bed warm, and protected from draughts, whether
in a kennel or in the house.

In the house a good warm corner can be contrived for the
sick-bed by hanging an old blanket or other covering over a
clothes-horse, and using this screen to surround the bed on the
sides exposed to door and windows. Do not put the screen too
close to the dog's bed, so that he does not feel shut in, but get
down on the floor yourself and feel where the draughts are
coming from, and then arrange your screen to stop them. I
stress this because I find that many owners who pooh-pooh the
idea of draughts in their houses are horrified when they are
persuaded to try resting on floor-level themselves!

If possible, use the dog's own bed, but this must depend on
the patient, e.g. if partly paralysed, or with a fractured pelvis,
the dog cannot get on to a raised bed; for such a patient several
layers of sacks or blankets, or a sack filled with wood-wool not
packed too tightly, make a good bed. Many layers of newspaper
under the sacks greatly help to preserve the warmth. Many
patients whose vitality is low tend to get chilled at night and in
the early hours of the morning, so it is well worth while to get
up once or twice in the night to renew hot water-bottles, but
try to keep an even temperature as far as possible. While I am

on this subject, may I remind you that hot water-bottles must be covered, and covered so that no kicking or scratching on the part of the patient can uncover them? Neglect of this precaution can result in nasty burns.

Quietness really means that the dog patient must not be disturbed more than is absolutely necessary. Frequent visits and unnecessary fussing and petting may do more harm than good. Attend to the patient at regular intervals, as determined by the needs to give medicine, food, etc., but in between *let him rest.*

If your dog is dangerously ill, try to arrange some way of peeping in at him frequently without having to go in to him and arouse him, perhaps from a healing sleep. If the dog is partly paralysed, or so weak that he is unable to move himself, remember to turn him over gently at least twice a day, so that he does not lie for hours in the same position.

Unless decreed otherwise by the veterinary surgeon in charge of the case, all sick animals should have plenty of fresh drinking water. A small quantity, renewed several times a day, will be fresher and more attractive to the patient than a large bowlful which is allowed to go stale before it is re-charged.

Owners are often worried if the sick dog does not take food for a day or two. Most animals can well bear a few days' self-imposed starvation and are often all the better for it. If your patient does not want food, coax him by all means but do not force him. If he is still on hunger-strike after several days have gone by, it may be advisable to try forced feeding, but never be in a big hurry over this.

If an animal is off-colour for only a few days little grooming need be attempted, but in dealing with a longer illness some attention to the toilet each day will make a lot of difference to the comfort of the patient. Eyes should be washed out each day with warm water, and the eyelids smeared with a little olive oil or liquid paraffin to prevent the hairs on the lids sticking down. The nose, if discharging, should be cleaned several times a day with a swab of cotton wool dipped into warm (not hot) water, and afterwards wiped with a little olive oil too. A similar cotton-wool swab in warm water should be wiped round the face and ears and also round the tail and back feathering each day. If necessary, wash any soiled fur with a cloth wrung out with cleansing solution and then dried off, rather than soak the feathering itself.

If you are keeping a record of the patient's temperature always remember that it must be taken before the patient is disturbed or excited in any way. Nervousness, excitement and exertion can quickly cause a rise in temperature and if your Collie is of a very excitable temperament you may get a wrong impression if you take his temperature after his morning toilet instead of before.

Giving medicine is important. If he is to have a dose, make sure that he gets it; be firm with him and let him see that you intend him to have it. Tablets can often be given in food or in a tit-bit of meat or chocolate (one of my patients, a Peke, always takes his tablets in marmalade!) if it is easier. Crush the tablets and give the dog the resulting powder on the back of his tongue. Firm pressure with your fingers just behind the big canine teeth will usually make any dog open his mouth. Press upwards, keeping the dog's lips between his teeth and your fingers, and when his mouth is well opened throw in the dose.

If the patient has been put on to some drug which you are directed to 'give every four hours', or some similar direction, do please give the dose at the proper intervals. Many in use at the present time depend for their value on keeping the level of the drug in the patient's blood constant all the time. And the timing of doses is worked out to achieve this result. If this blood level is allowed to fall too soon, or becomes irregular, that may undo all the good that has been, or can be, done by the medicine.

If these notes give any helpful ideas or useful advice towards easing the lot of the animal patient and helping the 'nurse in charge' they will have achieved their object.

# CHAPTER 17

# THE ALLIED BREEDS

## THE SMOOTH COATED COLLIE

IT IS almost wrong to include the Smooth Coated Collie in this chapter, for he is not really an 'Allied Breed' but exactly the same breed. For the Smooth differs from the Rough only in coat. He is just the same typical Collie; in fact, often more typical, for it is not easy to cover up a fault in a Smooth and therefore the top winners are often structurally more perfect specimens than many of their long-coated brethren! It may be possible to get away with a structural defect in a Rough, for his wealth of coat may hide the defect and hoodwink the judge. This cannot be done with a Smooth, so this variety must have faultless conformation, with great spring of rib and plenty of heart room, and if his quarters are not well turned, or his shoulder badly placed, then the faults will be obvious at a glance. Probably because of this essential of perfect conformation before a Smooth can be considered as a show proposition, it is rare that we find an unsound Smooth in the ring, almost all moving freely and gracefully, looking as though they could do a day's work.

Throughout its history the Smooth has, unfortunately, lagged a long way behind the Rough in popularity, both as a show prospect and as a companion, and certainly the added beauty of the heavily coated Rough can be the only reason for this, for in every other respect, both physically and in character, they are identical. In fact, at every phase of their history they have carried a large proportion of Rough blood, though the early years of this century were the days in which the Smooth was at its peak and when the strains were more clearly defined. Even in that period there was a great drawing on the blood of the Rough, and the outstanding Smooth of the time, Ch. Canute Perfection, was by the Rough dog Count of Moreton.

Several times during its history the Smooth has been in such low water as to be near extinction. After the First World War things were very low, and again immediately after the recent war. Each time, however, a small band of stalwarts has saved them. Again the crossing with the Rough became essential if any of the variety were to remain at all, and here it is interesting to note that puppies from such a cross are always either Rough or Smooth, never having an 'in-between' coat. Puppies from a Rough x Smooth mating are registerable with the Kennel Club in their appropriate breed and can be shown as such, there being no need to register the puppies as either cross or inter-bred.

The history of the Smooth as a show dog runs side by side with that of the Rough, except that the first classes for Smooths were scheduled only in 1877, and even after that date both coats were frequently shown together as either Sheepdogs or Collies, and in fact today we often get classes for Collies Rough or Smooth. A number of breeders who were already well known in Roughs added Smooths to their Kennels in those early days, and there has always been a number who kept exclusively to Smooths.

There have been many Smooths who have carried the Collie name into high places, but undoubtedly the one who did the breed most good by her outstanding wins in Variety competitions and in the big, Best-in-Show, ring was that lovely blue merle, Ch. Laund Lynne. This bitch was an absolute picture, standing almost unmoving, in the centre of the ring, gazing with adoration at her owner, Mr. W. W. Stansfield, with all parts of her rigid except the very tip of her tail, which moved constantly from side to side. Her wonderful showmanship gained her many high places and her most outstanding achievement was the winning of the award for Best Non-Sporting exhibit at the Kennel Club's Championship Show. In addition to her wonderful show career, during which she was rarely beaten, she could work either sheep or cattle and was often to be seen working the hedges whilst her owner waited on the other side with his gun.

Today the Smooths are gradually increasing in number, and are again to be had in all the three colours in which we know the Roughs. For very many years there were no sable and white Smooths, but these have come back since the war and at a number of recent shows have turned up in at least equal numbers with the other two colours.

Our illustration of this breed shows today's most winning dog, Mr. Farrington's Ch. Wythenshawe Windhover.

For those who do not want the bother of a long-coated dog, but who still hanker after a Collie, the Smooth is undoubtedly the answer.

## THE SHETLAND SHEEPDOG

Doubtless readers are familiar with the Shetland pony, the diminutive counterpart of the Shire horse. So then is the *Toonie*, or *Peerie*, dog of the Islands a race of diminutive dogs—Collies, in fact, seen through the wrong end of a telescope!

The Shetland Sheepdog is (as a literal translation of one of his Gaelic names has it) a '*Fairy Dog*' and it would be hard to find a more appropriate name. The Sheltie, as he is affectionately called, is exactly like his bigger brother, the Collie, except in size. His markings and colour are the same—all shades of sable—and though he is small he is by no means a toy. He is a sturdy dog, an upstanding little creature, full of gaiety and life, ready for fun and with great courage when it is required. He is exceedingly intelligent and always most anxious to please.

In the Shetland Islands, where the ponies, cattle and sheep are small, so too must the dog which cares for them be scaled to size. In the beginning the desire of the Island shepherds for a small dog (which had to be nimble and in which the main essential was good work) colour and type were immaterial, and the only things they set out to establish were working ability and size. The little dog had to be fleet of foot, to skirt his flock with speed, or, if necessary, to gallop over the backs of the closely packed sheep. He had to be sensible and reliable. Gradually, however, people began to see his potentialities in other directions, and both in the Islands themselves and on the Scottish mainland, with stock brought from the Islands by the fishermen, a great attempt was made to establish this clever little worker in type as well. To this end the cross with the show Collie was made, on many occasions, and in the early history of the breed as a show dog most of the specimens

N

exhibited were half Collie. These attempts were so successful that the *Peerie* dog quickly became known as the Shetland Collie. Although at the time when the first Shetlands were exhibited they carried such a large infusion of Collie blood, the Collie fraternity strongly opposed the name of Shetland Collie, and the Kennel Club upheld their arguments, refusing to recognize the breed under this name. So Shetland Sheepdogs they became; now, familiarly, Shelties.

Today, bred to type though he has been for many years, and established in that type from the wonderful assortment of oddities from which he originally descended, he has nevertheless retained all his working ability. Over and over again a puppy taken straight from a show Kennel and put to work will show immediate ability for the task. The early, constant companionship of these little dogs with their shepherd owners gave them a great understanding of humans which has never left them, and this today makes them the ideal working partner. The great intelligence of this breed is demonstrated almost daily where we have wonderful examples of the work done by these dogs in Obedience competitions and working trials. The Sheltie is a reticent dog, but there is no doubt that, properly taught, they can learn almost anything. Their happy disposition and, above all, their innate desire to please, coupled, it must be admitted, with the knowledge that they are in the limelight—a knowledge, in fact, that they are important people—has certainly helped to make the Sheltie the great force it is today in Obedience competitions.

To the need of the day for a 'big dog in a little space', the Sheltie is undoubtedly the answer. He has all the delightful traits of his big brother—in a 14 in. frame! He is the perfect companion, gay and alert, removing one's mind from the cares of the day, full of life and energy, happy and bright, yet ready always to accommodate himself to your mood, full of sympathy, and with a heart full of loyalty. He is a good guard, and so very beautiful to look at! He is, too, hardy and adaptable; in fact, the dog of today!

Since the publication of the first edition of this book the little Sheltie has forged ahead with such leaps and bounds that he now warrants a book all to himself, and he is fully dealt with by the author in a companion volume, *The Shetland Sheepdog*.

OWNERS' NAMES AT TIME OF WINNING C.C.s.

DATE IS THAT OF GAINING TITLE

Colour Key: T—Tricolour.  S—Sable.  BM—Blue merle.

| Dog's Name and Owner and Breeder | Colour | Family | Sire | Dam |
|---|---|---|---|---|
| Alphington Brown Girl, Ch. b. 1960<br>O. Mrs. A. E. Newbery<br>B. Mrs. E. M. Drury | S | 1 | Ch. Alphington Sociable | Inchgower Sun Queen |
| Alphington Chris, d.<br>O., Mr. P. Chave<br>B. Mrs. H. M. Vinnicombe | S | 1 | Reformer Rubio | Leonie of Ladypark |
| Alphington Nigger King, Ch. d. 1950<br>O. Mrs. A. E. Newbery<br>B. Mrs. A. E. Newbery | T | 1 | Alphington Land Boy | Alphington Honeymoon |
| Alphington Sociable, Ch. d. 1956<br>O. Mrs. A. E. Newbery<br>B. Mrs. Vinnicombe | S | 1 | Ch. Liberty of Ladypark | Leonie of Ladypark |
| Alphington Sunboy, d.<br>O. Mrs. A. E. Newbery<br>B. Mrs. A. E. Newbery | S | 3 | Ch. Sombresextens from Shiel | Alphington Bold Lass |
| Antoc Tawny Tattoo, Ch. d. 1959<br>O. Mrs. A. Speding<br>B. Mrs. A. Speding | S | 13 | Ch. Westcarrs Whistler | Antoc Tawny Token |
| Arcot, Alexander of, Ch. d. 1960<br>O. Mrs. M. J. Tweddle<br>B. Mrs. M. J. Tweddle | S | 3 | Ch. Danvis Drifter | Ch. Antanette of Arcot |
| Arcot, Andrew of, Ch. d. 1959<br>O. Mrs. M. J. Tweddle<br>B. Mrs. M. J. Tweddle | T | 3 | Ch. Gunner of Glenturret | Ch. Antanette of Arcot |
| Arcot, Anna of, Ch. b. 1960<br>O. Mrs. M. J. Tweddle<br>B. Mrs. M. J. Tweddle | S | 3 | Danvis Dale | Lanette of Arcot |
| Arcot, Antanette of, Ch. b. 1956<br>O. Mrs. M. J. Tweddle<br>B. Mr. J. H. Stokes | S | 3 | Ascot of Arcot | Annabell of Arcot |

| Dog's Name and Owner and Breeder | Colour | Family | Sire | Dam |
|---|---|---|---|---|
| Arranbeck, Acrobat of, d. ...<br>O. Mr. V. Hanson<br>B. Miss J. R. Lee | S | 8 | Eden Examine | Titania of Arranbeck |
| Artlesgreen Elsham Rebel, d.<br>O. Mr. A. L. Green<br>B. Mr. A. L. Green | S | 2 | Ch. Whitelea Why Boy | Lassie of Whitelea |
| Ashcombe Annabella, Ch. b. 1958<br>O. Mrs: Vinnicombe<br>B. Mrs. Vinnicombe | S | 1 | Ch. Liberty of Ladypark | Leonie of Ladypark |
| Bapchild Floss, Ch. b. 1950<br>O. Mr. F. Brown<br>B. Mr. G. Roberts | T | 3 | Waldorn of Waldemar | Redevalley Rosette |
| Bellrenia, Sensation of, d.<br>O. Mr. P. H. Prosser<br>B. Mr. W. Phillips | S | 12 | The Rajah | Queenie's Pride |
| Beulah's Blanco-y-Negro, Ch. d. 1955<br>O. Mrs. N. K. George<br>B. Mrs. N. K. George | T | 10 | Beulah's Knight o' Nights | Ch. Beulah's Silver Mantilla |
| Beulah's Gold Sun Fu Five, d.<br>O. Mrs. N. K. George<br>B. Mrs. N. K. George | S | 3 | Ch. Beulah's Golden Sunfu Son | Beulah's Night Wonda |
| Beulah's Golden Conquest, Ch. d. 1949<br>O. Mrs. N. K. George<br>B. Mrs. N. K. George | S | 1 | Beulah's Nightvictorious | Beulah's Golden Favorita |
| Beulah's Golden Flora, Ch. b. 1949<br>O. Miss P. M. Grey<br>B. Mrs. N. K. George | S | 1 | Ch. Beulah's Golden Futureson | Beulah's Golden Kiska |
| Beulah's Golden Fu-Betta, b.<br>O. Mrs. N. K. George<br>B. Mrs. N. K. George | S | 10 | Ch. Beulah's Golden Fusonkin | Beulah's Golden Mity-Sweet |
| Beulah's Golden Fusonkin, Ch. d. 1950<br>O. Mrs. N. K. George<br>B. Mrs. N. K. George | S | 1 | Ch. Beulah's Golden Futureson | Beulah's Golden Kiska |
| Beulah's Golden Futureson, Ch. d. 1947<br>O. Mrs. N. K. George<br>B. Mrs. N. K. George | S | 10 | Ch. Beulah's Golden Future | Ch. Beulah's Golden Feather |

| Name | | Sex | No. | Sire | Dam |
|---|---|---|---|---|---|
| ... ..., N. K. George | | | | | |
| B. Mrs. N. K. George | | | | | |
| Beulah's Golden MityClan, Ch. d. 1961 | .. | S | 3 | Ch. Beulah's Golden Mity Sol | Beulah's Gold Sun-Fusonia |
| O. Mrs. N. K. George | | | | | |
| B. Mrs. N. K. George | | | | | |
| Beulah's Golden Mity Sol, Ch. d. 1956 | .. | S | 10 | Ch. Beulah's Golden Mityatam | Beulah's August Princess |
| O. Mrs. N. K. George | | | | | |
| B. Mrs. N. K. George | | | | | |
| Beulah's Golden Soldorida, b. | .. | S | 3 | Ch. Beulah's Golden Mity Sol | Beulah's Night Fu-Nelda |
| O. Mrs. N. K. George | | | | | |
| B. Mrs. N. K. George | | | | | |
| Beulah's Golden Sunfu Son, Ch. d. 1953 | .. | S | 10 | Ch. Beulah's Golden Fusonkin | Beulah's August Princess |
| O. Mrs. N. K. George | | | | | |
| B. Mrs. N. K. George | | | | | |
| Beulah's Night Fame, Ch. 1947 | .. | T | 10 | Beulah's Nightvictorious | Beulah's Golden Fantasy |
| O. Mrs. J. Lowe | | | | | |
| B. Mrs. N. K. George | | | | | |
| Beulah's Nightglamorous, b. | .. | T | 1 | Beulah's Nightvictorious | Beulah's Night Black and Beautiful |
| O. Miss C. Molony | | | | | |
| B. Mrs. N. K. George | | | | | |
| Beulah's Nightglorious, Ch. d. 1950 | .. | T | 1 | " | " |
| O. Mrs. N. K. George | | | | | |
| B. Mrs. N. K. George | | | | | |
| Beulah's Nightgorgeous, b. | .. | T | 1 | " | " |
| O. Mrs. N. K. George | | | | | |
| B. Mrs. N. K. George | | | | | |
| Beulah's Night-so-Neat, Ch. b. 1953 | .. | T | 1 | Shiel's Beulah's Golden Viceroy | Shiel's Beulah's Night Flower |
| O. Mrs. N. K. George | | | | | |
| B. Miss M. Osborne | | | | | |
| Beulah's Silver Maravella, Ch. b. 1956 | .. | BM | 3 | Ch. Beulah's Silver Don Marjo | Beulah's Night Wonda |
| O. Mrs. N. K. George | | | | | |
| B. Mrs. N. K. George | | | | | |
| Beulah's Silver Medialuna, Ch. b. 1952 | .. | BM | 10 | Beulah's Silver Don Glorio | Beulah's Night Vivid |
| O. Mrs. N. K. George | | | | | |
| B. Mrs. N. K. George | | | | | |
| Beulah's Silver Mee Onea, Ch. b. 1957 | .. | BM | 10 | Beulah's Knight o' Nights | Beulah's Silver Meramare |
| O. Mrs. N. K. George | | | | | |
| B. Mrs. N. K. George | | | | | |
| Beulah's Silver Don Marjo, Ch. d. 1952 | .. | BM | 10 | Beulah's Silver Don Glorio | Beulah's Night Vivid |
| O. Mrs. N. K. George | | | | | |
| B. Mrs. N. K. George | | | | | |

## CHALLENGE CERTIFICATE WINNERS 1946—APRIL 9, 1960—(Cont.)

| Dog's Name and Owner and Breeder | Colour | Family | Sire | Dam |
|---|---|---|---|---|
| Beulah's Silver Don Mero, d. .. .. | BM | 10 | Beulah's Silver Don Glorio | Beulah's Night Vivid |
|   O. Mrs. N. K. George | | | | |
|   B. Mrs. N. K. George | | | | |
| Beulah's Silver Mantilla, Ch. b. 1952 .. | BM | 10 | ,, | ,, ,, ,, |
|   O. Mrs. N. K. George | | | | |
|   B. Mrs. N. K. George | | | | |
| Blue Motif, d. Ch. 1958 .. .. | BM | 10 | Motley of Mariemeau | Dream Girl of Bryher |
|   O. Miss Hope and Mr. Davis | | | | |
|   B. Mrs. E. Blatchford | | | | |
| Blue Starlight, b. .. .. .. | BM | 3 | Lyncliffe Landseer | Raybreck Blue Bloom |
|   O. Mr. D. Smart | | | | |
|   B. Mr. R. T. Wiggins | | | | |
| Bridholme Crosstalk Silver Rambler, Ch. d. 1962 | BM | 4 | Ch. Westcarrs Blue Minoru | Silver Flame |
|   O. Mr. F. Clegg, Mr. G. Archer | | | | |
|   B. Mrs. Caygill | | | | |
| Bridholme, Matchless of, d. .. .. | S | 13 | Ch. Leonertes of Ladypark | Bridholme Lightworth Sable Lady |
|   O. Mr. F. Clegg | | | | |
|   B. Mr. F. Clegg | | | | |
| Bridholme Penalston Panelope, Ch. b. 1958 .. | S | 2 | Longfellow of Ladypark | Merry Meg |
|   O. Mr. F. Clegg | | | | |
|   B. Mrs. M. Alston | | | | |
| Campsieglen Wendy, Ch. b. 1950 .. .. | T | 1 | Lyncliffe Lancer | Helengowan Sequence |
|   O. Mr. J. Richmond | | | | |
|   B. Mrs. McAdam | | | | |
| Chapelburn, Ivor, Ch. d. 1948 .. .. | S | 2 | Waldo of Waldemar | Eden Estella (late Chapelburn Golden Gleam) |
|   O. Mr. and Mrs. McAdam | | | | |
|   B. The Misses Stewart | | | | |
| Cherry Lady, Ch. b. 1962 .. .. | S | 6 | Good Gift | Lady Elizabeth |
|   O. Mr. R. Adamson | | | | |
|   B. Mr. R. Adamson | | | | |
| Corbieux, Cezar of, Ch. d. 1949 .. | S | 5 | Waldo of Waldemar | Golden Queen of Bellrenia |
|   O. Mr. R. Ditchburn | | | | |
|   B. Mr. B. Wildsmith | | | | |
| Coverdale's Janson, d. .. .. | S | 13 | Coverdale's Black Tarquin | Coverdale's Golden Janice |

| Name / Owner / Breeder | | Sire | Dam |
|---|---|---|---|
| O. Mr. and Mrs. L. P. Green<br>B. Mr. and Mrs. L. P. Green | S 1 | Coverdale's McShan | Ch. Coverdale's Lady Jayne |
| Coverdale's Lady Shan, Ch. b. 1961<br>O. Mr. T. J. Gardiner<br>B. Mr. and Mrs. L. P. Green | | | |
| Cragenure Chancellor, d.<br>O. Mr. W. Williamson<br>B. Mr. Peter Bell | S 8 | Ch. Gunner of Mariemeau | Cragienure Crystal |
| Craigfern Ranger, d.<br>O. Mr. J. Addis<br>B. Mr. J. Allen | S 11 | Lethellen Landlord | Allenrob Lassie |
| Crannyglen, Commander of, d.<br>O. Mrs. V. Wheeler<br>B. Mrs. V. Wheeler | S — | Lochson of Ladypark | Gibson Girl |
| Cressbrook, Amyone, of, b.<br>O. Mrs. P. Smith<br>B. Mrs. P. Smith | T 8 | Laudable of Ladypark | Sabina of Cressbrook |
| Cronway Cuspidor, d.<br>O. Mr. J. H. Northway<br>B. Mr. J. H. Northway | S 1 | Ch. Lochinvar of Ladypark | Cronway Cadence |
| Cronway Cynosure, b.<br>O. Mr. J. H. Northway<br>B. Mr. J. H. Northway | S 1 | ,, ,, | ,, ,, |
| Daddystown, Lass of, b.<br>O. Mrs. T. Beattie<br>B. Mrs. T. Beattie | S 4 | Jerry's Choice | Biddy of Daddystown |
| Daddystown, Foxlyn Poppy of, b.<br>O. Mr. C. Freeman<br>B. Mrs. T. Beattie | S 4 | Don of Oldpark | Lass of Daddystown |
| Daddystown, Cherry of, b.<br>O. Mrs. T. Beattie<br>B. Mr. T. Prenter | S 13 | Don of Oldpark | Mariemeau Ladyship |
| Danethorpe Crossfox Chic, b.<br>O. Mr. H. Underwood<br>B. Mr. and Mrs. Nesbitt | S 6 | Orangefield Playboy | Crossfox Colleen |
| Danethorpe Silver Dew, Ch. b. 1951<br>O. Mr. H. Underwood<br>B. Mrs. I. M. Bishop | BM 3 | Ch. Beulah's Nightglorious | Beulah's Silver Wave |

199

| Dog's Name and Owner and Breeder | Colour | Family | Sire | Dam |
|---|---|---|---|---|
| Danethorpe Wistful of Wessingvil, Ch. b. 1953 .. <br> O. Mr. H. Underwood <br> B. Mr. J. D. Thompson | S | 5 | Ch. Lochinvar of Ladypark | Wessingvil Kay's Playmate |
| Danvis Daytime, b. .. <br> O. Mr. T. Purvis <br> B. Mr. T. Purvis | T | 5 | Ch. Cezar of Corbieux | Ch. Danvis Deborah |
| Danvis Deanna, b. Ch. 1960 <br> O. Mr. T. Purvis <br> B. Mr. T. Purvis | S | 5 | Danvis Diadem | Danvis Daphne |
| Danvis Deborah, Ch. b. 1953 <br> O. Mr. T. Purvis <br> B. Mr. T. Purvis | T | 5 | Ch. Gunner of Mariemeau | Danvis Delta |
| Danvis Derna, b. Ch. 1960 .. <br> O. Mr. T. Purvis <br> B. Mr. T. Purvis | S | 5 | Laudable of Ladypark | Ch. Danvis Deanna |
| Danvis Devotion, b. <br> O. Mrs. M. Williams <br> B. Mr. T. Purvis | S | 5 | Ch. Lochinvar of Ladypark | Ch. Danvis Deborah |
| Danvis Diadem, d. .. <br> O. Mr. T. Purvis <br> B. Mr. T. Purvis | S | 5 | Ch. Lochinvar of Ladypark | Ch. Danvis Deborah |
| Danvis Drifter, Ch. d. 1956 .. <br> O. Mr. T. Purvis <br> B. Mr. P. Bell | S | 2 | Cragienure Chancellor | Eden Golden Queen of Riglea |
| Danvis Driver, Ch. d. 1956 .. <br> O. Mr. T. Purvis <br> B. Mr. T. Purvis | S | 5 | Ch. Danvis Drifter | Danvis Daphne |
| Danvis Dyllorna, Ch. b. 1955 <br> O. Mr. T. Purvis <br> B. Mr. T. Purvis | S | 5 | Ch. Lochinvar of Ladypark | Ch. Danvis Deborah |
| Deb's Happy Marquis, Ch. d. 1958 .. <br> O. Mrs. T. A. Combe <br> B. Mrs. T. A. Combe | S | 4 | Shencolne Happy Wanderer | Clayswood Debutante |
| Delwood Betty, Ch. b. 1951.. <br> O. Mrs. A. Bishop | S | 2 | Laund Limitless | Delwood Suzanne |

| Name | Owner / Breeder | | Class | No. | Sire | Dam |
|---|---|---|---|---|---|---|
|  | O. Mrs. Wilberforce<br>B. Capt. N. C. Bloom | .. | T | 2 | Chapelburn Ronald | Chapelburn Morag |
| Dewshill Dynamite, Ch. d. 1947 | O. Mr. R. Wiggins<br>B. Mr. J. Lennox | .. | S | 2 | Cornriggs Colin | Chapelburn Morag |
| Dewshill Defence, d. | O. Mr. J. Lennox<br>B. Mr. J. Lennox | .. | S | 2 | Ch. Glenlusset Thane | St. Inan's Starlight |
| Doon Flowergirl, b. .. | O. Mr. J. Pollock<br>B. Mr. A. Hunter | .. | S | 2 | Dryfesdale Decider | Dryfesdale Mayblossom |
| Dryfesdale Delilah, b. | O. Mr. E. Watt<br>B. Mr. E. Watt | .. | S | 1 | Dunsinane Alaric of Arranbeck | Rinth Recluse |
| Dunsinane, Defender of, Ch. d. 1959 | O. Mrs. A. F. Chatfield<br>B. Mr. I. Clarke | .. | S | 2 | Killartry Rex | Biddy of Daddystown |
| Eden Edwina, b. .. | O. Mr. F. Robson<br>B. Mrs. T. Beattie | .. | S | 4 | Chapelburn Ronald | Eden Effigy |
| Eden Elation, Ch. b. 1949 .. | O. Mr. F. Robson<br>B. Mr. F. Robson | .. | S | 1 | Eden Extra Model | Eden Elisbeth |
| Eden Enchanting, Ch. b. 1948 .. | O. Mr. F. Robson<br>B. Mr. F. Robson | .. | S | 8 | Eden Excellent | Eden Effigy |
| Eden Endearing, Ch. b. 1949 | O. Mr. F. Robson<br>B. Mr. F. Robson | .. | S | 1 | Don of Oldpark | Gay Jewel |
| Eden Erasmic, Ch. b. 1952 .. | O. Mr. A. A. Hayward<br>B. Messrs. J. and A. McCleary | .. | S | 1 | Ch. Legend of Ladypark | Eden Eldorina |
| Eden Esmeralda, Ch. b. 1959 | O. Mr. F. Robson<br>B. Mr. F. Robson | .. | S | 1 | Eden Excellent | Eden Effigy |
| Eden Estrella, Ch. b. 1950 .. | O. Mr. F. Robson<br>B. Mr. F. Robson | .. | S | 1 |  |  |

## CHALLENGE CERTIFICATE WINNERS 1946—APRIL 9, 1960—(Cont.)

| Dog's Name and Owner and Breeder | Colour | Family | Sire | Dam |
|---|---|---|---|---|
| Eden Evolution, d. .. .. .. .. <br> O. Mr. F. Robson <br> B. Mr. F. Robson | S | 1 | ,, ,, | ,, ,, |
| Eden Examine, d. .. .. .. .. <br> O. Mr. H. Horsfield <br> B. Mr. F. Hirst | S | 5 | Lyncliffe Lancer | Seagull |
| Eden Raybreck Dynamic .. .. .. <br> O. Mr. F. Robson <br> B. Mr. R. Wiggins | T | 3 | Ch. Dewshill Dynamite | Raybreck Blue Select |
| Eden Rip of Ladywell, Ch. d. 1951 .. <br> O. Mr. F. Robson <br> B. Mr. R. March | S | 10 | Ch. Lochinvar of Ladypark | Ch. Lena of Ladypark |
| Eden Vandason of Marobiny, Ch. d. 1952 .. <br> O. Mr. F. Robson <br> B. Mrs. M. Green | S | 1(s) | Ch. Chapelburn Ivor | Vanda of Greenwood |
| Ellington Elena, b. .. .. .. <br> O. Mrs. F. Morris <br> B. Mrs. F. Fishpool | S | 6 | Eden Excellent | Ellington Marros Sensation |
| Failsmuir Golden Rosa, b. .. .. .. <br> O. Mrs. M. Fail <br> B. Mrs. M. Fail | S | 1(s) | Ascot of Arcot | Cramlington Queen |
| Fieldbloom, Serene of, b. .. .. <br> O. Mr. M. H. Long <br> B. Mr. M. H. Long | S | — | Heir of Fieldbloom | Beauty of Fieldbloom |
| Frienell Buff, d. .. .. .. <br> O. Mr. F. Daw <br> B. Mrs. R. James | S | 4 | Herald of Mariemeau | Mariemeau Frienell Freda |
| Gatebeck Butterscotch, d. Ch. 1958 .. <br> O. Mrs. B. M. Allen <br> B. Mrs. B. M. Allen | S | 1 | Lover of Ladypark | Beauty of Marnabrooke |
| Glenacre, Amber Lad of, Ch. d. 1953 .. <br> O. Mr. T. Rimmer <br> B. Mr. T. Rimmer | S | 3 | Eden Expander | Jubilee Joy |
| Glenlusset Superb, Ch. d. 1953 .. .. <br> O. Mr. W. C. Tew | S | 2 | Ch. Chapelburn Ivor | Glenlusset Debutante |

| Name | Owner / Breeder | Sex | No. | Sire | Dam |
|---|---|---|---|---|---|
| | O. Mr. W. C. Tew | | | | |
| | B. Mr. W. C. Tew | | | | |
| Glenmist, Lovely Lady of, Ch. b. 1960 | O. Mr. F. Mitchell / B. Mr. F. Mitchell | S | 2 | Rifflesee Royalist | Ch. Sapphire of Glenmist |
| Glenmist, Rifflesee Reward of, Ch. b. 1958 C. D. | O. Mr. F. Mitchell / B. Dr. and Mrs. Collins | S | 2 | Ch. Lad of Ladypark | Ch. Rose of Ladypark |
| Glenmist, Sapphire of, Ch. b. 1958 | O. Mr. F. Mitchell / B. Mr. F. Mitchell | S | 2 | Ch. Liberty of Ladypark | Ch. Rifflesee Reward of Glenmist, C. D. |
| Glenmist, Sceptre of, b. | O. Mr. F. Mitchell / B. Mr. F. Mitchell | S | 2 | ,,      ,, | ,,      ,,      ,, |
| Glenmist, Spellbinder of, Ch. b. 1961 | O. Mrs. B. Mayland / B. Mr. F. Mitchell | S | 2 | ,,      ,, | ,, |
| Glenturret, Gunner of, Ch. d. 1957 | O. Mr. D. McPherson / B. Mr. D. McPherson | S | 2 | Ch. Gunner of Mariemeau | Vanity of Glenturret |
| Glenturret, Vanity of, b. | O. Mr. D. McPherson / B. Mr. P. Bell | S | 2 | Cragienure Chancellor | Eden Golden Queen of Riglea |
| Hallmarsh Bloom, b. | O. Mr. T. Marshall / B. Mr. T. Marshall | S | 1 | Meanwood Magnate | Helengowan Sapphire |
| Harpole Suzette, b. | O. Mrs. W. Nutt / B. Mr. C. H. Banks | S | 9 | Merrion Sapper | Ham Green Wendy |
| Heightlyn Firefly, d. | O. Miss H. Ratcliffe / B. Miss H. Ratcliffe | S | 11 | Laund Beulah's Golden Laird | Killartry Linda |
| Helengowan Cornriggs Catriona, Ch. b. 1949 | O. Mr. and Mrs. McAdam / B. Mr. F. J. Jarvis | S | 2 | Cornriggs Colin | Dulwych Decorous |
| Helengowan Sapphire, b. | O. Mr. T. Marshall / B. Mr. and Mrs. McAdam | S | 1 | Ch. Chapelburn Ivor | Helengowan Shirley |

| Dog's Name and Owner and Breeder | Colour | Family | Sire | Dam |
|---|---|---|---|---|
| Helengowan Starboy, Ch. d. 1948<br>O. Mr. and Mrs. McAdam<br>B. Mr. and Mrs. McAdam | S | 1 | Ch. Chapelburn Ivor | Helengowan Shirley |
| Helengowan Superb, d.<br>O. Mr. and Mrs. McAdam<br>B. Mr. and Mrs. McAdam | S | 1 | ,, | ,, |
| Helengowan Superior, Ch. d. 1950<br>O. Mr. and Mrs. McAdam<br>B. Mr. and Mrs. McAdam | S | 1 | ,, | ,, |
| Helengowan Spray of Gold, b.<br>O. Mr. and Mrs. McAdam<br>B. Mr. and Mrs. McAdam | S | 1 | Helengowan Success | Cragienure Colia |
| Helengowan Success, d.<br>O. Mr. and Mrs. McAdam<br>B. Mr. and Mrs. McAdam | S | 1 | Ch. Helengowan Superior | Stanheath Lady Rose |
| Helengowan Caber Sheila, b.<br>O. Mrs. and Mrs. McAdam<br>B. Mr. J. Richmond | T | 1 | Ch. Chapelburn Ivor | Ch. Campsieglen Wendy |
| Hewburn Irene, b.<br>O. Mr. B. Hewison<br>B. Mr. J. Cook | S | 1 | Longmeadow Lancer | Whitelea Winniepoo |
| Hewburn Countess, Ch. b. 1955<br>O. Mr. B. Hewison<br>B. Mrs. J. Greathead | S | 10 | Ch. Lena's Golden Son | Copper of Ladywell |
| Hildlane Merry Monarch, d.<br>O. Mrs. H. Goodwin<br>B. Mrs. T. A. Combe | S | 13 | Ch. Deb's Happy Marquis | Channonz April Dawn |
| Inglebrook's Wen Genny, Ch. b. 1959<br>O. Mr. and Mrs. J. Fendley<br>B. Mr. D. Rippon | S | 3 | Ch. Mywicks Model Examiner | Brooklea Wendy |
| Killartry, Valour of, d.<br>O. Miss Winkworth<br>B. Miss de Bell Ball | S | 11 | Thane of Mariemeau | Vanity of Killartry |
| Lady Laurienne, b.<br>O. Mr. S. Llewellyn | S | 13 | Ch. Lochinvar of Ladypark | Llyngarth Jen |

| Name | Owner / Breeder | Sire | S | No. | Dam |
|---|---|---|---|---|---|
| *(name continued from previous page)* | O. … and Mrs. Collins<br>B. Miss P. M. Grey | | | | |
| Ladypark, Landrover of, d. | O. Miss P. M. Grey<br>B. Miss P. M. Grey | Ch. Lochinvar of Ladypark | S | 2 | Dawn Duchess of Ladypark |
| Ladypark, Lena of, Ch. b. 1951 | O. Mr. R. March<br>B. Miss P. M. Grey | Lucky of Ladypark | S | 10 | Lilac of Ladypark |
| Ladypark, Legend of, d. Ch. 1957 | O. Miss P. M. Grey<br>B. Miss P. M. Grey | Libretto of Ladypark | S | 2 | Ch. Maid of Ladypark |
| Ladypark, Leonertes of, Ch. d. 1957 | O. Mr. G. Archer<br>B. Mr. L. Richardson | Ch. Lochinvar of Ladypark | S | 1 | Ch. Eden Estrella |
| Ladypark, Liberty of, Ch. d. 1954 | O. Miss P. M. Grey<br>B. Miss P. M. Grey | Libretto of Ladypark | S | 1 | Lindy Lou of Ladypark |
| Ladypark, Lilt of, Ch. b. 1953 | O. Miss P. M. Grey<br>B. Mr. R. March | Ch. Lochinvar of Ladypark | S | 10 | Ch. Lena of Ladypark |
| Ladypark, Limpid of, Ch. 1955 | O. Miss P. M. Grey<br>B. Miss P. M. Grey | Libretto of Ladypark | S | 1 | Lindy Lou of Ladypark |
| Ladypark, Linty of, b, | O. Miss P. M. Grey<br>B. Mr. F. Robson | Ch. Beulah's Golden Futureson | S | 1 | Eden Eldrena |
| Ladypark, Lionheart of, d. | O. Miss P. M. Grey<br>B. Miss P. M. Grey | Lumley of Ladypark | S | 1 | Lindy Lou of Ladypark |
| Ladypark, Little Mary of, b. | O. Miss P. M. Grey<br>B. Miss P. M. Grey | Ch. Lochinvar of Ladypark | S | 1 | Lucibel of Ladypark |
| Ladypark, Lochson of, d. | O. Mr. R. Adamson<br>B. Mr. B. J. Hewison | Ch. Lochinvar of Ladypark | S | 5 | Wessingvil Kay's Playmate |
| Ladypark, Lottery of, b. Ch. 1957 | O. Miss P. M. Grey<br>B. Mr. T. Purvis | Ch. Lochinvar of Ladypark | S | 5 | Ch. Danvis Deborah |

| Dog's Name and Owner and Breeder | Colour | Family | Sire | Dam |
|---|---|---|---|---|
| Ladypark, Lochinvar of, Ch. d. 1949<br>O. Miss P. M. Grey<br>B. Miss P. M. Grey | S | 1 | Eden Examine | Ch. Beulah's Golden Flora |
| Ladypark, Lovely of, Ch. b. 1958<br>O. Miss P. M. Grey<br>B. Miss P. M. Grey | S | 1 | Ch. Legend of Ladypark | Lindy Lou of Ladypark |
| Ladypark, Loyal of, Ch. d. 1955<br>O. Miss P. M. Grey<br>B. Miss P. M. Grey | S | 2 | Ch. Lochinvar of Ladypark | Dawn Duchess of Ladypark |
| Ladypark, Lucretia of, b.<br>O. Miss P. M. Grey<br>B. Miss P. M. Grey | S | 2 | Ch. Lochinvar of Ladypark | Lucibel of Ladypark |
| Ladypark, Lucifer of, d.<br>O. Mr. F. Daw<br>B. Miss P. M. Grey | S | 2 | ,, ,, ,, | ,, ,, |
| Ladypark, Maid of, Ch. b. 1952<br>O. Miss P. M. Grey<br>B. Mr. E. Lee | S | 2 | Ch. Lochinvar of Ladypark | Laird's Rose |
| Ladypark, Rose of, Ch. b. 1950<br>O. Dr. and Mrs. Collins<br>B. Mr. E. Lee | S | 2 | | |
| Larkena Rexley of Larkfield, Ch. d. 1955<br>O. Mr. and Mrs. Parrott<br>B. Mr. K. W. Brown | S | 2 | Gamston Golden Example | Gamston Marietta |
| Laird's Galway Sun, Ch. d. 1951<br>O. Mr. E. Lee<br>B. Mr. E. Lee | S | 2 | Ch. Lochinvar of Ladypark | Laird's Rose |
| Landula Liana, Ch. b. 1958<br>O. Mrs. G. Lancaster<br>B. Mrs. G. Lancaster | S | 1 | Landula Lochinvar | Landula Leonora |
| Laund Beulah's Golden Starr, d.<br>O. Mr. W. W. Stansfield<br>B. Mrs. N. K. George | S | 1 | Ch. Beulah's Golden Futureson | Beulah's Golden Kiska |
| Laund Ebony of Killartry, Ch. d. 1948<br>O. Mr. W. W. Stansfield | T | 1 | Laund Dewshill Banner | Alphington Sweet Lady |

| | | | | |
|---|---|---|---|---|
| O. Mr. A. Thomas<br>B. Mrs. B. Cockroft | | | | |
| Lena's Golden Son, d.<br>O. Mr. R. March<br>B. Mr. R. March | S | 10 | Ch. Lochinvar of Ladypark | Ch. Lena of Ladypark |
| Leamtop Lustre, Ch. b. 1956<br>O. Mr. T. Hately<br>B. Mr. T. Hately | S | 1 | Wizard of Wessingville | Lady of Ladypark |
| Lovely Romance, Ch. b. 1956<br>O. Mrs. L. Reed<br>B. Mrs. L. Reed | S | 1 | Ch. Summer Night's Achievement | Penny of Kierlance |
| Longmeadow Lancer, d.<br>O. Mr. T. Tomlinson<br>B. Mr. J. Carrington | S | 1 | Eden Examine | Glamour Girl |
| Lyncliffe Lady, b.<br>O. Mrs. L. Cooper<br>B. Mr. F. Hirst | T | 5 | Lyncliffe Lancer | Seagull |
| Lyncliffe Blue Lady, Ch. b. 1948<br>O. Mrs. K. Cliffe<br>B. Mrs. K. Cliffe | BM | 1 | Am. Ch. Beulah's Silver Don Mario | Leyland Lima |
| Lyncliffe Lorenzo, d.<br>O. Mrs. K. Cliffe<br>B. Mrs. K. Cliffe | S | 3 | Lyncliffe Loadstar | Ch. Lyncliffe Lucinda |
| Lyncliffe Lucinda, Ch. b. 1950<br>O. Mrs. K. Cliffe<br>B. Mr. R. Hill | T | 3 | King Raq of Hirspen | Fine Lady |
| Lyncliffe Luzita, b, Ch. 1960<br>O. Mrs. K. Cliffe<br>B. Mrs. K. Cliffe | S | 3 | Ch. Lyncliffe Thyland Lad | Lyncliffe Lavenda |
| Mariemeau, Crystal of, b.<br>O. Mr. F. Daw<br>B. Mrs. R. James | S | 4 | Thane of Mariemeau | Mariemeau Colleen |
| Mariemeau, Maureen of, b.<br>O. Mr. F. Daw<br>B. Mrs. R. James | S | 4 | " | Mariemeau Colleen |
| Mariemeau, Gunner of, Ch. d. 1949<br>O. Mr. D. McPherson<br>B. Mrs. R. James | S | 5 | " | Patricia of Mariemeau |

## CHALLENGE CERTIFICATE WINNERS 1946—APRIL 9, 1960—(Cont.)

| Dog's Name and Owner and Breeder | Colour | Family | Sire | Dam |
|---|---|---|---|---|
| Marnabrooke, Rhapsody of, b. .. .. O. Mrs. N. Ashworth B. Mr. L. Richardson | S | 1 | Ch. Lochinvar of Ladypark | Ch. Eden Estrella |
| Marros Dominican, d. .. .. O. Mr. V. Hanson B. Mr. V. Hanson | S | 6 | Laund Beulah's Golden Laird | Marros Madonna |
| Matkin Mercury, Ch. d. 1950 .. O. Messrs. Matthews and King B. Messrs. Matthews and King | S | 6 | Seftonian Sepia | Crossfox Chota |
| Milburndene, Emperor of, d. .. O. Mrs. M. Milburn B. Mrs. M. Milburn | S | 2 | Wearmouth Lucky Lukey of Ladypark | Lambert's Milady |
| Milburndene, Maestro of, d. .. O. Mrs. M. Milburn B. Mrs. M. Milburn | S | 2 | Ch. Lena's Golden Son | Mischief of Milburndene |
| Milburndene, Masterpiece of, d. .. O. Mrs. M. Milburn B. Mrs. M. Milburn | S | 1 (s) | Maharajah of Milburndene | Madonna of Milburndene |
| Milburndene, Meteor of, d. .. O. Mrs. M. Milburn B. Mrs. M. Milburn | S | 2 | Ch. Lena's Golden Son | Mischief of Milburndene |
| Moodisburn Laura of Glenturret, b. .. O. Mr. and Mrs. Beattie B. Mr. D. McPherson | S | 1 | Ch. Gunner of Mariemeau | Dryfesdale Dauntless |
| Mywicks Fashioness, Ch. b. 1951 .. O. Mr. J. Mycroft B. Miss K. Plaster | S | 2 | Eden Examine | Homeward Treasure |
| Mywicks Golden Princess, Ch. b. 1950 O. Mr. J. Mycroft B. Mr. J. Mycroft | S | 5 | Rimington Kitticholm Pilot | Rimington Panda |
| Mywicks Meadow Lancer, Ch. d. 1956 .. O. Mr. J. Mycroft B. Mr. J. Mycroft | S | 4 | Mywicks Monitor | Shoinemaw Sheena |
| Mywicks Model Examiner, Ch. d. 1955 .. O. Mr. J. Mycroft | S | 5 | Eden Examine | Mywicks Pandaloo |

| Name | | No. | Sire | Dam | Owner | Breeder |
|---|---|---|---|---|---|---|
| Mywicks Sheildon Marigold | S | 4 | Ch. Mywicks Meadow Lancer | Mywicks My Lady Fair, Ch. b. 1960 | O. Mr. J. Mycroft | B. Mr. J. Mycroft |
| Chloe of Naragansette | S | 10 | Ch. Chapelburn Ivor | Naragansette, Claren of, Ch. b. 1955 | O. Mr. H. F. McLaren | B. Mr. H. F. McLaren |
| Ladylove of Ladypark | S | 1 | Ch. Selstoma Safeguard | Naragansette, Forth of, Ch. d. 1957 | O. Mr. H. F. McLaren | B. Mr. H. F. McLaren |
| Dulwych Debutante | T | 2 | Chapelburn Stormer | Netherkeir Dulwych Dancing Lady, b. | O. Mr. A. Watt | B. Mr. F. J. Jarvis |
| ,, | T | 2 | ,, | Netherkeir Dulwych Diolite, Ch. d. 1950 | O. Mr. A. Watt | B. Mr. F. J. Jarvis |
| Silver Lassie | BM | 2 | Beulah's Nightvictorious | Nygaria Silver Major, d. | O. Mr. F. Wright | B. Mrs. M. B. Kendall |
| Slow Starter from Shiel | S | 1 | Ch. Summernight's Achievement | Overmist, Lancelot of, d. | O. Mr. W. Higgins | B. Miss Whiteley |
| Ch. Sapphire of Glenmist | S | 2 | Rifflesee Royalist | Pattingham Gay Lady of Glenmist, Ch. b. 1961 | O. Mrs. M. Franklin | B. Mr. F. Mitchell |
| Ch. Pattingham Lullaby | S | 1 | Ch. Lochinvar of Ladypark | Pattingham Kismet, d. | O. Mrs. M. Franklin | B. Mrs. M. Franklin |
| Danethorpe Laugh of Ladypark | S | 1 | Libretto of Ladypark | Pattingham Lullaby, Ch. b. 1955 | O. Mrs. M. Franklin | B. Mrs. M. Franklin |
| Pattingham Golden Lydia | S | 1 | Pattingham Kismet | Pattingham Patrick, d. | O. Mrs. M. Franklin | B. Mrs. M. Franklin |
| Danethorpe Laugh of Ladypark | S | 1 | Ch. Liberty of Ladypark | Pattingham Prelude, Ch. b. 1959 | O. Mrs. M. Franklin | B. Mrs. M. Franklin |

| Dog's Name and Owner and Breeder | Colour | Family | Sire | Dam |
|---|---|---|---|---|
| Pattingham Priscilla, Ch. b. 1958 ..    O. Mrs. M. Franklin    B. Mrs. M. Franklin | S | 10 | Pattingham Kismet | Pattingham Danethorpe Dark Dinny |
| Poppystown Pearlie, b.    O. Mr. G. Dransfield    B. Mr. G. Dransfield | S | 3 | Ch. Legend of Ladypark | Poppystown Superior |
| Prue's Golden Regina, Ch. b. 1955    O. Mr. and Mrs. L. Green    B. Mr. W. Rackett | S | 1 | Shiel's Beulah's Golden Viceroy | Cathanbrae Gaiety |
| Ravensglen Portia, b.    O. Mrs. B. A. Lloyd    B. Mrs. K. Anderson | S | 10 | Ch. Liberty of Ladypark | Luna Lyra of Ladypark |
| Raybreck Golden Gloria, Ch. b. 1949    O. Mr. R. T. Wiggins    B. Mr. R. T. Wiggins | S | 3 | Laund Beulah's Golden Laird | Glorious Gift |
| Rhodelands Boy, Ch. d. 1959    O. Mr. P. A. Ball    B. Mr. P. A. Ball | T | — | Ch. Mywicks Meadow Lancer | Seftonian Sunshade |
| Rhodelands Lucky Boy, d. Ch. 1957    O. Mr. P. A. Ball    B. Mr. A. Hayward | BM | — | Ch. Dewshill Dynamite | Seftonian Blue Princess |
| Rifflesee Regalia, b.    O. Mr. G. Roberts    B. Mrs. A. F. Chatfield | S | 2 | Ch. Liberty of Ladypark | Ch. Rifflesee Regality of Dunsinane |
| Rifflesee Regality of Dunsinane, Ch. b. 1957    O. Mrs. A. F. Chatfield    B. Dr. and Mrs. K. G. Collins | S | 2 | Ch. Lad of Ladypark | Ch. Rose of Ladypark |
| Rifflesee Resplendence, Ch. d. 1954    O. Dr. and Mrs. Collins    B. Dr. and Mrs. Collins | S | 2 | „ | |
| Selstoma Safeguard, Ch. d. 1952    O. Mr. Morley    B. Mr. T. Tomlinson | S | 6 | Eden Examine | Danethorpe Dairymaid |
| Selstoma Sequence, Ch. d. 1952    O. Mr. T. Tomlinson | S | 6 | Longmeadow Lancer | Danethorpe Dabchick |

| | | | Sire | Dam |
|---|---|---|---|---|
| B. Mr. T. Tomlinson<br>Selstoma Whitelea Wildcat, Ch. b. 1953<br>O. Mr. T. Tomlinson<br>B. Mr. G. Archer | S | 1 | Rimington Kiitieholm Pilot | Lassie's Return |
| Shearcliffe Golden Queen, Ch. b. 1951<br>O. Mr. J. S. Broderick<br>B. Mrs. J. Spray | S | 1 | Lyncliffe Loadstar | Lyncliffe Lady Rinth |
| Sheildon Marquis, d.<br>O. Mrs. M. Lothian<br>B. Mrs. M. Lothian | S | 4 | Ch. Mywicks Meadow Lancer | Sheildon Shani |
| Sheildon Sequin, b. Ch. 1958<br>O. Mr. G. Wadell<br>B. Miss M. Hannay | S | 4 | Ch. Loyal of Ladypark | Sheildon Fantasia |
| Shiel, Silvacymbal from, b.<br>O. Miss M. Osborne<br>B. Miss M. Osborne | BM | 10 | Ch. Westcarrs Blue Minoru | Ch. Silvaseabear from Shie |
| Shiel, Silvasceptre from, Ch. b. 1955<br>O. Miss M. Osborne<br>B. Miss M. Osborne | BM | 10 | Ch. Westcarrs Blue Minoru | Silvaseagull from Shiel |
| Shiel, Silvaseabear from, Ch. b. 1952<br>O. Miss M. Osborne<br>B. Miss M. Osborne | BM | 10 | Westcarrs Black Bisley | Lilac of Ladypark |
| Shiel, Silvaseagull from, b.<br>O. Miss M. Osborne<br>B. Miss M. Osborne | BM | 10 | Beulah's Silver Don Mero | Ch. Silvaseabear from Shiel |
| Shiel, Silvastarjoy from, b.<br>O. Mrs. Newbery<br>B. Miss M. Osborne | BM | 10 | Ch. Sombresextens from Shiel | Ch. Silvaseabear from Shiel |
| Shiel, Silvastartime from, b.<br>O. Mrs. J. Turner<br>B. Miss M. Osborne | BM | 10 | ,,  ,, | ,,  ,, |
| Shiel, Sombresextens from, Ch. d. 1954<br>O. Mrs. A. E. Newbery<br>B. Mrs. Saxby | T | 2 | Shiel's Beulah's Golden Viceroy | Charmagne of Nygaria |
| Shiel, Squad Commander from, d.<br>O. Mr. J. A. McLeary<br>B. Miss M. Osborne | S | 10 | Sword of State from Shiel | Snow Warning from Shiel |

## CHALLENGE CERTIFICATE WINNERS 1946—APRIL 9, 1960—(Cont.)

| Dog's Name and Owner and Breeder | Colour | Family | Sire | Dam |
|---|---|---|---|---|
| Singabeam Sheen-of-Gold, Ch. b. 1959 <br> O. Mr. A. A. Carter <br> B. Mr. A. A. Carter | S | 1 | Ch. Legend of Ladypark | Singabeam Stargirl |
| Skellvale, Statesman of, Ch. d. 1960 <br> O. Mr. P. Rodford <br> B. Mr. A. Atkinson | S | 2 | Ch. Legend of Ladypark | Ch. Sundown of Skellvale |
| Skellvale Sundown of, Ch. b. 1959 <br> O. Mr. A. Atkinson <br> B. Mr. P. Rodford | S | 2 | Wizard of Wessingvil | Sensation of Skellvale |
| Southwardedge, Statesman of, Ch. d. 1959 <br> O. Mr. R. Ingley <br> B. Mrs. D. Horton | S | 1 | Ch. Legend of Ladypark | Salute of Southwardedge |
| Stanheath Lady Rose, b. <br> O. Mr. J. Keenan <br> B. Mr. J. Keenan | S | 2 | Chapelburn Supreme | Chapelburn Sheila |
| Sudborough Lochdorna, Ch. b. 1954 <br> O. Mr. G. Archer <br> B. Mrs. J. W. Allen | S | 13 | Ch. Lochinvar of Ladypark | Sudborough Lassie |
| Summernight's Achievement, Ch. d. 1951 <br> O. Mr. W. Higgins <br> B. Mr. A. G. Summerscales | S | 9 | Lyncliffe Landseer | Lassie of Hildern |
| Tideswell Blue Prince, Ch. d. 1953 <br> O. Mrs. N. K. George <br> B. Mrs. J. Harrison | BM | 10 | Ch. Dewshill Dynamite | Beulah's Silver Magdalena |
| Ugony's Golden Gloria, Ch. b. 1952 <br> O. Miss M. Young <br> B. Miss E. M. Woods | S | 1 | Ch. Lad of Ladypark | Alphington Landgirl |
| Ugony's Golden Gypsy, Ch. b. 1955 <br> O. Miss M. Young <br> B. Miss M. Young | S | 1 | Ch. Beulah's Golden Fusonkin | Earlshall Ugony's Golden Sheila |
| Ugony's Golden Son o' Lad of Rifflesee, Ch. d. 1952 <br> O. Miss M. Young <br> B. Miss M. Young | S | 1 | Ch. Lad of Ladypark | Golden Rod of Wooden |
| Ugony's Golden Fabelita, Ch. b. 1956 <br> O. Miss M. Young | S | 2 | Ralda's Beulah's Golden Fable | Shencolne Solitaire |

| Name | Reg. | No. | Sire | Dam | Owner / Breeder |
|---|---|---|---|---|---|
| *(name cut off)* | | | | | O. Miss M. Young — B. Mrs. J. Hill |
| Valtura, Ladye Fayre of, b. | S | 1 | Ch. Eden Vandason of Marobiny | Eden Eldora | O. Mr. A. Hurley — B. Mr. F. Robson |
| Viscount Pilot, Ch. d. 1959 | S | 3 | Rimington Kittieholm Pilot | Audrey's Choice | O. Mr. A. E. Atack — B. Mr. A. E. Atack |
| Walbrooke Stormy Petrel, Ch. d. 1955 | S | 2 | Ch. Lochinvar of Ladypark | Tessa of Riglea | O. Miss M. Dorsey — B. Miss M. Dorsey |
| Waldemar, Waldorn of, d. | S | 13 | Ch. Walford of Waldemar | Pool's Bett | O. Mrs. W. M. Thompson — B. Mr. S. Royal |
| Waldemar, Walhost of, d. | S | 6 | Waldorn of Waldemar | Yvette of Waldemar | O. Mrs. W. M. Thompson — B. Mrs. W. M. Thompson |
| Walwyn, Weldon of, d. | S | 3 | Welkim of Walwyn | Whatagem of Wearmouth | O. Mrs. Shield — B. Mrs. Shield |
| Warrenholme Black Prince, Ch. d. 1952 | T | 1 | King Bob of Hirspen | Surprise of Bramblecott | O. Mr. F. Bristow — R. Mr. F. Bristow |
| Wearmouth, Welcome of, b. | S | 3 | Wearmouth Lucky Lukey of Ladypark | Waitress of Wearmouth | O. Mr. R. Stothard — B. Mr. R. Stothard |
| Wearmouth, Whatastar of, Ch. d. 1956 | S | 3 | Lucky Laddie of Rokertop | Whatagirl of Wearmouth | O. Mr. R. Stothard — B. Mr. R. Stothard |
| Wearmouth, Whatabird of, b. | S | 3 | Whataspec of Wearmouth | Whatagirl of Wearmouth | O. Mr. R. Stothard — B. Mr. R. Stothard |
| Wessingvil, Wizard of, d. | S | 5 | Ch. Lochinvar of Ladypark | Wessingvil Kay's Playmate | O. Mr. T. Heatley — B. Mr. J. D. Thompson |
| Westcarrs Blue Minerva, b. | BM | 10 | Rifflesee Royalist | Lobelia of Ladypark | O. Miss C. Molony — B. Miss C. Molony |

CHALLENGE CERTIFICATE WINNERS 1946—APRIL 9, 1960—(Cont.)

| Dog's Name and Owner and Breeder | Colour | Family | Sire | Dam |
|---|---|---|---|---|
| Westcarrs Blue Minoru, Ch. d. 1955<br>O. Miss C. Molony<br>B. Miss C. Molony | BM | 10 | Rifflesee Royalist | Lobelia of Ladypark |
| Westcarrs Blue Myboy, d.<br>O. Miss C. Molony<br>B. Miss C. Molony | BM | 10 | Mywicks Monitor | Westcarrs Blue Minerva |
| Westcarrs Blue Mygirl, Ch. b. 1959<br>O. Miss C. Molony<br>B. Miss C. Molony | BM | 10 | ,, | ,, ,, ,, |
| Westcarrs Walker, d.<br>O. Mr. B. Lakeman and Mrs. D. Mortiboy<br>B. Miss C. Molony | S | 1 | Ch. Westcarrs Whistler | Ch. Westcarrs Whitethroat |
| Westcarrs Whistler, Ch. d. 1953<br>O. Miss C. Molony<br>B. Miss C. Molony | S | 1 | Ch. Lochinvar of Ladypark | Beulah's Nightglamorous |
| Westcarrs Whitethroat, Ch. b. 1951<br>O. Miss C. Molony<br>B. Miss C. Molony | S | 1 | Ch. Beulah's Golden Futureson | Beulah's Nightglamorous |
| Westcarrs Willing, b.<br>O. Miss C. Molony<br>B. Miss C. Molony | S | 1 | Ch. Westcarrs Whistler | Ch. Westcarrs Whitethroat |
| Westcarrs Willow b.<br>O. Mr. F. Parkin<br>B. Miss C. Molony | S | 1 | ,, ,, | ,, ,, |
| Whitelea, Girley of, Ch. b. 1954<br>O. Mr. G. Archer<br>B. Mr. G. Archer | S | 13 | Rimington Kitticholm Pilot | Ch. Sudborough Lochdorna |
| Whitelea Walter, d.<br>O. Mr. G. Archer<br>B. Mr. G. Archer | S | '1 | Rimington Kitticholm Pilot | Lassie's Return |
| Whitelea Watastra, Ch. b. 1960<br>O. Mr. and Mrs. A. T. Jeffries<br>B. Mr. G. Archer | T | 13 | Whitelea Why Boy | Ch. Sudborough Lochdorna |
| Whitelea Why, Ch. b. 1948 | S | 7 | Whitelea Whit | Backwoods Fashioness |

| Dog's Name | Colour | Family | Sire | Dam |
|---|---|---|---|---|
| O. Mr. Richardson and Miss Wright | | | | |
| B. Mr. J. Nally | | | | |
| Whitelea Why Gal, Ch. b. 1953 | S | 1 | Whitelea Why Lad | Whitelea Wyne |
| O. Mr. Richardson and Miss Wright | | | | |
| B. Mrs. G. Lancaster | | | | |
| Wild Amber Rose, b. | S | 1 A | Amber Prince | Gay Jewel |
| O. Messrs. J. and J. A. McLeary | | | | |
| B. Messrs. J. and J. A. McLeary | | | | |
| Wittonpark, Melody of, b. | S | 1 | Ch. Selstorna Safeguard | Cragienure Christine |
| O. Mr. and Mrs. H. Jackson | | | | |
| B. Mr. and Mrs. H. Jackson | | | | |
| Woodlands Wanderer, Ch. d. 1949 | S | 1 | Lyncliffe Lancer | Foxlyn Ruby |
| O. Mr. A. Hayward | | | | |
| B. Mr. C. Freeman | | | | |

It will be noticed that there are four dogs in the above list whose dams cannot, at the moment, be related to any family. These are the two Irish-bred winners, Serene of Fieldbloom and Commander of Crannyglen, both of whom trace back to a bitch, Clanrole Daisy, born about 1927, and the two Rhodelands, Boy and Lucky Boy, who go back to Yellow Primrose (about 1910). The author would very much appreciate any information on these two bitches, also on an unregistered bitch, Mountshannon Mona, also born about 1920.

## CHALLENGE CERTIFICATE WINNERS APRIL 10, 1960—JUNE 2, 1962

| Dog's Name and Owner and Breeder | Colour | Family | Sire | Dam |
|---|---|---|---|---|
| Arcot, Abelle of, b. | S | 3 | Ch. Alexander of Arcot | Lanette of Arcot |
| O. Mrs. M. Tweddle | | | | |
| B. Mrs. M. Tweddle | | | | |
| Beulah's Golden Mister Fu, d. | S | 10 | Beulah's Gold Sun Fu Five | Beulah's August Princess |
| O. Mrs. N. K. George | | | | |
| B. Mrs. N. K. George | | | | |
| Bririch Silver Dream, Ch. b. 1963 | BM | 3 | Crosstalk Silver Star | Bririch Merry Mischief |
| O. Mrs. V. Streeter | | | | |
| B. Mrs. V. Streeter | | | | |
| Carramar Blue Ballerina, b. | BM | 10 | Ch. Rhodelands Boy | Westcarrs Blue Myrobella |
| O. Mr. J. Sargeant | | | | |
| B. Mr. J. Sargeant | | | | |
| Coverdales Filipepi, Ch. d. 1963 | S | 3 | Coverdale's McShan | Coverdales Golden Gesture |
| O. Mr. and Mrs. L. P. Green | | | | |
| B. Mr. G. Richards | | | | |

| Dog's Name and Owner and Breeder | Colour | Family | Sire | Dam |
|---|---|---|---|---|
| Danvis Damascus, Ch. d. 1961 | S | 5 | Ch. Gunner of Glenturret | Danvis Delsia |
|   O. Mr. T. Purvis | | | | |
|   B. Mr. T. Purvis | | | | |
| Danvis Dorabelle b. | S | 5 | Ch. Alexander of Arcot | Ch. Danvis Derna |
|   O. Mr. T. Purvis | | | | |
|   B. Mr. T. Purvis | | | | |
| Danvis Sheba of Simbastar, Ch. b. 1961 | S | SL | Ch. Mywicks Meadow Lancer | Leecroft Ladyfair |
|   O. Mr. T. Purvis | | | | |
|   B. Mrs. Illingworth | | | | |
| Deloraine Distinctive, Ch. b. 1965 | S | I | Sheik of Glenmist | Pattingham Polka |
|   O. Mrs. F. Jefferies | | | | |
|   B. Mrs. F. Chapman | | | | |
| Deloraine Don Juan, Ch. d. 1964 | S | I | Panto of Shencolne | Pattingham Polka |
|   O. Mrs. F. Jefferies | | | | |
|   B. Mrs. F. Chapman | | | | |
| Dunsinane, Dorgano Demander of, Ch. d. 1963 | S | 6 | Ch. Defender of Dunsinane | Foxshot Charmer |
|   O. Mrs. A. Chatfield | | | | |
|   B. Mrs. Mylett | | | | |
| Dunsinane, Deena of, b. | S | 2 | Laudable of Ladypark | Dancer of Dunsinane |
|   O. Mrs. A. Chatfield | | | | |
|   B. Mrs. E. M. Tomlinson | | | | |
| Dunsinane, Emric Epithet of, Ch. b. 1961 | S | 2 | Ch. Defender of Dunsinane | Lady of Dunsinane |
|   O. Mrs. A. Chatfield | | | | |
|   B. Mr. T. Pearce | | | | |
| Duntiblae Doorknocker, Ch. b. 1962 | S | I | Ch. Liberty of Ladypark | Westcarrs What |
|   O. Mr. and Mrs. J. R. Cochrane | | | | |
|   B. Mr. and Mrs. J. R. Cochrane | | | | |
| Ewdenvale, Stately Scot of, Ch. d. 1963 | S | I | Ch. Leonertes of Ladypark | Landula Lady Luck |
|   O. Mr. J. A. Pilcher | | | | |
|   B. Mr. J. A. Pilcher | | | | |
| Fellview Shepherd Boy, Ch. d. 1963 | S | I | Ch. Leonertes of Ladypark | Wendy of Fellview |
|   O. Mr. T. Wall | | | | |
|   B. Mr. T. Wall | | | | |
| Glenmist, Debonair of, Ch. d. 1962 | S | 2 | Pattingham Kismet | Starlet of Glenmist |

| Name / Owner / Breeder | Sire | Code | No. | |
|---|---|---|---|---|
| ... O. Mr. J. Mycroft and Mr. D. Rippon<br>B. Mr. D. Rippon | Ch. Mywicks Meadow Lancer | | 3 | Brooklea Wendy |
| Jefsire Strollaway, Ch. d. 1961<br>O. Mr. and Mrs. A. T. Jeffries<br>B. Mr. and Mrs. A. T. Jeffries | Ch. Gunner of Glenturret | S | 13 | Jefsire Satin Sensation |
| Jefsire Tudor Queen, Ch. b. 1962<br>O. Mr. E. J. Gutteridge<br>B. Mr. P. Sharp | Ch. Jefsire Strollaway | S | 13 | Ch. Jefsire Amber Linnet |
| Larkena Rabelias, Ch. d. 1962<br>O. Mr. J. Parrot<br>B. Mr. J. Parrot | Larkena Royalist | S | 2 | Lavish of Ladypark |
| Lochview Lovely, b.<br>O. Mrs. A. Leckie<br>B. Mrs. A. Leckie | Netherkeir Torchfire | S | 1 | Lochview Beauty |
| Lowerpark Black Buccaneer, Ch. d. 1963<br>O. Mrs. L. Westby<br>B. Mrs. L. Westby | Carramar Midnight Raider | T | 13 | Lowerpark Blue Polar |
| Lowerpark Blue Cloud of Glenmist, Ch. d. 1961<br>O. Mrs. L. Westby<br>B. Mr. F. Mitchell | Lowerpark Blue Lancer | BM | 13 | Blue Beauty of Glenmist |
| Manorlake, Midnight Minx of, b.<br>O. Miss C. Molony<br>B. Mr. B. Lakeman | Ch. Westcarrs Whistler | T | 10 | Miss Minx of Manorlake |
| Meerhay, Copper Gleam from, d.<br>O. Mrs. A. P. Payne<br>B. Miss D. M. Young | Copper Glow from Meerhay | S | 1 | Ugony's Rippling Glint |
| Milburndene, Minuet of, b.<br>O. Mrs. M. Milburn<br>B. Mrs. M. Milburn | Model of Milburndene | S | 2 | Moonshine of Milburndene |
| Mywicks Satine of Simbastar, Ch. b. 1963<br>O. Mr. J. Mycroft<br>B. Mrs. Illingworth | Ch. Mywicks Meadow Lancer | T | ? | Leecroft Ladyfair |
| Narragansette, Ferry of, d.<br>O. Mr. J. McLaren<br>B. Mr. J. McLaren | Ch. Forth of Narragansette | S | 10 | Ch. Claren of Narragansette |
| Normansfield Defender, d.<br>O. Mr. N. Abell<br>B. Mr. N. Abell | Ch. Defender of Dunsinane | S | 1 | Normansfield Sable Lady |

217

## CHALLENGE CERTIFICATE WINNERS APRIL 10, 1960—JUNE 2, 1962—(Cont.)

| Dog's Name and Owner and Breeder | Colour | Family | Sire | Dam |
|---|---|---|---|---|
| Pattingham Gay Cascade of Glenmist, Ch. b. 1961 | S | SL | Pattingham Patrick | Ch. Lovely Lady of Glenmist |
| O. Mrs. M. Franklin | | | | |
| B. Mr. F. Mitchell | | | | |
| Pattingham Playful, d. | S | 1 | Pattingham Kismet | Pattingham Golden Lydia |
| O. Mr. G. Hammond | | | | |
| B. Mrs. M. Franklin | | | | |
| Selstoma Saruto, b. | S | 6 | Ch. Legend of Ladypark | Selstoma Treena |
| O. Mr. F. Wright | | | | |
| B. Mr. T. Tomlinson | | | | |
| Shearcliffe Vampire, Ch. d. 1963 | S | 8 | Ch. Mywicks Meadow Lancer | Shearcliffe Tessa |
| O. Mr. J. Broderick | | | | |
| B. Mr. J. Broderick | | | | |
| Shiel, Satu from, b. | S | 1 | Ch. Mywicks Meadow Lancer | Tonbeauly's Tara |
| O. Miss M. Osborne | | | | |
| B. Miss M. Osborne | | | | |
| Skellvale, Sovereign of, Ch. d. 1963 | S | 6 | Ch. Statesman of Skellvale | Ellington Erasmic |
| O. Mr. P. Rodford | | | | |
| B. Mrs. Fishpool | | | | |
| Swatterscarrs Crosstalk Silver Rain, b | BM | 4 | Ch. Westcarrs Blue Minoru | Black Ricky |
| O. Mrs. A. Gibbs | | | | |
| B. Mrs. A. Caygill | | | | |
| Swatterscarrs Soraya, b. | T | 4 | Longscar Kaiser of Kinreen | Swatterscarrs Shona |
| O. Mrs. A. Gibbs | | | | |
| B. Mrs. A. Gibbs | | | | |
| Swintonian Model, Ch. b. 1961 | T | 1 | Ch. Mywicks Meadow Lancer | Movaneen |
| O. Mr. J. Franey | | | | |
| B. Mr. J. Franey | | | | |

## CHALLENGE CERTIFICATE WINNERS JUNE 3, 1962—MAY 1, 1965

| Dog's Name and Owner and Breeder | Colour | Family | Sire | Dam |
|---|---|---|---|---|
| Beulah's Night Don Salvador, Ch. d. 1965 | T | 3 | Ch. Beulah's Blanco-y-Negro | Beulah's Golden Soldorida |
| O. Mrs. N. K. George | | | | |
| B. Mrs. N. K. George | | | | |
| Beulah's Night Society, b. | T | 3 | " | " |
| O. Mrs. N. K. George | | | | |

B. Mr. G. Archer

| | | | | Sire | Dam |
|---|---|---|---|---|---|
| Carramar Blue Prince, d. | .. | .. | BM | 10 | Ch. Rhodelands Boy | Westcarrs Blue Myrobella |
| O. Mr. J. Sargeant | | | | | | |
| B. Mr. J. Sargeant | | | | | | |
| Carramar Blue Tweed, Ch. d. 1966 | .. | | BM | 10 | Ch. Carramar Boy Blue | Carramar Black Opal |
| O. Mr. J. Sargeant | | | | | | |
| B. Mr. J. Sargeant | | | | | | |
| Carramar Boy Blue, Ch. d. 1962 | .. | | BM | 10 | Ch. Rhodelands Boy | Westcarrs Blue Myrobella |
| O. Mr. J. Sargeant | | | | | | |
| B. Mr. J. Sargeant | | | | | | |
| Clanayre Chiffon Princess, Ch. b., 1964 | .. | | S | 1 | Ch. Jetsfire Strollaway | Ch. Deloraine Distinctive |
| O. Mrs. F. Jefferies | | | | | | |
| B. Mrs. F. Jefferies | | | | | | |
| Corviross Silver Joy, b. Ch. 1966 | .. | | BM | 4 | Clayswood Don Nickolas | Ch. Crosstalk Silver Belle |
| O. Mrs. Coombe | | | | | | |
| B. Mr. Job and Mr. Corbishley | | | | | | |
| Crosstalk Silver Belle, Ch. b., 1964.. | .. | | BM | 4 | Ch. Westcarrs Blue Minoru | Black Rickey |
| O. Mr. L. Casely | | | | | | |
| B. Mrs. A. Caygill | | | | | | |
| Danvis Clanreoch Carmen, b. | .. | | T | 5 | Danvis Dooley | Danvis Damozel |
| O. Mr. T. Purvis | | | | | | |
| B. Mr. C. Wray | | | | | | |
| Danvis Dooley, d. Ch. 1967 | .. | | S | 5 | Danvis Dale | Ch. Danvis Derna |
| O. Mr. T. Purvis | | | | | | |
| B. Mr. T. Purvis | | | | | | |
| Danvis Duffer, Ch. d., 1964.. | .. | | S | 5 | Ch. Danvis Damascus | Ch. Danvis Derna |
| O. Mr. T. Purvis | | | | | | |
| B. Mr. T. Purvis | | | | | | |
| Deloraine Decorative, Ch. b., 1964 | .. | | S | 1 | Sheik of Glenmist | Pattingham Polka |
| O. Mrs. F. Jefferies | | | | | | |
| B. Mrs. F. Chapman | | | | | | |
| Dunsinane Avara of Aberthorne, Ch. b. 1965 | .. | | S | 10 | Defiant of Dunsinane | Desire of Dunsinane |
| O. Mrs. A. Chatfield | | | | | | |
| B. Mr. J. Tait | | | | | | |
| Dunsinane, Darling of, Ch. b., 1963 | .. | | S | 2 | Ch. Liberty of Ladypark | Ch. Rifflesee Regality of Dunsinane |
| O. Mrs. A. Chatfield | | | | | | |
| B. Mrs. A. Chatfield | | | | | | |

# CHALLENGE CERTIFICATE WINNERS JUNE 3, 1962 —MAY 1, 1965—(Cont.)

| Dog's Name and Owner and Breeder | Colour | Family | Sire | Dam |
|---|---|---|---|---|
| Dunsinane, Deborah of, Ch. b., 1963 | S | SL | Ch. Mywicks Meadow Lancer | Lecroft Ladyfair |
| O.  Mrs. A. Chatfield | | | | |
| B.  Mrs. Illingworth | | | | |
| Dunsinane, Moondrift of, d. | BM | 10 | Ch. Carramar Boy Blue | Donna Jetta of Dunsinane |
| O.  Mrs. A. Chatfield | | | | |
| B.  Mrs. A. Chatfield | | | | |
| Elmways Heath Princess, b. | S | 4 | Janlynn's Golden Laird | Frienell Bess |
| O.  Mr. and Mrs. G. Lampard | | | | |
| B.  Mr. and Mrs. G. Lampard | | | | |
| Fourjoys Blue Peter, d. Ch. 1968 | BM | 4 | Ch. Bridholme Crosstalk Silver Rambler | Swattercarrs Sultana |
| O.  Mr. B. Harland | | | | |
| B.  Mr. B. Harland | | | | |
| Franwyns Jefsfire Harvest, Ch. b., 1962 | S | 1 | Ch. Jefsfire Strollaway | Starlight of Southwardedge |
| O.  Mr. F. Davies | | | | |
| B.  Mr. and Mrs. Jeffries | | | | |
| Franwyns Jefsfire Starmaker, d. | S | 1 | ,, | ,, |
| O.  Mr. F. Davies | | | | |
| B.  Mr. and Mrs. Jeffries | | | | |
| Glencorse Gloria, b. Ch. 1967 | S | 1 | Glencorse Grenadier | Blue Dolphin |
| O.  Mr. A. Semple | | | | |
| B.  Mr. A. Semple | | | | |
| Glenmist, Glamour Boy of, d. | S | 2 | Ch. Pattingham Pacemaker | Leading Lady of Glenmist |
| O.  Miss Young and Mrs. Payne | | | | |
| B.  Mr. F. Mitchell and Mr. J. Mottram | | | | |
| Glenmist, Starlet of, Ch. b. 1965 | S | 2 | Ch. Liberty of Ladypark | Ch. Rifflesee Reward of Glenmist C.D. |
| O.  Mrs. B. Mayland | | | | |
| B.  Mr. F. Mitchell | | | | |
| Glenmist Golden Legacy, Ch. d. 1965 | S | 2 | Ch. Debonair of Glenmist | Ch. Sapphire of Glenmist |
| O.  Mr. F. Mitchell | | | | |
| B.  Mr. F. Mitchell | | | | |
| Glenriver, Golden Primrose of, b. | S | 1 | Ch. Gunner of Glenturret | Sarrise of Glenriver |
| O.  Mr. J. S. Prudhoe | | | | |
| B.  Mr. P. Prudhoe | | | | |
| Glenriver Presentation, b. | S | 1 | Ch. Danvis Damascus | Glenriver Merry Girl |
| O.  Mr. P. Prudhoe | | | | |

## CHALLENGE CERTIFICATE WINNERS JUNE 3, 1962—MAY 1 1965—(Cont.)

| Dog's Name and Owner and Breeder | Colour | Family | Sire | Dam |
|---|---|---|---|---|
| Narragansette, Noah of, d. .. .. .. <br> O. Mr. P. McLaren <br> B. Mr. P. McLaren | S | 1 | Ferry of Narragansette | Netherkeir Vanity |
| Pattingham Gay Legend of Glenmist, Ch. d., 1963 <br> O. Mrs. M. Franklin <br> B. Mr. F. Mitchell | S. | 2 | Ch. Debonair of Glenmist | Ch. Sapphire of Glenmist |
| Pattingham Pacemaker, Ch. d., 1964 .. .. <br> O. Mrs. M. Franklin <br> B. Mrs. M. Franklin | S | 2 | Pattingham Kismet | Ch. Pattingham Gay Lady of Glenmist |
| Pattingham Pheasant, Ch. b., 1965 .. .. <br> O. Mrs. M. Franklin <br> B. Mrs. M. Franklin | S | 1 | Ch. Duntiblae Dog Watch | Ch. Pattingham Prelude |
| Pride of Twym, d. .. .. .. .. <br> O. Mr. W. R. Cooper <br> B. Mrs. J. Musson | S | 3 | Ashcombe Alan | Westhoe Lassie (unr.) |
| Ralvera's Meadow Maid, Ch. b., 1965 .. .. <br> O. Mr. J. Fendley <br> B. Mr. J. Fendley | S. | 1 | Ch. Mywicks Meadow Lancer | Coverdale's Golden Dawn |
| Ralvera's Meadow Marquis, Ch. d., 1964 .. .. <br> O. Mr. J. Fendley <br> B. Mr. J. Fendley | S | 1 | Ch. Duntiblae Dog Watch | Ch. Ralvera's Meadow Maid |
| Rowdina Dramatic of Dunsinane, Ch. d., 1965 .. <br> O. Mrs. Winwood <br> B. Mrs. A. Chatfield | S | SL | Ch. Dorgano Demander of Dunsinane | Ch. Deborah of Dunsinane |
| Shearcliffe, Wishful, Ch. b., 1964 .. .. <br> O. Mr. J. Broderick <br> B. Mr. J. Broderick | T | 8 | Ch. Defender of Dunsinane | Shearcliffe Tessa |
| Selstoma Sandpiper, Ch. d., 1964 .. .. <br> O. Mr. T. Tomlinson <br> B. Mr. T. Tomlinson | S | 6 | Oakbrook Gay Laird | Selstoma Sandpiper of Dindella |
| Siloams Sheba, b. Ch. 1966 .. .. .. <br> O. Mr. J. Winstanley <br> B. Mr. J. Winstanley. | S | 4 | Ch. Danvis Damascus | Siloams Natasha Secundus |
| Son of Good Gift, d. .. .. .. .. <br> O. Mr. T. Herron <br> B. Mr. D. Moorhead | S | 4 | Good Gift | Bride's Blossom |
| Tilehouse Thistle, Ch. b. 1965 .. .. .. | BM | 4 | Ch. Lowerpark Black Buccaneer | Crosstalk Silver Joy |

O. Miss D. M. Young
B. Miss D. M. Young

NOTE.—The three Ch. litter-sisters out of Leecroft Ladyfair cannot, at present, be tied into any family. They go back to Kinnerley Allegro (ex the unregistered Seedley Lassie) and it is information on this latter bitch that I would be glad to receive.

## CHALLENGE CERTIFICATE WINNERS MAY 2, 1965—MAY 31, 1966

| Dog's Name and Owner and Breeder | Colour | Family | Sire | Dam |
|---|---|---|---|---|
| Antoc Day Dream Ch. 1968 .. .. S | | 13 | Ch. Debonair of Glenmist | Antoc Tawny Lyric |
|   O. Mrs. A. Speding | | | | |
|   B. Miss. C. Speding | | | | |
| Antoc Vicar of Bray, d. Ch. 1966 .. | S | 13 | Ch. Larkena Vanara Golden Victor | Antoc Rose Marie |
|   O. Mrs. A. Speding | | | | |
|   B. Mrs. A. Speding | | | | |
| Delwood Donabrus Kildonan, b. .. | S | 1 | Ch. Mywicks Meadow Lancer | Delwood Belle |
|   O. Miss Bell and Mr. Johns | | | | |
|   B. Mrs. M. Nicolson | | | | |
| Chateauroux Lysander, Ch. d., 1965 .. | S | 2 | Ch. Chateauroux Caesar | Chateauroux Princess |
|   O. Mrs. F. Arthur | | | | |
|   B. Mrs. F. Arthur | | | | |
| Dunsinane Amazon of Aberthorne, b. Ch. 1967 .. | S | 10 | Dunsinane Abbot of Aberthorne | Allison of Aberthorne |
|   O. Mrs. A. Chatfield | | | | |
|   B. Mr. J. Tait | | | | |
| Duntiblae Dog Watch, Ch. d. 1965 .. | S | 4 | Ch. Mywicks Meadow Lancer | Ch. Duntiblae Doorknocker |
|   O. Mr. and Mrs. J. Cochrane | | | | |
|   B. Mr. and Mrs. J. Cochrane | | | | |
| Kingsville, Dream Baby of, b. Ch. 1967 .. | T | 4 | Bririch Silver Spray | Kingsville Corviross Gay Silver |
|   O. Mr. and Mrs. Westwell | | | | |
|   B. Mr. T. Evans | | | | |
| Mofson, Morning Dew of, b. .. | S | 6 | Golden Boy of Mofson | Lady of Dreadon |
|   O. Mr. R. Adamson | | | | |
|   B. Mr. R. Adamson | | | | |
| Narragansette, City of, . .. | S | 13 | Noah of Narragansette | Crest of Narragansette |
|   O. Mr. P. McLaren | | | | |
|   B. Mr. P. McLaren | | | | |
| Pattingham Peacable, b. Ch. 1966 .. | S | 2 | Ch. Duntiblae Dogwatch | Pattingham Peaceful |
|   O. Mrs. M. Franklin | | | | |
|   B. Mrs. M. Franklin | | | | |

| Dog's Name and Owner and Breeder | Colour | Family | Sire | Dam |
|---|---|---|---|---|
| Plantons Paulette, b. .. .. .. | S | 1 | Glenriver Sungod | Glenriver Presentation |
| O. Mr. E. Scarffe | | | | |
| B. Mr. M. Siddle | | | | |
| Rokeby, Romney of, b. Ch. 1966 .. .. | S | 13 | Dazzler of Dunsinane | Witchcraft of Rokeby |
| O. Mr. and Mrs. Eglin | | | | |
| B. Mr. and Mrs. Eglin | | | | |
| Southwardedge, Shepherd of, d. .. .. | S | 1 | Ch. Statesman of Skellvale | Sheila of Southwardedge |
| O. Mrs. M. Horton | | | | |
| B. Mrs. M. Horton | | | | |
| Yeldust, Duke of, d. Ch. 1967 .. .. | S | 2 | James from Ugony | Ugony's Golden Pepi |
| O. Mrs. A. Studley | | | | |
| B. Mrs. A. Studley | | | | |

| Dog's Name and Owner and Breeder | Colour | Family | Sire | Dam |
|---|---|---|---|---|
| Arcot, Alida of, b. Ch. 1969 .. .. | S | 2 | Arkle of Arcot | Looknowe Brandywyne |
| O. Mrs. M. Tweddle | | | | |
| B. Mrs. I. Baker | | | | |
| Asoka Clayswood Blue Venture, d. Ch. 1968 | BM | 6 | Lacemaker of Ladypark | Clayswood Blue Slippers |
| O. Mrs. M. Litton | | | | |
| B. Mr. G. Tams | | | | |
| Bellacoyle Golden Shandy, b. .. .. | S | 1 | Ch. Larkena Vanara Golden Victor | Bellacoyle Alpine Gold |
| O. Mrs. M. Orr | | | | |
| B. Mrs. T. Webb | | | | |
| Bellacoyle Silver Cora, b. .. .. | BM | 1 | Bellacoyle Beauty | Rowsbur Silver Heather |
| O. Mr. A. G. Cowley | | | | |
| B. Mrs. T. Webb | | | | |
| Beulah's Silver Don Mariolo, d. Ch. 1968.. | BM | 3 | Beulah's Silver Don Antonio | Beulah's Night Savilla |
| O. Mrs. N. George | | | | |
| B. Mr. N. Ward | | | | |
| Burwydne Brendenbury, b. Ch. 1969 .. | S | 10 | Burwydne Brave Ruler | Burwydne Gay Gal |
| O. Mr. S. Grassby | | | | |
| B. Mr. F. Buckle | | | | |
| Cathanbrae Ladypark Lavender Blue, b. Ch. 1969.. | BM | 6 | Lacemaker of Ladypark | Clayswood Blue Slippers |
| O. Mrs. T. Taylor | | | | |
| B. Mr. G. Tams | | | | |
| Chateauroux Caesar, d. Ch. 1967 .. .. | S | 2 | Ch. Jefsfire Stollaway | Chateauroux Lady Corzet |
| O. Mrs. F. Arthur | | | | |

b. ...rs. ... Arthur

Cheryldene Blue Lilac, b. Ch. 1971 .. .. BM 10 — Bririch Silver Spray — Donna Julie of Dunsinane
O. Mrs. D. Lockett
B. Mrs. D. Lockett

Cheryldene Moonskater of Dunsinane d. Ch. 1969 .. BM 10 — Ch. Carramar Boy Blue — Cheryldene Blue Lilac
O. Mrs. A. Chatfield
B. Mrs. D. Lockett

Clickham Bririch Bewitcher, b. .. .. S 2 — Ch. Defender of Dunsinane — Bririch Sweet Sue
O. Mr. D. Smith
B. Mrs. V. Hickson

Cressbrook, Ares of, d. .. .. S 2 — Ch. Mywicks Meadow Lancer — Affinity of Cressbrook
O. Mrs. C. Smith
B. Mrs. C. Smith

Danvis Camanna Golden Sensation d. Ch. 1969 .. S 3 — Ch. Danvis Duffer — Danvis Lestine Lochwinnock
O. Mr. T. Purvis
B. Mrs. M. A. Hassocks

Deburgh Rose Marie of Rokeby, b. Ch. 1970 .. S 13 — Dazzler of Dunsinane — Witchcraft of Rokeby
O. Miss V. Morris
B. Mr. and Mrs. J. Eglin

Deloraine Dinah-Mite, b. Ch. 1967 .. .. S 1 — Ch. Duntiblae Dogwatch — Pattingham Polka
O. Mrs. F. Chapman
B. Mrs. F. Chapman

Donabrus Kylmeryl, b. .. .. T 1 — Delwood Dynamite — Donabrus Kilmuir
O. Mrs. M. Nicolson
B. Mrs. M. Nicolson

Dorgano Double Ace of Rokeby d. .. S 13 — Ch. Royal Ace of Rokeby — Dorgano Delishus
O. Mr. and Mrs. J. Eglin
B. Mr. and Mrs. D. Mylett

Dunsinane, Amazon of Aberthorne, b. Ch. 1967 .. S 10 — Dunsinane Abbot of Aberthorne — Allison of Aberthorne
O. Mrs. A. Chatfield
B. Mr. J. Tait

Dunsinane Rosalinda of Rokeby, b. Ch. 1967 .. S 1 — Dazzler of Dunsinane — Ch. Romney of Rokeby
O. Mrs. A. Chatfield
B. Mr. and Mrs. J. Eglin

Duntiblae Detective, d. .. .. S 2 — Ch. Larkena Vanara Golden Victor — Duntiblae Dunfoolin'
O. Mr. and Mrs. J. S. G. Cochrane
B. Mr. and Mrs. J. S. G. Cochrane

Duntiblae Dogstar, d. Ch. 1969 .. .. S 2 — Ch. Duntiblae Dogwatch — Duntiblae Dolly Mixture
O. Mr. and Mrs. J. S. G. Cochrane
B. Mr. and Mrs. J. S. G. Cochrane

P

## CHALLENGE CERTIFICATE WINNERS JUNE 1, 1966—MAY 31, 1969—(Cont.)

| Dog's Name and Owner and Breeder | Colour | Family | Sire | Dam |
|---|---|---|---|---|
| Duntiblae Dundrum, d. .. .. | S | 1 | Ch. Pattingham Pacemaker | Ch. Duntiblae Doorknocker |
| O. Mr. and Mrs. J. S. G. Cochrane | | | | |
| B. Mr. and Mrs. J. S. G. Cochrane | | | | |
| Edgemont Ballerina, b. .. .. | S | 4 | Ch. Royal Ace of Rokeby | Edgemont Elite of Rushmead |
| O. Mr. N. K. Greenhalgh | | | | |
| B. Mr. N. K. Greenhalgh | | | | |
| Fellview Consort, d. Ch. 1969 .. | S | 1 | Ch. Selstoma Sandpiper | Fellview Amanda |
| O. Mr. T. Wall | | | | |
| B. Mr. T. Wall | | | | |
| Firestone Marciano, d. Ch. 1970 .. | S | 2 | Ch. Jefsfire Lucky-by-Name | Firestone Mystic Princess |
| O. Mr. and Mrs. F. Plimmer | | | | |
| B. Mr. and Mrs. F. Plimmer | | | | |
| Fourjoys Blue Danny, d. Ch. 1968 .. | BM | 4 | Ch. Bridholme Crosstalk Silver Rambler | Fourjoys Black Magic |
| O. Mr. and Mrs. B. Harland | | | | |
| B. Mr. B. Harland | | | | |
| Fourjoys Blue Minstrel of Whitelea, d. Ch. 1970 | BM | 10 | Ch. Bridholme Crosstalk Silver Rambler | Tilehouse Twiglet |
| O. Mr. W. Richmond | | | | |
| B. Mr. B. Harland | | | | |
| Franwyns Dale, d. Ch. 1967 .. | S | 1 | Chateauroux Ideal | Ch. Franwyns Jefsfire Harvest |
| O. Mr. and Mrs. F. Davies | | | | |
| B. Mr. and Mrs. F. Davies | | | | |
| Geoffdon New Romance, b. Ch. 1968 .. | S | 2 | Leecroft Lover Boy of Dunsinane | Geoffdon Joyful |
| O. Mr. G. Mildon | | | | |
| B. Mr. G. Mildon | | | | |
| Glyngarth Fair Offer, b. Ch. 1968 .. | S | 1 | Chateauroux Ideal | Glyngarth Meadow Mystic |
| O. Mr. and Mrs. I. G. Tuck | | | | |
| B. Mr. and Mrs. W. R. Cooper | | | | |
| Gorjess Black Jester, d. .. .. | T (U.S.A.) | | Gorjess Black Arab | Gorjess Blue Mistral |
| O. Mrs. D. J. Everett | | | | |
| B. Mrs. J. Harns | | | | |
| Janiveer's Damsel of Dunsinane, b. .. | S | 4 | Ralvera's Meadow Maestro | Rushmead Amanda |
| O. Mr. P. Thornton | | | | |
| B. Miss C. Holden | | | | |
| Jefsfire Gay Return, b. Ch. 1969 .. | S | 2 | Jefsfire Fury | Saadiacre Jefsfire Gay Tweed |
| O. Mr. and Mrs. A. Jeffries | | | | |
| B. Mrs. Wigglesworth | | | | |
| Jefsfire Happy By Name, d. Ch. 1967 .. | S | 2 | Ch. Mywicks Meadow Lancer | Jefsfire Fashion |

| | | | | |
|---|---|---|---|---|
| Jefsfire Gold Token, Ch. 1969<br>O. Mr. and Mrs. A. Jeffries<br>B. Mr. & Mrs. Jeffries | S | 2 | Ch. Danvis Duffer | Jefsfire Starlight |
| Jefsfire High Regard, d. Ch. 1970<br>O. Mr. A. Tukes<br>B. Mr. and Mrs. A. T. Jeffries | S | 2 | Jefsfire High Return | Jefsfire Gay Return |
| Jefsfire Phares Forever Amber, b. Ch. 1967<br>O. Mr. and Mrs. A. T. Jeffries<br>B. Mr. and Mrs. A. Jeffries | S | 13 | Ch. Jefsfire Lucky By Name | Ch. Jefsfire Amber Linnet |
| Jefsfire Ready Maid, b. Ch. 1970<br>O. Mr. and Mrs. Sharpe<br>B. Mr. and Mrs. A. Jeffries | S | 2 | Jefsfire Gold Token | Jefsfire Bewitched |
| Larkena Rabais, d. Ch. 1968<br>O. Mr. and Mrs. A. Jeffries<br>B. Mr. J. Parrott | S | 1 | Ch. Larkena Vanara Golden Victor | Ivanmoor Lilac Lady |
| Laund Livia, b. Ch. 1968<br>O. Mr. A. Lindsey<br>B. Mrs. A. Bishop | S | 2 | Ch. Duke of Yeldust | Laund Lesley |
| Lochkaren Loretta of Ystap, b. Ch. 1967<br>O. Mrs. A Bishop<br>B. Mr. and Mrs. F. Mitchell | S | 2 | Ch. Pattingham Pacemaker | Leading Lady of Glenmist |
| Manorlake Anna of Arcot, b.<br>O. Mrs. P. Giles<br>B. Mr. B. Lakeman | S | 3 | Achieve of Arcot | Abelle of Arcot |
| Pattingham Kingani Iolanthe, b. Ch. 1967<br>O. Mrs. M. Tweddle<br>B. Mrs. M. Franklin | S | 1 | Ch. Pattingham Pacemaker | Landula Loetta |
| Pattingham Playbox, b. Ch. 1968<br>O. Mr. J. Hernenway<br>B. Mr. M. Franklin | T | 2 | Ch. Larkena Vanara Golden Victor | Geoffdon Briar Rose |
| Pattingham Ptarmigan, d.<br>O. Mr. G. Mildon<br>B. Mrs. M. Franklin | S | 1 | Ch. Pattingham Pacemaker | Ch. Pattingham Pheasant |
| Rokeby, Ramsey of, d. Ch. 1969<br>O. Mrs. M. Franklin<br>B. Mr. and Mrs. J. Eglin | S | 13 | Dazzler of Dunsinane | Ch. Romney of Rokeby |
| Rokeby, Rosalie of, b. Ch. 1969<br>O. Mr. and Mrs. J. Eglin<br>B. Mrs. L. Wagstaffe | S | 6 | Ch. Royal Ace of Rokeby | Dentonian Donna Anna |

227

## CHALLENGE CERTIFICATE WINNERS JUNE 1, 1966—MAY 31, 1969—(Cont.)

| Dog's Name and Owner and Breeder | Colour | Family | Sire | Dam |
|---|---|---|---|---|
| Rokeby, Royal Ace of, d. Ch. 1967 <br> O. Mr. and Mrs. J. Eglin <br> B. Mr. and Mrs. J. Eglin | S | 13 | Dazzler of Dunsinane | Ch. Witchcraft of Rokeby |
| Rokeby, Witchcraft of, b. Ch. 1969 <br> O. Mr. and Mrs. J. Eglin <br> B. Mr. and Mrs. J. Eglin | T | 13 | Prospecthill Rustler of Rokeby | Retta of Rokeby |
| Sandiacre String of Pearls, b. Ch. 1969 <br> O. Mrs. S. M. Wigglesworth <br> B. Mr. C. R. Chambers | S | 2 | Ch. Royal Ace of Rokeby | Colrenes Seawitch of Sandiacre |
| Shearcliffe Barbarian of Dunsinane, d. <br> O. Mrs. A. Chatfield <br> B. Mr. J. Broderick | S | 5 | Ch. Dorgano Dubonnet of Dunsinane | Shearcliffe Vena |
| Shearcliffe Blue Sonnet of Dunsinane, b. Ch. 1968 <br> O. Mrs. A. Chatfield <br> B. Mr. A. Yates | BM | 3 | Ch. Carramar Boy Blue | Shearcliffe Silver Star |
| Shirdale, Saveen of, b. <br> O. Mrs. E. Griffiths <br> B. Mrs. E. Griffiths | S | 13 | Jefsfire Chateauroux Fellow | Superfine Scimitar |
| Silvafox Squire, d. <br> O. Mr. A. North <br> B. Mr. A. North | S | 13 | Dazzler of Dunsinane | Silvafox Shani |
| Skellvale, Shane of, d. Ch. 1969 <br> O. Mr. P. Rodford <br> B. Mr. P. Rodford | S | 1 | Ramsey of Rokeby | Susan of Skellvale |
| Tameila Blue Peter from Valebridge, d. Ch. 1969 <br> O. Mr. D. W. Hurrel <br> B. Mrs. M. Gawder | BM | 4 | Esemaich Silver Chieftain | Vanity Fair from Valebridge |
| Tilehouse Tonto, d. Ch. 1967 <br> O. Mrs. I. Combe <br> B. Mrs. I. Combe | T | 4 | Ch. Lowerpark Black Buccaneer | Ch. Corviross Silver Joy |
| Valebridge, Vanity Blue from, b. Ch. 1967 <br> O. Mrs. M. Gander <br> B. Mrs. M. Gander | BM | 4 | Esemaich Silver Chieftain | Vanity Fair from Valebridge |
| Witchknowe Wilma, b. <br> O. Mrs. M. Brown <br> B. Mrs. M. Brown | S | 1 | Monkreddan Glen Grant | Dewshill Doodle |
| Wrenarve, Whimsey of, b. | S | 1 | Ch. Lowerpark Black Buccaneer | Wild Honey of Wrenarve |

## CHALLENGE CERTIFICATE WINNERS JUNE 1, 1969—DECEMBER 31, 1972

| Dog's Name and Owner and Breeder | Colour | Family | Sire | Dam |
|---|---|---|---|---|
| Aberthorne, Acrogen of, b.  ..  ..  .. <br> O.  Mrs. S. Toothill <br> B.  Mr. J. Tait | S | SL | Defiant of Dunsinane | Anna of Acrogen |
| Aberthorne, Actress of, b. Ch. 1972 .. <br> O.  Mr. J. Tait and Miss Skilbeck <br> B.  Mr. J. Tait | S | SL | Defiant of Dunsinane | Anna of Acrogen |
| Antoc Pickpocket, d.  ..  ..  .. <br> O.  Mrs. A. Speding <br> B.  Mrs. A. Speding | S | 13 | Pattingham Pacesetter | Antoc Rosemarie |
| Antoc the Boy Friend, d. Ch. 1972.. <br> O.  Mrs A. Speding <br> B.  Mrs A. Speding | S | 13 | Glamour Boy of Glenmist | Ch. Antoc Daydream |
| Asoka Gay Mist, b. Ch. 1971  .. <br> O.  Mrs. Green <br> B.  Mrs. Litton | BM | 4 | Ch. Asoka Clayswood Blue Venture | Ch. Kingsville Corviross Gay Silver |
| Beaublade Barrister, d. Ch. 1972  .. <br> O.  Mr. & Mrs. D. Clarke <br> B.  Mr. & Mrs. D. Clarke | S | 1 | Ch. Larkena Vanara Golden Victor | Beaublade Duntiblae Doch-an'-Doris |
| Beaublade Black Fascinator, d. Ch. 1973 .. <br> O.  Mr. & Mrs. D. Clarke <br> B.  Mr. & Mrs. D. Clarke | T | 1 | Ch. Larkena Vanara Golden Victor | Beaublade Duntiblae Doch-an-Doris |
| Beaublade Bettinavare, b.  .. <br> O.  Mr. & Mrs. D. Clarke <br> B.  Mr. & Mrs. D. Clarke | S | 1 | Ch. Jefsire High Regard | Beaublade Duntiblae Doch-an'-Doris |
| Betcherrygah Bridgett, b. Ch. 1972 .. <br> O.  Mr. N. Burt <br> B.  Mr. D. Horridge | S | 6 | Ch. Chateauroux Flawless | Selstoma Sparkle |
| Bilbar Anromeda of Temaur, b.  .. <br> O.  Mr. & Mrs. Fleetwood <br> B.  Mr. & Mrs. W. Smith | T | 2 | Leecroft Lover Boy of Dunsinane | Antigone of Cressbrook |
| Brettonpark Vanity Fair, b. Ch. 1970 .. <br> O.  Mr. & Mrs. Duncan <br> B.  Mr. & Mrs. Duncan | S | SL | Dazzler of Dunsinane | Brettonpark Gaiety Girl |
| Bririch Gold Edition, d. Ch. 1970 .. <br> O.  Mr. & Mrs. Hickson <br> B.  Mr. & Mrs. Hickson | S | 3 | Ch. Royal Ace of Rokeby | Bririch Golden Belita |

# CHALLENGE CERTIFICATE WINNERS JUNE 1, 1969—DECEMBER 31, 1972—(Cont.)

| Dog's Name and Owner and Breeder | Colour | Family | Sire | Dam |
|---|---|---|---|---|
| Bririch Gold Emblem, d. Ch. 1971 | S | 3 | Ch. Royal Ace of Rokeby | Bririch Golden Belita |
| O. Mr. & Mrs. Hickson | | | | |
| B. Mr. & Mrs. Hickson | | | | |
| Bririch Idcam Amanda, b. Ch. 1972 | S | 13 | Ch. Ramsey of Rokeby | Dorgano Devastate |
| O. Mr. & Mrs. Hickson | | | | |
| B. Mrs. Atterton | | | | |
| Carramar Pretty Polly, b. | BM | 10 | Clickham Silver Snow Star | Ch. Carramar Pollyanna |
| O. Mrs. J. Sargeant | | | | |
| B. Mrs. J. Sargeant | | | | |
| Cathanbrae Dark 'n Dainty, b. | T | 1 | Ch. Ramsey of Rokeby | Ch. Cathanbrae Golden Rust Queen |
| O. Mrs. T. Taylor | | | | |
| B. Mrs. T. Taylor | | | | |
| Cathanbrae Golden Rust Queen, b. Ch. 1971 | S | 1 | Duke of Dantena | Pixie Girl Vanity |
| O. Mrs. T. Taylor | | | | |
| B. Mr. Hyde | | | | |
| Cathanbrae High and Mighty, d. | S | 1 | Ch. Ralvera's Donna's Dale | Ch. Cathanbrae Golden Rust Queen |
| O. Mrs. T. Taylor | | | | |
| B. Mrs. T. Taylor | | | | |
| Cathanbrae Ralvera's Donna's Daydream, Ch. 1971 | S | 1 | Ch. Ralvera's Meadow Marquis | Ralvera's Delightful Donna |
| O. Mrs. T. Taylor | | | | |
| B. Mr. R. Fendley | | | | |
| Cathanbrae Willow Pattern, d. Ch. 1974 | BM | 6 | Knight Marksman of Rokeby | Ch. Cathanbrae Ladypark Lavender Blue |
| O. Mrs. T. Taylor | | | | |
| B. Mrs. T. Taylor | | | | |
| Chateauroux Katherina, b. Ch. 1971 | S | 2 | Chateauroux Ideal | Madame de Pompadour |
| O. Mr. Arthur | | | | |
| B. Mrs. Arthur | | | | |
| Clayswood Blue Bonnet, b. Ch. 1972 | BM | 1 | Corviross Silver Easter | Beauty's Lady Fine |
| O. Mrs. V. Green | | | | |
| B. Mrs. Clay | | | | |
| Clickham Ciraveen Black Cavan, d. Ch. 1972 | T | 3 | Ch. Clickham Night Superior | Bririch Blue Belle of Ciraveen |
| O. Mr. D. Smith | | | | |
| B. Mr. & Mrs. Cheetham | | | | |
| Clickham Night Superior, d. Ch. 1971 | T | 3 | Ch. Carramar Blue Tweed | Clickham Bririch Night Glamour |
| O. Mr. D. Smith | | | | |
| B. Mr. D. Smith | | | | |
| Clanayre Claudine, b. Ch. 1972 | S | 1 | Clanayre Venture | Clanayre Featherway |
| O. Mrs. F. Iefferies | | | | |

| Dog / Owner / Breeder | Sex | No. | Sire | Dam |
|---|---|---|---|---|
| O. Mr. G. Clements — B. Mr. J. Mycroft | | | | Little Liason of Ladypark |
| **Duntiblae Degree, d. Ch. 1972** — O. Mr. & Mrs. Cochrane — B. Mr. & Mrs. Cochrane | S | 6 | Ch. Duntiblae Dogstar | Duntiblae Clickham Candy Floss |
| **Duntiblae Delayed, d.** — O. Mrs. Trueby — B. Mr. & Mrs. Cochrane | S | 2 | Ch. Duntiblae Dogstar | Cavatina Cleopatra |
| **Dunsinane, Cavatina Cool Delilah of, b. Ch. 1973** — O. Mrs. A. Chatfield — B. Mr. M. W. Grace | S | 1 | Ch. Jelshre Falkenor of Joywil | Dencoak Mona Lisa |
| **Dunsinane, Dencoak Delilah of, b. Ch. 1972** — O. Mrs. A. Chatfield — B. Mr. D. Watson | S | SL | Brettonpark Highlander of Dunsinane | Leecroft Louise |
| **Dunsinane, Drum Major of, d.** — O. Mrs. A. Chatfield — B. Mrs. B. Cockroft | S | 1 | Brettonpark Highlander of Dunsinane | Ch. Rosalie of Rokeby |
| **Dunsinane Radar of Rokeby, d. Ch. 1971** — O. Mrs. A. Chatfield — B. Mr. & Mrs. J. Elgin | S | 6 | Ch. Dorgano Double Ace of Rokeby | Ch. Witchcraft of Rokeby |
| **Dunsinane Robinhood of Rokeby, d. Ch. 1973** — O. Mrs. A. Chatfield — B. Mr. & Mrs. J. Eglin | S | 13 | Dazzler of Dunsinane | Shearcliffe Blue Star |
| **Dunsinane, Shearcliffe Black Belle of, b. Ch. 1970** — O. Mrs. A. Chatfield — B. Mr. J. Broderick | T | 3 | Ch. Carramar Boy Blue | Sheena of Silvermoor |
| **Edronal Lady Selena of Devon, b** — O. Mrs. & Miss Page — B. Mrs. Stunt | S | 2 | Glamour Boy of Glenmist | Fellview Fable |
| **Fellview Fern, b.** — O. Mr. T. Wall — B. Mr. T. Wall | S | 1 | Chateauroux Cap'n Scrunch | Fellview Bracken |
| **Fellview Monarch, d. Ch. 1973** — O. Mr. T. Wall — B. Mr. T. Wall | S | 1 | Ch. Fellview Consort | Niteshade of Rokeby |
| **Fernmoss Nite Lark of Rokeby, b. Ch. 1973** — O. Miss S. Hulme — B. Mr. & Mrs. J. Eglin | T | 13 | Ch. Clayswood Asoka Blue Venture | Ch. Westlynn Witchcraft |
| **Geoffdon Westlynn's Wayside Boy, d. Ch. 1971** — O. Mr. G. Mildon — B. Mr. & Mrs. Westwood | S | 1s | Ch. Ramsey of Rokeby | |

231

| Dog's Name and Owner and Breeder | Colour | Family | Sire | Dam |
|---|---|---|---|---|
| Grancoats Blue Destiny, b. .. .. | BM | 4 | Sir Liaz of Kempdelph | Grancoats Blue Minette |
| O. Mr. & Mrs. Westwell | | | | |
| B. Mr. & Mrs. Westwell | | | | |
| Grennynes Blue Angel, b. .. .. | BM | 4 | Sean of Grennynes | Silver Dawn of Grennynes |
| O. Mr. & Mrs. Parkinson | | | | |
| B. Mr. & Mrs. Parkinson | | | | |
| Hunnycombe Sundew, b. .. .. | S | 13 | Hunnycombe Statesman | Hunnycombe Serenade |
| O. Mr. Paterson | | | | |
| B. Mrs. A. Smith | | | | |
| Janlynn's Blue Marquis, d. Ch. 1971 | BM | | Bellacoyle Beauty | Brackenmist Silver Dollar |
| O. Miss Hope & Mr. Davies | | | | |
| B. Miss Hope & Mr. Davies | | | | |
| Janlynn's Blue Maskerade, d. .. | BM | | Bellacoyle Beauty | Brackenmist Silver Dollar |
| O. Mrs. G. H. Gale | | | | |
| B. Miss Hope & Mr. Davies | | | | |
| Jefsfire Gold Token, d. Ch. 1970 .. | S | 2 | Ch. Danvis Duffer | Jefsfire Starlight |
| O. Mr. & Mrs. Jeffries | | | | |
| B. Mr. & Mrs. Jeffries | | | | |
| Jefsfire High Return, d. Ch. 1970 .. | S | 1 | Jefsfire Chateauroux Fellow | Ch. Jefsfire Paterdale Charmer |
| O. Mr. & Mrs. Jeffries | | | | |
| B. Mr. & Mrs. Jeffries | | | | |
| Jefsfire Lucky Lea, b. Ch. 1972 .. | T | 15 | Ch. Jefsfire Lucky By Name | Beaudeer Cherry Bee |
| O. Mr. & Mrs. Jeffries | | | | |
| B. Mr. K. Tombs | | | | |
| Jefsfire Ready Maid, b. Ch. 1970 .. | S | 2 | Ch. Jefsfire Gold Token | Jefsfire Bewitched |
| O. Mr. & Mrs. Jeffries | | | | |
| B. Mr. & Mrs. Jeffries | | | | |
| Jimarlyns Rejoice of Rokeby, d. Ch. & Irish Ch. 1972 | S | 6 | Dorgano Double Ace of Rokeby | Ch. Rosalie of Rokeby |
| O. Mr. J. Davidson | | | | |
| B. Mr. & Mrs. J. Eglin | | | | |
| Joywil, Jefsfire Falkenor of, d. Ch. 1971 .. | S | 2 | Ch. Royal Ace of Rokeby | Jefsfire Dawn Edition of Glenmist |
| O. Mr. & Mrs. Atherton | | | | |
| B. Mr. & Mrs. Jeffries | | | | |
| Kilgoreys Princess Isobel, b. .. .. | S | 1 | Aspasia's Some Blarney | Esemaich Fairest Faith |
| O. Mr. & Mrs. K. Baskett | | | | |
| B. Miss S. Moore | | | | |

| Name | | Reg. | No. | Sire | Dam |
|---|---|---|---|---|---|
| Landula Lian, d. | .. | S | | Landula Cavalier | Menju Charmer |
| O. Mrs. G. Lancaster | | | | | |
| B. Mr. & Mrs. Smith | | | | | |
| Laund Lara, b. | .. | S | 2 | Ch. Royal Ace of Rokeby | Ch. Laund Livia |
| O. Mrs. A. Bishop | | | | | |
| B. Mrs. A. Bishop | | | | | |
| Laund Lucigard, d. Ch. 1972 | .. | S | 2 | Ch. Jefsfire High Regard | Laund Luciano |
| O. Mrs. A. Bishop | | | | | |
| B. Mrs. A. Bishop | | | | | |
| Laund Luscombe, d. Ch. 1970 | .. | T | 2 | Ch. Royal Ace of Rokeby | Ch. Laund Livia |
| O. Mrs. A. Bishop | | | | | |
| B. Mrs. A. Bishop | | | | | |
| Loorbeer Leman, b. | .. | S | 1 | Spanish Silk of Simbastar | Lorber Lafayette |
| O. Mrs. J. Ward | | | | | |
| B. Mrs. A. Teale | | | | | |
| Leecroft Timbury's Daydream, b. | .. | S | 3 | Leecroft Liston | Inglebrooks Star Lady |
| O. Mrs. B. Cockcroft | | | | | |
| B. Mr. & Mrs. Billington | | | | | |
| Leepark Glenbarry, d. Ch. 1971 | .. | S | SL | Leepark Venture | Linnet of Leepark |
| O. Mrs. J. Cable | | | | | |
| B. Mrs. J. Cable | | | | | |
| Leverpark Laughan Larilan, d. Ch. 1972 | .. | S | 2 | Rushmede Dandini of Dunsinane | Remlaw Royalist of Leverpark |
| O. Mr. & Mrs. Vaughan | | | | | |
| B. Mr. & Mrs. Vaughan | | | | | |
| Lowerpark Silver Dollar, d. | .. | BM | 10 | Lowerpark Hamish | Lowerpark Silver Flora |
| O. Mrs L. Westby | | | | | |
| B. Mrs. L. Westby | | | | | |
| Lynway Some Loving, d. | .. | S | 1 | Sandiacre Softly Softly | Lynway Sugar Sugar |
| O. Mrs. & Miss Clarke | | | | | |
| B. Mrs. & Miss Clarke | | | | | |
| Narrangansette, Athol of, d. | .. | S | 1 | Ch. Fellview Concord | Balmaceuwan Bella Donna |
| O. Mr. P. McLaren | | | | | |
| B. Mr. J. Stewart | | | | | |
| Narrangansette, Snogarth of, d. Ch. 1970 | .. | S | 13 | Netherkeir Torchfire | Jefsfire Satin Symphony |
| O. Mr. P. McLaren | | | | | |
| B. Mr. P. McLaren | | | | | |
| Narrangansette, Theda of, b. Ch. 1974 | .. | S | 13 | Netherkeir Torchfire | Phares Golden Girl of Narragansette |
| O. Mr. P. McLaren | | | | | |
| R. Mr. P. McLaren | | | | | |

# CHALLENGE CERTIFICATE WINNERS JUNE 1, 1969—DECEMBER 31, 1972—(Cont.)

| Dog's Name and Owner and Breeder | Colour | Family | Sire | Dam |
|---|---|---|---|---|
| Panorama's Sweet Nightingale, b.<br>O. Mrs. A. Gibbs<br>B. Mrs. A. Hassock | S | 3 | Ch. Danvis Duffer | Danvis Lestine Lochwinnock |
| Pattingham Peat Moss, d.<br>O. Mr. H. Nelson<br>B. Mrs. M. Franklin | S | 1 | Ch. Pattingham Pacemaker | Pattingham Playtop of Fleetbrook |
| Pattingham Prosper, d.<br>O. Mrs. M. Franklin<br>B. Mrs. M. Franklin | S | 2 | Ch. Geoffdon Westlynn's Wayside Boy | Pattingham Peat |
| Pattingham Sandiacre Sincerity<br>O. Mrs. M. Franklin<br>B. Mrs. S. Wigglesworth | S | SL | Ch. Royal Ace of Rokeby | Ch. Sandiacre Request of Rokeby |
| Pelido Copper Beech, d. Ch. 1972<br>O. Mr. & Mrs. P. Burtenshaw<br>B. Mr. & Mrs. P. Burtenshaw | S | 1 | Leecroft Lover Boy of Dunsinane | Pelido Hunnycombe Saffron |
| Ravensbeck Moonlight of Antoc, b. Ch. 1973<br>O. Mrs. A Speding<br>B. Mrs. P. House | T | SL | Antoc Griffin | Ravensbeck Cherry Ripe |
| Rokeby, Rauno of, d. Ch. 1972<br>O. Mr. & Mrs. J. Eglin<br>B. Mr. & Mrs. J. Eglin | S | 13 | Ch. Ramsey of Rokeby | Ch. Witchcraft of Rokeby |
| Rokeby, Ravissant of, b. Ch. 1971<br>O. Mr. & Mrs. J. Eglin<br>B. Mr. & Mrs. J. Eglin | S | 6 | Dorgano Double Ace of Rokeby | Ch. Rosalie of Rokeby |
| Rokeby, Rose Noble of, b.<br>O. Mr. & Mrs. Purdie<br>B. Mr. & Mrs. J. Eglin | S | 13 | Ch. Rauno of Rokeby | Sharval Racine of Rokeby |
| Rossheath Seeker of Skellvale, d.<br>O. Mr. H. Linley<br>B. Mr. P. Rodford | S | 1 | Ch. Ramsey of Rokeby | Susan of Skellvale |
| Sandiacre Request of Rokeby, b. Ch. 1971<br>O. Mrs. S. Wigglesworth<br>B. Mr. & Mrs. J. Eglin | S | SL | Dorgano Double Ace of Rokeby | Ch. Rosalie of Rokeby |
| Sandiacre Secondhand Rose, b. Ch. 1970<br>O. Mrs. S. Wigglesworth<br>B. Mrs. S. Wigglesworth | S | SL | Dazzler of Dunsinane | Jefsfire Fashionette |
| Shipelle Charmer, b.<br>O. Mrs. Shipley | S | 2 | Ch. Thistleblue Bluelands Boy | Shipelle Tomasa Twitchet |

| Dog's Name and Owner and Breeder | Colour | Family | Sire | Dam |
|---|---|---|---|---|
| B. Mrs. J. Sykes | | | | |
| Tameila Vanity Blue, b. Ch. 1973 | BM | 1 | Tameila Mooncloud | Tilehouse Blue Shade |
| O. Mrs. A. Hodgson | | | | |
| B. Mrs A. Hodgson | | | | |
| Thistleblue Bluelands Boy, d. Ch. 1970 | T | 10 | Ch. Jetsfire Lucky By Name | Thistleblue Petrova |
| O. Mr. L. Casely | | | | |
| B. Mr. & Mrs. Rainbow | | | | |
| Tilehouse Tala, b. | BM | 10 | Ch. Tilehouse Tonto | Colareta Blue Nanetta |
| O. Mrs. I. Combe | | | | |
| B. Mrs. I. Combe | | | | |
| Ugony, Mystic Maid from, b. Ch. 1971 | S | 1 | Ch. Antoc Vicar of Bray | Pippa from Ugony |
| O. Mrs. Markey | | | | |
| B. Miss D. Young | | | | |
| Westlynn's Star, b. Ch. 1970 | S | 1s | Ch. Ramsey of Rokeby | Ch. Westlynns Witchcraft |
| O. Mrs. D. Wallis | | | | |
| B. Mr. & Mrs. Westwood | | | | |
| Westlynn's Witchcraft, b. Ch. 1970 | S | 1s | Ch. Royal Ace of Rokeby | Westlynn's Wild Venture |
| O. Mr. & Mrs. Westwood | | | | |
| B. Mr. & Mrs. Westwood | | | | |
| Witchknowe Wilma, b. | S | 1 | Monkreddan Glen Grant | Dewshill Doodle |
| O. Mrs. M. Brown | | | | |
| B. Mrs. M. Brown | | | | |

Please will you read carefully the preface to the seventh edition, and then try your best to find me the information I still seek. Thank you.

## CHALLENGE CERTIFICATE WINNERS JANUARY 1, 1973—JUNE 30, 1974

| Dog's Name and Owner and Breeder | Colour | Family | Sire | Dam |
|---|---|---|---|---|
| Abbelane Gloriana b. | S | 8 | Ch. Dunsinane Radar of Rokeby | Georgetta of Abbelane |
| O. Mrs. H. Newey | | | | |
| B. Mrs. H. Newey | | | | |
| Antoc April Love, b. | S | 13 | Ch. Antoc the Boy Friend | Antoc High Society |
| O. Mrs. A. Speding | | | | |
| B. Mrs. A. Speding | | | | |
| Antoc Midnight Cowboy, d. Ch. 1973 | T | SL | Antoc Griffin | Ravensbeck Cherry Ripe |
| O. Mrs. A. Speding | | | | |
| B. Mrs. P. House | | | | |
| Bhyllsacre Dream Girl, b. Ch. 1974 | S | 13 | Ch. Antoc Vicar of Bray | Antoc Make Believe |
| O. Mrs. I. Cozens | | | | |
| B. Mrs. I. Cozens | | | | |

| Dog's Name and Owner and Breeder | Colour | Family | Sire | Dam |
|---|---|---|---|---|
| Bririch Black Keino, d. .. .. | T | 4 | Ch. Thistleblue Bluelands Boy | Ch. Bririch Blue Chiffon |
| O. Mr. & Mrs. E. Hickson | | | | |
| B. Mr. & Mrs. E. Hickson | | | | |
| Bririch Blue Chiffon, b. Ch. 1973 .. | BM | 4 | Bririch Black Courier | Grennyne's Blue Angel |
| O. Mr. & Mrs. E. Hickson | | | | |
| B. Mr. & Mrs. G. Parkinson | | | | |
| Bririch Gold Jeanette, b. .. .. | S | 13 | Ch. Bririch Gold Edition | Ch. Bririch Ideam Amanda |
| O. Mr. & Mrs. E. Hickson | | | | |
| B. Mr. & Mrs. E. Hickson | | | | |
| Bririch Gold Lance, d. .. .. | S | 13 | Ch. Bririch Gold Edition | Ch. Bririch Ideam Amanda |
| O. Mr. & Mrs. E. Hickson | | | | |
| B. Mr. & Mrs. E. Hickson | | | | |
| Bririch Night Enchantment, b. Ch. 1974 .. | T | 1 | Ch. Royal Ace of Rokeby | Bririch Gold Belita |
| O. Mr. & Mrs. E. Hickson | | | | |
| B. Mr. & Mrs. E. Hickson | | | | |
| Carramar Pollyanna, b. Ch. 1973 .. | T | 10 | Ch. Carramar Boy Blue | Carramar Black Opal |
| O. Mrs. J. Sargeant | | | | |
| B. Mrs. J. Sargeant | | | | |
| Carsina Country Boy, d. .. .. | T | 4 | Ch. Thistleblue Bluelands Boy | Duntiblae Detonator |
| O. Mrs. G. Parker | | | | |
| B. Mrs. G. Parker | | | | |
| Cathanbrae Gold and Gay, b. .. | S | 1 | Ch. Ramsey of Rokeby | Ch. Cathanbrae Golden Rust Queen |
| O. Mrs. T. Taylor | | | | |
| B. Mrs. T. Taylor | | | | |
| Cathanbrae Smokey Joe, d. .. | BM | 6 | Ch. Antoc Midnight Cowboy | Ch. Cathanbrae Ladypark Lavender Blue |
| O. Mrs. T. Taylor | | | | |
| B. Mrs. T. Taylor | | | | |
| Cathanbrae Willow Pattern, d. Ch. 1973 .. | BM | 6 | Knight Marksman of Rokeby | Ch. Cathanbrae Ladypark Lavender Blue |
| O. Mrs. T. Taylor | | | | |
| B. Mrs. T. Taylor | | | | |
| Corydon Quinault, d. .. .. | T | 13 | Ch. Ramsey of Rokeby | Corydon Qui Vive |
| O. Mr. & Mrs. J. Blake | | | | |
| B. Mr. & Mrs. J. Blake | | | | |
| Danvis Jefsfire Johnny Walker, d. .. | T | 13 | Lynway Some Loving | Ch. Jefsfire Lucky Lea |
| O. Mr. T. Purvis | | | | |
| B. Mr. & Mrs. A. T. Jeffries | | | | |

B. Miss A. Warman

Dolbrad Enchanting Gold, b. .. .. S 13 | Dolbrad Secret Ace | Dolbrad Enchantress
  O. Mr. G. Doel
  B. Mr. G. Doel

Erjon Erl-King, d. .. .. S 13 | Knight Porter of Rokeby | Rare Chance of Rokeby
  B. Mrs. D. L. Jones
  O. Mrs. D. L. Jones

Glenryck Blue Jay, d. .. .. BM 2 | Grancoats Blue Destiny | Goldcrest Evensong
  O. Mrs. E. Eccleston
  B. Mrs. E. Eccleston

Janlynn, Glenalan Night Shadow of, d. Ch. 1974 .. T 2 | Mywicks Dusky Star | Dundrennan Blue Mink
  O. Miss M. Hope & Mr. M. Davies
  B. Mr. & Mrs. A. Jones

Janlynn, Shearcliffe Blue Starlet of, b. Ch. 1974 .. BM 3 | Brayston Premier | Ch. Shearcliffe Blue Sonnet of Dunsinane
  O. Miss M. Hope & Mr. M. Davies
  B. Mrs. A. Chatfield

Johrenda Sheldean Mystic Magic, d. Ch. 1974 .. T 10 | Ch. Royal Ace of Rokeby | Sheldean Rough Bracken
  O. Mr. & Mrs. B. Grassby
  B. Mr. S. Stuart

Kayroy Keepsake, b. .. .. S 5 | Westlynn's Bags-a-Swank | Rixown Roma
  O. Mrs. K. Conroy
  B. Mrs. K. Conroy

Laughan Larinka b. .. .. S 3 | Leecroft Lover Boy of Dunsinane | Remlaw Royalist of Laughan
  O. Mr. & Mrs. L. Vaughan
  B. Mr. & Mrs L. Vaughan

Lornevale Mystic Lady of Leawyn, b. .. T 3 | Ch. Clickham Night Superior | Blue Violet of Leawyn
  O. Mr. J. P. Woolnough
  B. Mr. J. A. Yates

Lowerpark Lucinda, b. .. .. S 3 | Lowerpark Bonanza | Lowerpark Lawlass
  O. Mrs. L. Westby
  B. Mrs. L. Westby

Lynway, Ragamuffin of Shymlea at, d. .. S 1 | Rainpark Razzmataz | Rainpark Barley Sugar
  O. Mrs. A. M. & Miss M. M. Clarke
  B. Mr. A. E. Tutly

Lynway Shadey Affair, b. .. .. S 6 | Lynway Some Loving | Regan of Rokeby
  O. Mrs. A. M. & Miss M. M. Clarke
  B. Mrs. A. M. & Miss M. M. Clarke

237

## CHALLENGE CERTIFICATE WINNERS JANUARY 1, 1973—JUNE 30, 1974—(Cont.)

| Dog's Name and Owner and Breeder | Colour | Family | Sire | Dam |
|---|---|---|---|---|
| Lynway Sundance, d. | S | 6 | Ch. Ramsey of Rokeby | Regan of Rokeby |
|   O. Mrs. A. M. & Miss M. M. Clarke | | | | |
|   B. Mrs. A. M. & Miss M. M. Clarke | | | | |
| Maivor, Top Score of, d. | S | SL | Ch. Thistleblue Bluelands Boy | Colrenes Edwina |
|   O. Mr. & Mrs. G. Keeling | | | | |
|   B. Mr. J. Redfern | | | | |
| Nellwyn's Black Beauty, b. Ch. 1973 | T | 13 | Ch. Royal Ace of Rokeby | Rokeby Lady Rhona of Scotforth |
|   O. Mr. K. Nelson | | | | |
|   B. Mr. K. Nelson | | | | |
| Pattingham Panacea, b. | S | 2 | Ch. Geoffdon Westlynn's Wayside Boy | Pattingham Petal |
|   O. Mrs. M. Franklin | | | | |
|   B. Mrs. M. Franklin | | | | |
| Piphoney Freelancer, d. | S | 2 | Jefsfire Jamie of Piphoney | Erjon Enchanted |
|   O. Mr. & Mrs. P. Norton | | | | |
|   B. Mr. & Mrs. P. Norton | | | | |
| Rokeby, Acorus Blue Grass of, b. Ch. 1974 | BM | 4 | Knight Avenger of Rokeby | Asoka Gay Mist |
|   O. Mrs. J. Eglin | | | | |
|   B. Mrs. V. Green | | | | |
| Rokeby, Niteshade of, b. | T | 13 | Ch. Ramsey of Rokeby | Ch. Witchcraft of Rokeby |
|   O. Mrs. J. Eglin | | | | |
|   B. Mrs. J. Eglin | | | | |
| Sandiacre Shakehands, d. Ch. 1974 | S | SL | Ch. Royal Ace of Rokeby | Ch. Sandiacre Secondhand Rose |
|   O. Mr. R. M. Shepherd | | | | |
|   B. Mrs. S. Wigglesworth | | | | |
| Shearcliffe, Allison of, b. Ch. 1974 | S | 1 | Shearcliffe Battleaxe | Coldernice Caprice |
|   O. Mr. J. Broderick | | | | |
|   B. Mrs. M. McCraicht | | | | |
| Shearcliffe Blossom, b. Ch. 1973 | T | 8 | Shearcliffe Bedazzle | Shearcliffe Black Ballyhoo |
|   O. Mr. J. Broderick | | | | |
|   B. Mr. J. Broderick | | | | |
| Zena's Pride, b. | S | 3 | Cavehill Laddie | Cavehill Border Gem |
|   O. Mr. R. Mclean | | | | |
|   B. Mr. D. Smyth | | | | |

# DIET SHEETS

## *At* 8 *Weeks of age*

7. 0 a.m.  Cereals or wholemeal bread with milk (about 1 large breakfast cup when mixed) plus ½ teaspoonful cod liver oil and ½ teaspoonful calcium phosphate.

11. 0 a.m.  6 oz. raw meat, chopped.

2. 0 p.m.  Drink of milk, with rusk or Lactol biscuit to chew.

5. 0 p.m.  As 11 a.m.

9.30 p.m.  Bowl of puppy meal (wholemeal) soaked with stock, gravy or milk. About ¾ pt. total volume.

## *At* 12 *Weeks*

7. 0 a.m.  As above, but increase quantity a little.

11. 0 a.m.  8 oz. raw meat.

5. 0 p.m.  8 oz. raw meat.

9.30 p.m.  As at 8 weeks but 1 pt. volume.

## 6 *Months*

7. 0 a.m.  As before. Increase cod liver oil and calcium to 1 teaspoonful each.

5. 0 p.m.  1 lb. raw meat.

9.30 p.m.  As before.

Continue on this diet as long as the puppy will take three meals, increasing the meat meal gradually to 1½ lb. At 8 months, discontinue calcium, but continue cod liver oil.

## *Adult Diet*

Breakfast. Cereals or wholemeal bread with milk or stock. 1 teaspoonful cod liver oil Main Meal. 1–1½ lb. raw meat, or other substitute. *See* Chapter 11.

## BREEDING TERMS AGREEMENT

AGREEMENT BETWEEN.................................

AND.........................................

Date....................

Mr........................having today taken over the
Collie bitch...................from Mr....................
on part-breeding terms, agrees to return to Mr..................
first and third pick* of the first litter, the bitch having been served
at no cost to Mr.............................., by one of
Mr........................'s dogs. In the event of an outside
stud dog having been used both parties to this agreement to share
the cost equally. Mr........................agrees to take
every possible care of the bitch during the terms of this agreement,
but he will not be held responsible for her death unless this is caused
by his negligence. When the puppies have been returned to Mr.
........................the transfer form for the bitch will be
handed over and she will become the unconditional property of
Mr........................

Signed......................

Signed......................

* Here can be inserted any terms one wishes; it need not be only
two puppies, it can be more or fewer or it can be spread over two
litters or more.

# APPENDIX 4

## LIST OF BREED CLUBS IN GREAT BRITAIN

AYRSHIRE COLLIE CLUB.—Mr. A. Hunter, 8 St. Inan's Road, Irvine, Ayrshire.

BRITISH COLLIE CLUB.—Mrs. B. Pender, 11 Scholes Drive, New Moston, Manchester 10.

COLLIE ASSOCIATION.—Mrs. Speding, Brook Cottage, Ripley, Christchurch, Hants. (Bransgore 72424.)

COLLIE CLUB OF WALES.—Mr. and Mrs. L. P. Green, Llechau Farm, Llanharry, nr. Pontyclun, Glam.

EAST ANGLIAN COLLIE ASSOC.—Mrs. P. M. Barnard, Washbay, Watering Lane, Kings Lynn, Norfolk.

IRISH COLLIE CLUB.—Mr. R. Gow, 409 Ballysillan Road, Belfast 14.

LANCASHIRE AND CHESHIRE COLLIE CLUB.—Mr. W. P. Turner, 32 Chorley Road, Hilldale, Parbold, nr. Wigan, Lancs.

LONDON AND PROVINCIAL COLLIE CLUB.—Mrs. L. Westby, Sunnyside, Toothill, Ongar, Essex. (Ongar 2767.)

LONDON COLLIE CLUB.—Mrs. M. Byrnes, Lennel House, Tudwick, Tiptree, Essex.

MIDLAND COLLIE CLUB.—Mr. A. T. Broadhead, 62 Milton Road, Fallings Park, Wolverhampton.

NORTHUMBERLAND AND DURHAM COLLIE CLUB.—Mr. A. P. Mather, 10 Bickford Terrace, Aycliffe Village, Co. Durham.

SCOTTISH COLLIE CLUB.—Mr. J. M. May, 36 Ash Road, Cumbernauld, Glasgow.

WEST OF ENGLAND COLLIE SOCIETY.—Miss M. Hope, Janlynn, Rectory Lane, Compton Martin, Bristol.

YORKSHIRE COLLIE CLUB.—Mrs. B. Cockroft, 49 Half House Lane, Hove Edge, Brighouse, Yorks.

Q

## APPENDIX 5

## PROGRESSIVE RETINAL ATROPHY (PRA)

In the late twenties, maybe in the early thirties also, an eye condition known as Progressive Retinal Atrophy existed fairly extensively in our breed, then appeared to die out. It existed also in many other breeds and is by no means confined to the Rough Collie.

The first scientific papers on this condition appeared in the mid-1940s, and since that time more and more research has been carried on with animals of all breeds.

Retinal Atrophy is a progressive degeneration of the nerve cells in the retina and the consequent degeneration of the blood vessels supplying these areas. There are various patterns in which this occurs. It may start at the edge of the retina or centrally. In our breed the central areas are affected first. A further variety is seen when the pigment layer (i.e. the outermost lining of the retina) is disturbed and clumps of pigment appear on the retina—this is seen in the Scotch Collie.

At the time of writing it cannot be stated definitely which is the method of inheritance in Collies, but it seems that the method of inheritance of the disease in Border Collies is quite different from those of the Rough.

Dr. K. Barnett (Cambridge University) has, in the past decade, made an intensive study of the condition in a great number of breeds, and in some of them the genetic pattern has been established, but, at the time of writing, this is not yet true of our breed.

The condition has been called 'night blindness'. This refers to a loss of vision at night and appears early in those cases where the periphery of the retina is first affected. It is usually a later sign where the disturbance occurs in the central area of the retina. In these cases the dog will have good vision until the retinal degeneration is advanced. It should also be stressed that Progressive Retinal Atrophy can be a sequel to a viral infection when no geneticpredisposition is present, but these different forms are distinguishable ophthalmologically.

In 1966 the British Veterinary Association/Kennel Club scheme for control of PRA was set up: in its early months it applied only to Elkhounds, but today it covers all breeds. As a result of this scheme it is now possible to have our dogs tested for a very nominal fee. In our breed a life-time 'clear certificate' cannot be issued until the animal is three years old, but in the meantime younger stock may, and should, be tested from the age of 12–14 months. If such animals, at the time of examination, show no signs of the disease, they will receive an 'interim' certificate, but it must be realised that Collies with such a certificate *must* be tested annually until they reach the age of three years.

I must point out very clearly that, at the time of writing, out of the thousands of qualified veterinary surgeons in the British Isles, only 17 are approved by the B.V.A. to carry out this examination, which is definitely a job for the specialist. Your approach here is to contact your own veterinary surgeon who will then make an appointment with the nearest 'referee', this being the name given to the qualified specialist. The cost is two guineas per dog. This small amount is possible only because the B.V.A./K.C. are subsidising the scheme so that, although with a young dog the final cost may amount to six guineas, there is really no excuse for us to say that we cannot afford to take advantage of the examination.

The examination is painless, simple and quick (there is no need for anaesthesia) and you will be told the result at once, so there is no agony of a prolonged wait as, for instance, in waiting the result of Hip Dysplasia X-rays.

When a 'clear' or 'interim' certificate is issued to you, this must be sent directly to the Kennel Club for ratification. The official certificate will then be issued, and in time the names of the 'clear' or 'interim' animals will be published in the *Kennel Gazette*. However, it is not everyone who sees this journal, and therefore I would appreciate receiving the names of all dogs receiving either certificate so that these may be published immediately in *Dog World*, this magazine having agreed to co-operate with us in every possible way.

It would also be of enormous benefit to the breed, and to my breed records, if you would trust me (in complete confidence if you so wish) with the names of any animals which cannot be passed, for then, maybe, a picture will begin to emerge, showing us the possible genetic pattern in our breed.

I beg you all, experienced breeder or complete novice, to treat this matter with the greatest seriousness, and to breed only from stock with a certificate. Naturally you cannot be expected to wait until your Collie, dog or bitch, is three years old before breeding with it, which is why we stress the advisability of asking for an 'interim' check. It is the only way we can have any hope of clearing our lovely breed of this scourge. It will take time, but if we are serious from now on we may have some hope of combating it.

Let us hope it will soon become the rule to see stock advertised from parents who have received a PRA certificate.

I am deeply indebted to one of the 'referees' for checking these notes for me and making suggestions and alterations to them.

APPENDIX 6

# TUBE FEEDING OF PUPPIES

In recent years a new means of hand-rearing puppies has been adopted. This is the 'tube feeding method'. It is absolutely ideal, particularly where (a) one is hand-rearing a whole litter, and (b) where a weakly puppy, not yet able to suckle, is helped 'over the hump'. In the first instance it is of exceptional value because it is so time saving.

The idea is to obtain a plastic pipe, specially made for the purpose, and obtainable through your veterinary surgeon or chemist. This is introduced into the puppy's stomach, attached to a hypodermic syringe (without its needle of course) and the milk slowly and gently fed through the tube direct into the stomach. This may sound alarming, and, first time of trying, it is, but the puppy very quickly learns to swallow the end of the tube, and this can then be marked off to show just how much of the tube must be inside the puppy, before the syringe full of milk is attached. There is only one thing to be certain about, make sure that the tube is, in fact, in the stomach, and not in the lungs. This can be very quickly noted before touching the plunger of the syringe, because if it should, by accident, have been introduced into the lung, bubbles will immediately arise up the pipe. The food is fed very slowly, but even so, it is vastly more speedy than is the ordinary method of bottle feeding a new-born puppy.

If you are trying to save a puppy which is not quite as strong as its litter mates, you will probably find that two or three good feeds from the tube will allow him to catch up to the point where he can hold his own with the rest of the family. However, I am not one who will always tube feed, just for speed, because I am sure that, where a puppy is strong enough to suckle from the bottle, it gains much by the extra exercise this entails him.

# COMPARATIVE FIGURES OF REGISTRATIONS
## AT THE KENNEL CLUB

It is interesting to note the tremendous increase in the popularity of the Rough Collie in the post-war years. In the last complete year before the war (1938) our registrations totalled 516. In the first full year after the war (1946) the total was 609. Then the registrations made very steady progress until in 1972 they reached an all time record of 6597.

| | | | |
|---|---|---|---|
| 1946 | 609 | 1960 | 2209 |
| 1947 | 834 | 1961 | 2801 |
| 1948 | 1026 | 1962 | 3074 |
| 1949 | 1182 | 1963 | 3245 |
| 1950 | 1322 | 1964 | 3775 |
| 1951 | 1445 | 1965 | 4033 |
| 1952 | 1349 | 1966 | 3957 |
| 1953 | 1360 | 1967 | 4495 |
| 1954 | 1563 | 1968 | 5064 |
| 1955 | 1436 | 1969 | 5736 |
| 1956 | 1695 | 1970 | 6086 |
| 1957 | 1757 | 1971 | 5750 |
| 1958 | 2131 | 1972 | 6597 |
| 1959 | 2371 | 1973 | 6211 |

# INDEX